THE NAME OF THE MOTHER

In this original and highly accomplished study, Marie Maclean studies the writings of social rebels and explores the relationship between their personal narratives and illegitimacy.

The case studies which Maclean examines fall into four groups:

- those which stress alternative family structures and 'female genealogies'
- those which pair female illegitimacy and revolution
- those which question the deliberate refusal of the name of the father by the legitimate
- those which study the revenge of genius on the society which excludes it

Skilfully interweaving feminist theory, French literary criticism, social and cultural history, deconstruction and psychoanalytic theory, Maclean traces the place of these personal narratives of illegitimacy in history and their use in theory, from Elizabeth I to Freud, Sartre and Derrida.

The Name of the Mother will be of vital interest and importance to any student of critical theory, feminist philosophy, French or cultural studies.

Marie Maclean is a Senior Research Fellow of Monash University and Fellow of the Australian Academy of the Humanities. She is also an advisory editor of *New Literary History* and her previous publications include *Narrative as Performance* (Routledge 1988).

THE NAME OF THE MOTHER

Writing illegitimacy

Marie Maclean

London and New York

First published 1994
by Routledge
11 New Fetter Lane, London EC4P 4EE

Simultaneously published in the USA and Canada
by Routledge
29 West 35th Street, New York, NY 10001

© 1994 Marie Maclean

Typeset in Bembo by
Ponting–Green Publishing Services,
Chesham, Buckinghamshire
Printed and bound in Great Britain by
T.J. Press (Padstow) Ltd, Cornwall

British Library Cataloguing in Publication Data
A catalogue record for this book is available from
the British Library

Library of Congress Cataloging in Publication Data
A catalog record for this book is available from the
Library of Congress

ISBN 0–415–10686–9

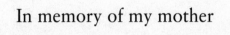

In memory of my mother

Contents

CONTENTS

Preface

Writers generalise from personal experience, but they also need to mythologise that experience in order to give it meaning. This mythologisation is one of the ways of justifying both existential necessity and existential choice. In writing this work, I am just as much a prey to this phenomenon as are Christiane Olivier and Dorothy Dinnerstein in their totally different readings of mother–child relationships. We each speak from our own lived context and our particular, and widely different, geographical and historical dilemmas.

I have come to distrust generalisations, and particularly those based on the assumption of the 'naturalness' of the so-called nuclear family, because I came from a radically different background. Born by the loving choice of a determinedly single mother in a period when this was generally not considered an option, I have found, particularly as my age and experience increased, that other people's reactions and assumptions were simply not mine, that discourse which appeared inevitable to those raised in a nuclear family was a matter of debate to me, and that, while some of my gendered positions were the same as those of other women, others were radically different.

It seemed to me worthwhile to examine the writing, the discourses and particularly the rebirth into the symbolic which occurs in the autobiographical or para-autobiographical texts of those to whom illegitimacy, real or assumed, becomes not a negative but a positive experience, not a disabling but an enabling context. My hypothesis was that there existed forms of 'minority-becoming' which could be traced in the personal writings of those who assumed the name of the mother, not as a burden but as a challenge.

Another assumption was that the writing of this 'minority-becoming' would take the form of a heteroglossia, a blending of the voices of gender, of class and of both familial and public discourses. It seemed to me that there were conclusions to be drawn from the fact that the fantasies of the 'normal' bourgeois child, the famous 'family romance', were the realities of the excluded. I saw a quiz about personality in a newspaper recently, which asked, *inter alia*, 'Would you like to be a. a love child b. a foundling c. an adulterine child d. an orphan?' My reaction was this: if, on the other hand, you are living day by day, albeit in the most pedestrian way, someone else's fantasy, then what will your fantasy be, and how will you live and write it? It is the relation between lived experience, social expectation and de-centred discourse, and the way in which they are related to shifting public and private mythologies, that provide the basis for my study.

I add a final 'postface' to this preface. Both the necessity and the difficulty of a different approach to family structures have been emphasised by the problems of indexing. The multiplicity of nomemclature has proved impossible to adapt to traditional taxonomy. In the end, I adopted the device of indexing my enormous cast under the name by which they were most commonly known.

I have an almost embarrassing number of people to thank for their encouragement and help in my project:

First and foremost my husband, Hector Maclean, who has supported my writing both personally and professionally, constituting himself researcher and proof-reader and keeping me going through some pretty bad times. Next, my friend Ross Chambers, who has generously made time to read and comment on each chapter in its first draft and, by his enthusiasm, convinced me of the importance of the work.

Thanks are due to Monash University and the Australian Research Council for grants which sent me to France and enabled me to employ my invaluable research assistants, Jenni Brown and James Cannon. Janice Price of Routledge provided constant encouragement and advice as the book developed. Special thanks to Marcelle Marini and Elena Pavis, whose affection and practical support made my last field-work in Paris possible. Of the many friends who gave me help and advice, I particularly mark my gratitude to Philip Anderson, Marie Rose Auguste, David Garrioch, Neil Levy, Neil Maclean, Sue Marson, Brian Nelson, Christine Planté, Vivianne Spiegel and Chris Worth.

Some parts of this work have appeared elsewhere in earlier versions:

A modified version of Chapter 1 as 'The Performance of Illegitimacy: Signing the Matronym', *New Literary History* 25, 1994, 95–107.

A very early version of a part of Chapter 5 as 'Revolution and Opposition: Olympe de Gouges and the *Déclaration des droits de la femme*', in *Literature and Revolution*, ed. D. Bevan, The Hague: Rodopi, 1989.

Parts of Chapter 5 as 'Revolution and Exclusion: the Other Voice' in *Discourse and Difference*, ed. A. Milner and C. Worth, Centre for General and Comparative Literature, Monash, 1990.

Parts of Chapter 6 as 'Flora Tristan: Pariah, Peregrina' *Romance Studies* 21, Winter 1992/Spring 1993, 7–14.

A modified version of Chapter 1 is forthcoming in *New Literary History*.

The author and publishers would like to thank Editions Gallimard for permission to reproduce lines from Jacques Prévert, 'Il ne faut pas . . .' in *Paroles* © Editions Gallimard on p. 186 of this book.

1

Performances of exclusion

Bastardy goes hand in hand with myth-making.[1] It is regarded as an exception to the rule, an ex-centric phenomenon, and the ex-centric always generates myths of excess, whether for good or for evil. This rule applies whether the myths are those of whole social groups, products of what Jung would call a 'collective unconscious',[2] or merely those of the individual psyche and its phantasms. This study will look at some of the personal narratives of illegitimacy and delegitimation, hoping to throw light on the relationship between the written texts and the phantasmic *mises en scène* which govern both individual performance and social prejudice.

Any reading of so-called reminiscences leaves one with a profound admiration for the human capacity to shape past events to present needs. Facts mutate in accordance with the laws of perspective. The constructive power of memory necessary to recreate a 'life' depends not only on the selective capacity for forgetting, but also on the structural demands and assertions of the stories it performs. Personal narrative is a discursive *mise en scène*, in which a self emerges from the shifting interplay of signifiers and utterances. The process of mythopoesis is also one of intertextuality, where the personal narrative, by the very fact of being written, is enmeshed in the dominant myths of a particular society. But the process works in two ways. On the one hand, the *mise en scène* of the letter, the memoir or the confession transforms a lived experience into a fiction, 'a more or less probable novel, but no longer history',[3] where the process of representation irrevocably transmutes life into art, even without any apparent cosmetic attempt by the writer. On the other hand, the myths produced can be so potent, and the

1

narrative structures so compelling, that fictional performances have 'real' consequences and life follows the path which myth has traced for it. Modern French culture offers a rich paradigm of such myths and anti-myths of bastardy, due in part to major historical shifts in the status of the illegitimate, and in part to a stronger polarisation of social prejudices and attitudes than those typical of, say, England in the same time-frame. We will be looking at a series of personal narratives of bastards or would-be bastards, ranging, for the most part, but not exclusively, over the 200-year history of modern France, and tracing a dramatic shift in the performance of exclusion.

The name: preconception or reconception

The privileged site of the personal narrative is the name, since a name is both the encapsulation of a past and the potential for a future. A name may be experienced as a compelling scenario, a legitimation which is at once a binding obligation and a self-fulfilling prophecy. Or again, it may be seen as one of many possible fictions, a nomination which can vary in performance. A proper name, Jacques Derrida suggested recently in a lecture, is something which both resists culture and enables it. In Western society the patronym embodies the forces of tradition and authority, it enables the dominant ideology and culture. As Gayatri Spivak remarks:

> the patronymic, in spite of all empirical details of the generation gap, keeps the transcendental ego of the dynasty identical in the eyes of the law. By virtue of the father's name the son refers to the father. The irreducible import-ance of the name and the law in his situation makes it quite clear that the question is not merely one of psycho-socio-sexual behaviour but of the production and consolidation of meaning.
>
> (1983: 169)

At the same time, by its very rigidity, the name of the father offers a potential site of resistance. It is a message which may always be disrupted by noise.[4] Our conception of self, in as far as it is patronymic, is an enabling *preconception*. The personal narrative afforded by a patronym seems 'real' and free of the taint of fiction, guaranteed as it is by the law of the Father.[5] On the other hand we may opt for *reconception*, a dangerous birth or rebirth into the way of the mother, always tainted by its excentricity. This fate or this choice will be crystallised in the proper name.

John Searle remarks that 'the uniqueness and immense pragmatic convenience of proper names in our language lie precisely in the fact that they enable us to refer publicly to objects without being forced to raise issues' (1969: 172), that they are in fact merely a convenient peg to hang things on. Debatable as such a transparency of the proper name would be in the case of the patronym, the question becomes even more vexed when the proper name becomes, so to speak, improper, and when it becomes an issue in its own right.[6]

What I want to consider are the implications of the substitution of the matronym (or of a pseudonym with maternal associations) for the traditional and conventionally accepted name of the father. The 'natural' site for such a substitution is of course that of illegitimacy. The 'natural' child is marked as culturally 'unnatural', and life and literature bear ample witness to the compulsive narrative of the 'bend sinister', both for good and evil. However, there is a fundamental paradox: the child who lives under a 'false' or unnatural name – since the name of the mother, in most Western societies, is that of *her* father or previous husband, and therefore not the right one – acquires thereby the freedom of the mask. The wearer of the mask may live the story of the mask, like the painter Eugène Delacroix, who gratefully and lovingly assumed the name of his mother's husband (see p.50); yet, by the very fact that this was not his father, he was already necessarily at one remove from the *pietas* and conformity he strove to present. The doubleness of the mask is inescapable whether one lives it as one's 'truth', or uses it to hide another story. Then again, the knowledge that a name can be a mask, that the 'sinister' escapes from the rightness, the fit of the patronym, may engender the freedom to choose or to change one's story. If one's personal narrative is perceived as a fiction, then other fictions may take its place. The bearer of a matronym in a patriarchal society has taken the first step towards seeing that a name is something which can be conferred, can be chosen or can, indeed, be created. The lack or refusal of a father's name is a form of social exclusion which can paradoxically be a form

3

of social liberation, conferring a real or imagined freedom from the law of the Father.

The signature

Any proper name benefits from the intertextuality of the nominal sequences to which it belongs and has a certain figurative force in its particular social context. But it acquires an extra energy, a life of its own, when it becomes a signature. Signing is the mark of both a contact and a contract. A signature as proof of a signer or addressor seems to authorise and guarantee. Yet what it guarantees is a text which has already escaped from its author's control, and which is subject to all the vagaries of transmission and reception. The varying possibilities of the signature and the shift in control from addressor to addressee may be seen in the whole range of para-autobiographical texts. As they are moved from the private to the public domain, they also move from the personal to the political. Once the notoriety of the author makes them objects of publication, distribution and exchange, their signature changes in value. Thus a personal diary, in which one is one's own addressee, is unsigned or its authorship is designated by the first name alone. The writer is entirely free to 'draw himself or to draw *something other* – or else to draw himself *as other*' (Derrida, 1990: 69). In Delacroix's *Journal*, Eugène originally controlled his own picture of Eugène. But when that *Journal* was posthumously published, it then acquired a signature with all the weight of the paintings and their reception behind it. We can only read the text in the light of those other texts, and in their light Eugène becomes irretrievably Delacroix. The signature of private letters, on the other hand, is the site of a one-to-one relationship, in which both the text and the name affixed to it are mediated by one particular addressee. A peculiar shift in perspective takes place when they are moved into the public paraliterary sphere. To take one notorious example, Baudelaire's *Correspondance*, over half of which was expertly geared with a view to the psychological blackmail of one particular addressee, his mother, now staggers under the signature of the author of *Les Fleurs du mal*. Re-signed, it signifies differently.

An authorial signature then, which makes a name the intermediary between public and private, empowers in as much as it acquires an identity *from* the texts it signs, just as it gives one to them. It disempowers in as much as it submits the signer to the judgement, and indeed the whim, of that unknown and un-controllable addressee, the general public. We always write with a certain audience in mind (which is part of what Derrida means when he says the addressee signs a text as effectively as does the author or addressor), but that audience may be at first no more than a projection of personal desire. The audience, however, becomes more defined with each text written and published, and so the signature acquires more definition and more power of its own. In the end an author is completely trapped by the expecta-tions engendered by his or her signature. The dilemma may be solved by assuming a pseudonym, which in time, of course, acquires a life of *its* own. So the signature is a marginal thing, a textual construct born of the author's imagination of the readers, and the readers' construction of the author. It is, as Jacques Derrida says in *The Ear of the Other*, the border between 'work' and 'life', between a 'system' and its 'subject'. He goes on: 'This border – I call it *dynamis* because of its strength, its power, its virtual and also mobile potential – is neither active nor passive, neither outside nor inside' (1982: 41).[7] Two texts of Derrida's, *Glas* and *The Ear of the Other*, contain almost the only theor-isations of the name of the mother. A discussion of the argument in *Glas* will be found in Chapter 10, while the ambiguities of the signature will be considered throughout. While I regard the contentions in the two texts as in essence powerful pieces of special pleading for the 'androgynous' self-generation of the (male) author, they contain, as always, masterfully suggestive ambiguities and possibilities of multiple interpretation, and their arguments must be taken very seriously.[8]

Delegitimation

Now, a number of writers and artists, in order to accede to this *dynamis*, this power of the name, have felt the need to shake off the constraining power of the name of the father. Picasso, for instance, at the moment of his accession to creative potential, chose to discard the name of the father who had trained him and assume that of his mother.[9] A signature is a public choice, even when that choice springs from private or even unconscious motivation. There is always a symbolic value in refusing the

5

story already written for one. It is the figurative equivalent of the breaking of the code or the infraction of artistic convention. Such infractions could give rise to a discussion of the whole vast subject of the choice and use of the pseudonym and the creation of a fictional signature (see Laugaa, 1986), but I wish to concentrate on one aspect, which I call *delegitimation*.

Delegitimation takes on different forms in different circumstances. It may involve publicly laying claim to actual illegitimacy and the proud assumption of the exclusion it entails. It may, on the other hand, be the proclamation of a symbolic illegitimacy by public rejection of the father's name, the father's values, or both. The particular delegitimation which consists of the assumption of the mother's name may itself be actual or symbolic. Thus, Baudelaire briefly assumes his mother's actual maiden name, though with variations, while Beyle (Stendhal or Brulard) and Labrunie (Nerval) choose a name or names with maternal associations. Again delegitimation has other possibilities for women than it has for men precisely because women's names are more fluid in any case. The deliberate assumption of the name of the mother may occur, but a secondary delegitimation, which involves the public rejection of the husband's name and either a reversion to the maiden name or the adoption of a pseudonym, is more frequent. Of course, a few rare cases like that of Olympe de Gouges, the revolutionary feminist, which we will examine in detail, may combine all three stages: the assumption of illegitimacy, the rejection of the husband's name, and the manufacture of a pseudonym based on the name of the mother. Delegitimation, in fact, has two sides: self-exclusion from a world one rejects and by which one is rejected, and self-inclusion in a world of the marginalised, which may be seen as potentially a social or creative utopia. It works on the boundary, moving between high and low, between the exception and the rule, exploiting the gaps, the lines of flight and the possibilities of sexual equivocation.

Some of the minor myths of antiquity show this liminal power of the transgressive and the marginal. (The major myths of bastardy will be dealt with in Chapter 2.) Starobinski draws a very interesting distinction, in *Stendhal pseudonyme*, between two forms of masking: that of Zeus, who remains the same old rapist beneath the mask (my wording), and that of Proteus, who is free to indulge in an endless chain of metamorphoses.

Proteus, the son of the sea, who lived on the boundary between land and water, had an infinite power of transformation until pinned down by virile strength (*Odyssey*, IV: 349). He has given a word to our language and become part of the discourse of difference.[10]

Another myth of the power of liminality, particularly of the form repesented by androgyny, is that of Tiresias, who alone knew the pleasures of both male and female sexuality, and revealed the jealously guarded secret that the female's pleasure was much greater than the male's. Tiresias lost his virility, embodied in his eyesight, but gained the power of prophecy. He has an exemplary value as the symbol of the boundary, the threshold not only between male and female but between human discourse and divine discourse.[11] The advantage of situating oneself on the boundary is a greater capacity to use transformation to one's own advantage or as part of a revolutionary programme.

The patronym and gender

It should be apparent that, in European society, the implications of the change, the choice or the creation of a name are different for men and for women. To men, in our culture, the name of the father is an irrevocable identity. Starobinski sees the refusal of the patronym as a murder in effigy of the father, because as he says:

> Our name awaits us in advance. It was there, before we knew it, like our body. The common illusion consists in thinking that our destiny and our truth are inscribed in it. Thus we confer on the name the dignity of an essence.
>
> (1961: 193)

It is notable that the 'we' here refers only to men, with no suggestion that the female perspective may be different. And yet this difference is reflected in the very process of delegitimation. For women in patriarchal society, a change of name used to be seen as natural if not inevitable. Whether they became brides of Christ or merely brides, 90 per cent of women have traditionally experienced at least two public names in their lifetime (not including the changes in personal appellation which accompany us all in private life). Women therefore had from the first a

7

certain protean quality. If one change is possible, then all other changes become thinkable.

A very ambivalent attitude to marriage resulted, one which still causes major problems to feminists. Was each new name to be seen as the death of an old identity or the birth of a new one? The question was answered as variously by men as by women. Some women adopted the prevalent male attitude whereby an identity was seen as fixed and centred in the patronym, and the loss of a name was seen as a form of castration, a loss of selfhood. The new name appeared merely as a symbol of woman's powerlessness, as she was transferred as property from one male to another. On the other hand, for many women the new name represented liberty of choice, and female freedom to choose was contrasted with male limitation to the patronym. Even in times of arranged marriages, the assumption of the new name meant the assumption of maturity, the step from being a child in one's father's house to being the mistress of one's own household. The new name was also the first step towards reproduction, again ambivalently viewed as either a burden or a source of power and authority. Thus, name-changing, status-changing and indeed shape-changing were linked. Women's lives lent themselves to multiple narratives. It is for this reason that the name of the mother means something other to me than to Naomi Segal, to whom 'the name of the mother and the no of the mother' represent 'the mother as authority in the world or as internalized superego' (1992: 9). I prefer to call this aspect the law of the Mother.

The marginalisation of women in a patriarchal society de-valued their essential multiplicity, which was contrasted with male unity and stability. This devaluation was, of course, com-pounded in the case of the illegitimate. In many cases the double exclusion was too heavy a burden to bear, but in other cases the transformation I spoke of occurred, and rejection by the father and lack of the father's name turned into a positive freedom from the law of the Father. The question-mark hanging over one's very identity led to a capacity to remake that identity. A name was not fixed; it could lead into the narrative of other possible worlds.

The capacity to resist the law of the Father repeats itself with startling similarity in the lives of the three very different female revolutionaries, Olympe de Gouges, Flora Tristan and Louise

Michel. I discuss them at length in later parts of this study. All I wish to point out here is how Olympe and Flora also exemplify the second stage of delegitimation. Freed by their illegitimacy from the paternal law, they were also resistant to that same law in the form of that surrogate for paternal authority, a husband. Both were attacked by the courts for the symbolic delegitimation which made them refuse to bear the married name.

The protean possibilities of the name were exploited by each to the full, but in different ways. Olympe de Gouges created a name which would fit the story she internalised and form her signature, the border between her life and her work. Thus, the first name, Olympe, her mother's second name, also stood for her insistence on equality with the highest in the land, the 'de' represented the nobility she was denied by the father who refused to recognise her, and the 'Gouges' was a version of the mother's surname, Gouze (see Groult in Gouges, 1986). The fiction she lived by was the utopian dream of the equality of male and female, high and low, where the only aristocracy was that of brain and beauty. Flora Tristan, on the other hand, may be said to have lived up to and fictionalised her given name, a shortened version of that of her father, who recognised her but conveniently forgot to legitimise his 'marriage'. She built a narrative about herself as female messiah, the new day and radiant beauty (Flora) who yet suffered and died for the sorrows of humanity (Tristan).

The positive and negative poles

These narratives could only be exploited because they were profoundly embedded in social thought. Indeed, it is sometimes surprising to see how the beliefs associated with earlier ideologies linger on into the modern social order. The medical and social doxa of a dictionary in 1833, for instance,[12] while presenting the conventional nineteenth-century picture of the bastard as criminal, unhealthy, depraved and degenerate, makes an immediate exception for the love children of the nobility, who are still seen as bringing a secret transfusion of energy to exhausted stock:

> For the children of *love*, if they are born with all its gifts, are more ardent, more witty, more lovable, when they

draw solely on their own genius, and are inspired by the same power which produced them.

(cit. Mozet, 1988: 10)

We find here in condensed form the narrative of the bastard as genius and regenerator, more handsome and more lusty than the common run of mortals. The love child is a confirmation of virility, the 'power which produced them', and a manifestation of the principle of natural energy. This echoes, almost word for word, the claim made by Leonardo four centuries earlier:

The man who uses coitus with contention and with deprecation makes irritable children and when the coitus is made with great love and great desire of the partners, then the child will be of great intellect, spirited and lively and lovable.

(Belt; cit. Eissler, 1961: 102)[13]

What has also remained constant is the essential doubleness of myths of the bastard:

However, and it is the mystery of origins and the part illegality plays in them, the bastard child is not only a transmitter of democracy but the transmitter of a certain superiority . . . because he makes available the intersection of two opposing principles – disruption and privilege – he is marked simultaneously by a minus sign and a plus sign.

(Paul-Lévy, 1981: 169)

The extreme polarisation of illegitimacy, whereby the bastard must always be the exception, either far above or far below the commonplace, is linked with the polarisation of the corresponding symbolism of the left hand and the right, the *dexter* and the *sinister*. The polarisation is also linked to the most pervasive of all binary oppositions, that between male and female.

Now the point of these examples is to show that the alterity of the female, and especially the double alterity of the illegitimate female, lends itself to multiple names and multiple narratives. The very flexibility of naming, and the rejection of the patriarchal order, give such women a protean quality. They are able, as Derrida says, to stage their signatures (1982: 43). This produces an ambivalent male reaction. On the one hand, the decentredness, the fluid potential of these women, is devalued as emptiness, as dissipation in all senses of the term, as an essential lack. They are condemned as harlots, as bad mothers and, of course, as bad artists. In reproducing biologically and also producing textually, they contravene the very laws of patriarchal culture. Yet, at the same time, many male writers endeavour, by different forms of delegitimation, to emulate the very emancipation from the law of the Father which they condemn in their female contemporaries. The delegitimatory tactics of Stendhal, Baudelaire and, in a different form, Sartre, bear witness to this.

Autography and autothanatography

The texts I have chosen in order to follow more closely the constitution or the consecration of the signature are mostly autobiographical or para-autobiographical works. These are, as I said earlier, a series of *mises en scène* which display a life for the purpose of creating a name, or envisage a death as an apotheosis. Derrida makes a very useful distinction between *autography* (which one could call myths to live by) and *autothanatography* (which one could call myths to die by) (1980: 291). What I wish to do in this study is to examine the personal texts of writers who have used or assumed the name of the mother in order to establish the relationship between the name and the signature and between life and narrative. Such texts also play on the shifting boundaries between legitimation and delegitimation and the way in which one may always be recuperated by the other. Delegitimation may function quite differently as a myth to live by, open to immediate social censure, and as a myth to die by, where consecration of the signature produces the inevitable relegitimation. The oppositional or the revolutionary can become canonised, or it can join the canon as the ideological context changes.

To take some examples, Flora Tristan's *Pérégrinations d'une paria* (Peregrinations of a Pariah) (1838) is a clear example of autography. As we shall see, the author, as she creates the text, creates simultaneously the key narratives, the dominating myths, that will shape not only her texts but her life. There is a continual circularity, a recycling of biography into fiction and fiction into biography. The *Pérégrinations*, by establishing an audience, also begins to shape a signature, and the author's

11

ostentatious delegitimation, by the public account of her quest for legitimacy, is aimed at a market as much as at a cause. On the other hand *L'Emancipation de la femme, ou Le Testament de la paria* (The Emancipation of Woman, or The Testament of the Pariah) is autothanatography, indeed partly apocryphal, since her ideas and intentions were reworked and embroidered after her death.[14] It is a myth to die by. Myths to die by may sometimes be mere obituaries, endeavouring to preserve the signature by presenting writers in the way in which they wish to be remembered. We could see Genet's *Journal du voleur* (The Thief's Journal) in such a light. However, autothanatography can become, and be intended to become, what Louis Marin calls an authenticating gospel, written for the express use not just of the general public but of the faithful who will ensure the final apotheosis.[15] *L'Emancipation de la femme* is such a text, transforming the narratives of the Christian religion to its own ends. Indeed the narrative of faith, sacrifice, redemption and assumption or beatification is the common model for autothanatographies. An anti-model, which still uses the myths of religion for its own ends, is Sartre's *Les Mots* (Words). It is worth examining this text not only as a parodied delegitimation, but as an anti-gospel, similar to the anti-myths of Mary which I discuss in Chapters 2 and 3. It establishes the priesthood of the writer even as it derides the tradition. The notorious power of others over the signature may be seen in terms of either crucifixion or beatification. In short, by exposing the myths of apotheosis *Les Mots* also uses them to its own ends, just as it exploits, while claiming to subvert, the law of the Father.

Theories and discourses

The studies which follow, after this first attempt at formulating theories of illegitimacy and the way in which they are interwoven with myth, will first consider some of the historical contexts in which such myths originate. Arising from this, there will be a critical examination of the relationship between psychoanalytic theories of the family and the 'family romance', and the narratives which engender them and which they engender. This will necessitate an assessment of some of the presuppositions behind the theories of the law of the Father and the name of the Father.

The case history of the 'female genealogy' of George Sand's family will be used to chart the movement in attitudes within one family from the seventeenth-century acceptance of patriarchally sanctioned illegitimacy, through the shift in values of the late eighteenth and early nineteenth centuries. This culminated, in Sand's case, in a deliberate personal delegitimation which asserted a woman's right to sexual and financial independence, but which ended in relegitimation and social conformity. This also leads into the very important distinction between illegitimacy as an oppositional force, contained by society but nevertheless individually enabling, and illegitimacy as a contribution to a revolutionary force that demands justice by changing the laws of society itself.

Three different revolutionaries are studied in detail. Resemblances between them, such as their sex and their status as bastards, merely emphasise the very different ways in which they write their exclusion. The variety of their lived experience, and of their mythical *mises en scène*, is matched by the varied forms taken by their entry into the symbolic, and the extraordinary heteroglossia of their discourses. Olympe de Gouges, hampered by her illiteracy and her need to use a scribe, chooses to express herself in the oral immediacy of theatrical dialogue and public rhetoric, and, in the process, makes the extraordinary protofeminist discovery of the power of linguistic gender-substitution to subvert man-made laws. Flora Tristan takes the 'Way of the Cross', and adapts her illiterate oral verve to the Saint-Simonian heretical discourses of friends like Constant and Ganneau as she produces her utopian visions and final transfiguration of both woman and bastard. Louise Michel, the most educated of the three, is the most radical in both action and discourse, fragmenting the structures of the patriarchal narrative, just as her faith in anarchy demands the fragmentation of patriarchal society.

The next section will move on from the socially excluded to the self-excluded, from the bastards to the *faux bâtards*, as the French call those who choose this form of delegitimation, and, perhaps not coincidentally, from female texts to male texts. Three case studies of those who chose the way of the mother, and, in different ways, the name of the mother, also reveal three very different modes of discourse, from the fragmentation and experiments with time shifts of Stendhal's *Vie de Henry Brulard* (Life of Henry Brulard) to the elegant irony of the young

13

Baudelaire/Dufaÿs, and then to the luxuriant anti-gospel of Sartre's *Les Mots*. All three are united in their vehement rejection not only of the father figures in their lives, but of bourgeois patriarchal structures.

Moving into the twentieth century, we also return, oddly enough, to one of the most ancient themes of bastardy, the literature of revenge. It is the form their revenge takes that distinguishes the writing of Genet and of Leduc. They dismember the name of the mother, her memory, the gender she bequeathed them, the society she left them in, but at the same time their painfully acquired mastery of the symbolic gives them the freedom to dismember, even more dramatically, the master tongue itself and the law of the Father.

Finally, I want to look at the critical discourse which is marked by what I call 'delegitimation by proxy'. The *locus classicus* seems to me the extraordinary self-identification of Sartre with Genet. Surely it must be unique in the annals of literature that the first volume of a writer's work should be written by another writer, yet Sartre's *Saint Genet* is sold as volume I of the *Complete Works of Jean Genet*, apparently with Genet's permission. The self-bastardisation it implies interiorises Sartre's rejection of bourgeois values, while at the same time the writing never escapes from the tradition of elegant academic discourse, in which he had been so carefully reared. As so often in the interwoven careers of Sartre and de Beauvoir, the whole phenomenon is paralleled in a series of delegitimations by proxy which mark Simone de Beauvoir's life and works, culminating in her strange master–mistress literary relationship with Violette Leduc. A more purely textual, but equally involved, identification is to be found in the Derrida/Hegel/Genet flowering and exfoliation of *Glas*. All these creative/critical works are yet another form of the ritual performance of exclusion.

All the writers I study have one thing in common: they want to have something of a liminal quality, to go beyond the limitations of their own gender, while retaining its advantages, and to enjoy the benefits of a double or multiple experience. The highly revealing entry in the large Robert dictionary, giving both *abâtardir* (to bastardise) and *efféminer* (to feminise) as the antonyms of *viriliser* (to virilise), shows not only the popular view of such a procedure, but also the perception of double gendering as a form of contamination, of creating the 'monster' constituted by the virile woman or the feminine man.

In writing illegitimacy and in defying the penalties of delegit-imation to seek its benefits, we see both men and women exploiting this multiplicity and doubleness and adopting a heteroglossia which includes shifts between different forms of gender-coded language, but also shifts in practices of naming. The signatures of these bastards and would-be bastards reflect the freedom, the 'illegitimacy' of the pseudonym, as well as the genealogy of difference of the matronym. As Laugaa remarks:

thinking of the genesis of the text in terms of the biological and symbolic model of a birth and a recognition (*naissance et reconnaissance*), the author projects him or herself into familial roles, occupying in turn the position of father, of mother, but also of child. This rotation of ages and sexes, these possible inversions of origin, are active in the practice of the pseudonym.

(1986: 292)

Personal myths, at first only private *mises en scène*, assume a new importance when incorporated in narrative which reaches the public domain. They are fed into the signature, since, as we have seen, a name always contains a story. The signature then assumes a life of its own, taking over more and more control as the interaction between author and reader comes into effect. Some personal myths derive only from obsessions springing from private traumas, but others are daydreams bred from social myth, one modern version of which is the psychoanalytic narrative. The interaction between social myth, personal myth and psychoanalytic myth will be the subject of the next chapter.

2

Myth and psychoanalysis: legitimate and illegitimate

A myth is originally not a fantasy or a falsity, but a narrative verified by faith, forming part of a corpus and reinforced by ritual. The corpus is tightly bound into culture and social structure which are legitimated by the narratives, just as the narratives are reconfirmed by ideology. Certain mythical structures, such as those of the major religions, still fulfil these criteria and function as living structures of public belief. In the present age, it is also generally agreed to admit to mythical status those obsessive narratives which spring from the unconscious and assume the role of personal systems of belief.

I am looking at the use of social and personal myth for three different purposes. The first and best known is that of the *legitimation* of social structures and traditions, a legitimation which often sees the imposition of founding narratives as received truths. In our society the narratives which have been imposed as founding myths have been linked to a patriarchal, phallologocentric, tradition. Whether the exposition of these phantasmatic structures by Freud and Lacan has served to uphold or to undermine that tradition, christened by Lacan the law of the Father, is a matter of heated debate, even among feminists. What is undisputed is the legitimating role that claims made in the name of science have played in establishing as 'truths' what are basically *écrits*, to use Lacan's term, that is, often inspired mixtures of clinical findings with narrative and, indeed, poetry.

These narratives may give both public and private access to a form of 'truth' inaccessible to science; but to claim, as does Anzieu (1977: 34), that Freud uses myth 'as a category to elucidate facts' is to remain strangely unaware of the necessarily

16

subjective role of the interpreter in such elucidation. In a circular progression, the interpreter legitimates, and often imposes, a view of the world already controlled by upbringing and gendering, and remains, on his own say-so, a prey to all the forces of obsession and repression (see Brenkman, 1992: 924–5). We will look at the myth of Oedipus and the wider corpus of stories to which it belongs as such a legitimatory narrative, from both a Freudian and a non-Freudian perspective.

Second, the drive towards *relegitimation* is closely linked to legitimation. This is the impulse which prompts those excluded by birth, race or sex from the legitimating reign of the law of the Father to endeavour to find a way back into the fold. This can take simple forms, such as the search for a father or paternal recognition, or more complex ones, such as elaborate shifts in the gender of discourse or in orientation of action. The simplest form of relegitimation for a woman is by marriage; indeed Boose (Boose and Flowers, 1989: 21) claims that, from the patriarchal point of view, all daughters are to some extent 'illegitimate' and remain so till marriage. The adoption of male mentors and models of discourse is the form of relegitimation of which academic women, and women writers generally, are most often accused and, indeed, have most often found necesssary. The paradigmatic case of Elizabeth I of England (see Chapter 3) will give us a clear example of a drastic relegitimation, involving both birth and gender, by which to judge this recurring impulse in other case studies. On the other hand, the male may be relegitimated by reputation and valour as well as by parental recognition. A number of the myths of paternity I study may be read ambivalently. While they encode bastardy in one form or another, they also act to recuperate it back to the patriarchal fold. Thus they are ultimately relegitimatory in nature.

However, the greatest emphasis in future chapters will be given to the third aspect, the impulse towards *delegitimation,* which I have described as the public assumption of either actual or imaginary bastardy for political or artistic purposes. What is particularly obvious in such cases is the use made of the ambivalence of myth to set up models of anti-myth, and the deliberate deconstruction of a number of maternal myths to reveal the models of the way of the mother and the name of the mother hidden behind their apparently legitimatory façades. The better-known the myth, and the more intense the structure

of belief attached to it, the easier it is to use it subversively.[1]
For example, the narratives of the Virgin Mary and the anti-
narratives to which they have given rise are central to our study
and to the signifying system of myth in Europe. We will see how
they recur in the personal mythology of delegitimation.

THE TRADITIONAL MYTHOLOGY OF THE
EXCEPTION

Myth may be used for many purposes. The function of any
mythical story was, in the first instance, to bear the burden of
belief. To sustain faith, myths must have an open structure,
open to all the possibilities of ongoing interpretability. As we
have seen, a social myth cannot function as myth unless it forms
part of a narrative corpus which has been initially underpinned
by faith and ritual (see Vickery, 1966).

Humankind has always felt the need for myths of ex-
centricity, of decentredness and the exception, because both the
heroic and the divine are figures of liminality, excluded from the
ways of common humanity and familial norms. In the search of
the bastard for a founding myth, it is easy to find stories in all
cultures where illegitimacy is inscribed as a shift into liminality
itself. This is particularly so in the archetype of the birth of the
divine child, since the child is legitimated not by the name of the
Father in a human genealogy, but by supernatural, extra-human
forces, which can only be activated by his own efforts. The
account of the ex-centric takes the form, in this case, of a
recurring myth which Lord Raglan identifies with that of the
'Hero of Tradition'. The importance of the archetype is seen in
the extent of its spread. It occurs in widely similar forms
throughout the world, and forms part of a larger mythical
corpus in each case. Since these are stories of the superlative,
and often the divine, they are narratives of the border, the zone
between inclusion and exclusion, the god and the human, the
natural and the unnatural.

There have been two major attempts to formulate the basic
motifs of these stories (see Dundes, 1965: 142–57), that of Von
Hahn in *Sagwissenschaftliche Studien* (1876) and the well-
known essay of Lord Raglan (1934). I will set out in parallel
tables the sequences they found, in order to show their simi-
larities and differences, and to demonstrate how both sequences

enact a to and fro between delegitimation and relegitimation. As in most narrative structures, not all the elements of a sequence apply to every hero concerned.

Von Hahn includes fourteen heroes in his table, seven from Greece (Perseus, Heracles, Oedipus, Amphion, Pelias, Lycastos and Theseus, of whom only Oedipus was born legitimately – though in very unusual circumstances, to which we will return); three from Germany (Wittich, the Saxon Siegfried – legitimate, but born in foreign captivity – and Wolfdietrich); Romulus of Rome, Cyrus of Persia, Key Chosrew of Bactria, and, from Indian mythology, Karna and Krishna (legitimate, but born in foreign captivity). Their stories rate scores of from seven to fourteen of the elements of the hero tale, but all share the elements of the hero's father being absent or hostile, his mother being persecuted or suffering because of his birth, exposure, upbringing by foster-parents, and eventual conquest of a kingdom. However, all the heroes are reviled in the end, and die an extraordinary death.

Of the twenty-one heroes Raglan discusses, with the notable exception of Jesus, the score ranges from twenty-two for Oedipus to thirteen for Robin Hood. His list is Oedipus,* Theseus,* Romulus,* Heracles,* Perseus,* Jason, Bellerophon, Pelops, Asclepius, Dionysus, Apollo, Zeus, Joseph, Moses, Elijah, Siegfried,* Arthur, Nyikang, Watu Gunung, Llew Llan- gwyffes, Robin Hood. (Those who appear also in Von Hahn's list are starred.) To these we can add Cuchulain, Parsifal and Merlin.

Otto Rank, in his *Der Mythus von der Geburt des Helden* (The Myth of the Birth of the Hero) (1909), adds the following stories: Sargon, King of Agade (Babylon, 2800 BC), Abraham, Judas, St Gregory, King Dârâb of Persia, Paris, Telephos, Gilgamesh, Zethos, Jesus, Zoroaster, Amenophis III of Egypt, Lohengrin, Ion.

The absent father

Of course, in the end the protagonist is effectively legitimised by consecration as a hero, inclusion in the pantheon of myth, or apotheosis. What is notable, however, is that these are all myths of paternal absence, in most of which the child is educated either by the mother or by a foster-parent of a much lower social class,

	VON HAHN		RAGLAN
DELEGITIMATION	1 The hero is of illegitimate birth	1 His mother is a royal virgin
	2 His mother is a princess	2 His father is a king and
	3 His father is a god or a foreigner	3 often a near relative of his mother
	4 Signs warning of his ascendance	4 Circumstances of conception unusual
		5 Often reputed son of a god
	5 He is exposed at birth	6 At birth, attempt to kill him
	6 Suckled by animals	7 He is spirited away
	7 Brought up by childless shepherd couple	8 Reared by foster-parents
RELEGITIMATION	8 He is high-spirited	9 Nothing known of childhood
	9 Seeks service in foreign land	10 On reaching manhood, he returns or goes to future kingdom
	10 Returns victorious and goes back to foreign land	11 After victory over king, giant, monster . . .
	11 Slays original persecutors, rules country, frees mother	12 he marries a princess and
		13 becomes king
	12 Founds cities	14 For a time he reigns and
		15 prescribes laws
DELEGITIMATION	13 The manner of his death is extraordinary	16 He loses favour with the gods and/or his subjects
	14 He is reviled because of incest and dies young	17 Is driven from throne and city
	15 Dies at the hand of an insulted servant	18 Meets with mysterious death
	16 Murders younger brother.	19 often at top of a hill
		20 His children do not succeed him
		21 His body is not buried
		22 He has one or more holy sepulchres.

often in a foreign land. It is necessary for the child to become a creature of the boundary, living at the divide between male and female gendering, between high and low, between native and foreign, between human and animal (in the seven cases of those suckled by animals) or between human and divine. What is also noticeable is the ex-centric position with regard to the name of the Father. In most cases the child does not bear the name of his true father; if he is inscribed in a genealogy it is that of his 'social' father, and although he rules a city he does not pass the power on to his sons. Both the double fathering of the hero of tradition, by divine father and social father, or by the father who casts him out and the father who fosters him, and his mothering by a royal virgin then give rise to further myths of their own. Some are myths of fathering, some of mothering, but many involve extended kinship rather than just the nuclear family.

The most striking cases of double fathering by the divine father and the social father are those of Zeus and Amphitryon as the fathers of Heracles, and God and Joseph as the fathers of Jesus. Any doubts about fathering the child of another are assuaged in Amphitryon's case by Zeus himself and in Joseph's by an angel of the Lord (Matthew I: 20–1). In both cases the divine child is inscribed in the genealogy of the social father; in fact Jesus' inscription in Joseph's family genealogy, the so-called Tree of Jesse (Matthew I) was an important factor in establishing his claim to be the Messiah.[2] The honouring of the social father in myth can be read as recognition of the fact that in most cultures, and unless he takes formal steps to disavow them, the mother's husband is accepted as the father of her children despite any underlying uncertainty. It does not, of course, prevent the divine child repudiating the social father in his quest for the divine father (Luke II: 48–9).

The Virgin Mother

On the maternal side, in many original hero tales the rape or supernatural impregnation of a royal virgin is merely an opening motif in the narrative. However, mothers do play an unusually important part in these stories, particularly in the sub-group, such as the stories of Theseus, Wittich, Parsifal and Cuchulain, where the abandoned or excluded mother must rear the child alone. However, it is principally with the cult of the Virgin

Mary that the tale of the virgin mother develops an importance of its own and is added to and extended over several centuries until it becomes a hero tale in its own right, and a myth which testifies to the remarkable powers of faith.

The original information in the Gospels merely gives Mary a fairly traditional role in the hero narrative. She is a young woman, espoused but still a virgin, who is impregnated by the Holy Ghost. The husband-to-be is convinced by the Angel's word of the divinity of the child, whose birth is accompanied by prophecies. A threat to its life from an angry king drives the family into exile. The child shows precocious powers. Both Mary and Joseph are soon repudiated by Him in the name of the absent Father, and her role thereafter is one of silence and mourning.

It was not until the second century AD, with the *Pseudo-evangelium Jacobi* (or *Gospel of James*), that the tale of Mary was elaborated to fit the hero archetype. She was said to have herself been the fruit of a miraculous birth, a story based on the very considerable Biblical tradition of women past the age of child-bearing being granted a miraculous conception. (This was gradually incorporated officially and became the doctrine of the Immaculate Conception, recognised by the Pope in 1854.) This divinely sanctioned conception of the virgin and her mother's name, Anne (Hannah), are based on the story told in the Book of Samuel of Samuel's conception and birth (see Warner, 1976: 31). The inspiration for this appropriation comes from the Gospel of St Luke (II: 46–55) where Mary's 'Magnificat' 'echoes both Hannah's hymn and the paean of Miriam, the sister of Moses, who struck her timbrel and danced for joy with the women of Israel when Pharaoh and his army were swallowed up by the Red Sea' (Warner, 1976: 13; see also Chapter 7 below).

Mary (Mariam) was later accorded 'royal' status, because she was also considered by the Church Fathers to belong to the line of David: 'Joseph, the son of David, betrothes the daughter of David, because the child cannot be enrolled in the name of its mother' (cit. Warner, 1976: 20). This 'royalty' was developed to the extent that she was shown, admittedly with the child in her arms, as the last fruit of the (masculine) genealogy of Jesse.

The deep popular need for a female centre of faith, a myth to complement the purely male model of the divine, ensured the further growth of the legend. The motifs of the Virgin's genealogy, her miraculous birth and her model childhood were

22

developed in the tenth century in the *Golden Legend* of Voraginus and in the Latin verse of Hroswitha of Gandersheim. The cult of St Anne and *her* mother, Esmeria, developed, both verbally and iconically, into a remarkable series of matriarchal texts to which we will return. Indeed, as Warner and Pontalis both show, the image of the matriarchal line and myths of double mothering, where the mother's function is delegated to the grandmother, foster-mother or nurse, received considerable impetus from the myth of St Anne.

The miraculous aspects of medieval versions of the Virgin's life mainly centred around her purity (as when her virginity is miraculously restored after childbirth) and chastity. Her normal married life and procreation of other children, described in the Gospels, were explained away by the celibate Fathers of the Church, and replaced by a total purity and freedom from the taint of sex from her conception to her death. As a natural final step, she too was granted an Assumption and an Ascension to take her rightful place as Queen of Heaven.

The extraordinary development of the myth of the Virgin Mother, and the very fervour of the cult devoted to her, meant, as I have said, that it was easy for anti-myths to develop, using the same name or some of the narrative elements. We will see how her myth was used, or abused, politically by Elizabeth I of England, by the revolutionary cult of Marianne or by the socialist cult of God the Mother. The name Mary or Marie, and its variants, as the name of the Mother *par excellence*, constantly recurs in the texts of the writers I will be examining.

The two brothers

One other parallel myth and much earlier story of double mothering and miraculous birth, which was more consciously used as a social myth of bastardy, is that of Abraham's engendering of Ishmael by his servant Hagar, after his wife Sarah had proved infertile. Sarah's encouragement of this use of her handmaiden to give her a surrogate son[3] was held to license Abraham's adoption of the bastard, which Sarah intended to call her own. Many adoptions of natural children and, in some cultures, the procreation by one father of multiple families, hark back to this precedent. This is the myth to which the story of Leonardo's birth and adoption adheres most closely. Ishmael begins, as it were, the bad press given to bastards when the Lord tells the pregnant Hagar:

> Behold thou art with child, and shalt bear a son, and shalt call his name Ishmael, because the Lord hath heard thy affliction. And he will be a wild man; his hand will be against every man, and every man's hand against him, and he shall dwell in the presence of [opposed to] all his brethren.
>
> (Genesis XVI: 11–13)

Sarah's persecution of Hagar culminates in Hagar's expulsion with her child into the desert, after Sarah, the first in a long line of aged mothers blessed by God, gives birth to her own miraculous child, Isaac, at the age of ninety. While both Ishmael and Isaac are promised prosperity and progeny, only the descendants of the son of the right hand, Isaac, are to be the chosen people. The descendants of the first-born son of the left hand, Ishmael, are put beyond the pale. Thus, this story of would-be double mothering, which turns into bitter resentment, is the archetype for the enormous literature which centres around the upbringing of two brothers, illegitimate and legitimate. The myth is in itself ambivalent, and a narrative which derives from it may be one of jealousy and revenge or one of devotion. Indeed, narratives of double mothering or fathering tend to engender tales of unbridled hate or of passionate love. We will see examples of both in the chapters which follow.

THE FREUDIAN ATTEMPT TO UNIVERSALISE THE PARTICULAR

Oedipal variants

The important thing to remember about archetypal stories such as that of the miraculous child is that they breed innumerable variants which are themselves then assimilated into a mythological or ideological system. Thus Freud's construction of a new myth from selected motifs of the myth of Oedipus has found enormous acceptance, because it found an ideological fit within the system of nineteenth- and early twentieth-century patriarchy (see Brenkman, 1992: 929). We can, of course, read the myth and its variants otherwise and exploit other ambiguities in the system.[4] The point I am trying to make is that the ambivalence of myth encourages multiple reading and reading against the grain. A poor peasant may read the tale of Joan of Arc as a personal message, whereas we may merely recognise a variant of the hero tale. As Freud indicates (see p.29), a bastard has a different stake in tales of the miraculous child from that of the legitimate child, who merely uses it as a daydream.

If, for instance, we venture into the set of variants of which Sophocles' *Oedipus Rex* is one, we will find that Oedipus' father, Laius, in some variants, is seen as the founding father of homosexuality. In his second marriage, he refuses heterosexual intercourse and leaves his wife Jocasta a virgin until she gets him drunk and 'has her will of him'. Obviously, a very different picture of Laius emerges. Now Freud actually records an 'absurd' dream in which his father becomes drunk and is taken to the watch-house. This shameful event is followed by a marriage, as a result of which Sigmund is born (SE V: 435–7).[5] Is this merely a coincidental recurrence of an archetype, or did Freud repress the unwanted part of the Oedipus story, only to have it return in a dream?[6] As Monique Schneider points out, 'A child born of the nuptial drunkenness of the father can only appear as the radical antithesis of the child of the master' (1985: 249). She sees Freud as setting up an intellectual genealogy in which masters and disciples play out an Oedipal relationship. This construct is endangered by the sordid realities of human reproduction.

The drunkenness episode in the original myth is carried one step further in the variant which suggests that Oedipus was really the divine child of Dionysus. This brings his story into line with that of the miraculous child who returns to slay his persecutors, but produces an interpretation at wide variance with the Freudian one. In these variants, the conformity of the Oedipus story to that of 'the hero of tradition' becomes far clearer.

If we explore the polyphony of mythical variants, it becomes clear that the suggestion postulated, in the wake of Freud, by scholars like Didier Anzieu in *Oedipe avant le complexe, ou de l'interpretation psychanalytique des mythes* (1966) that there is *one* basic underlying myth, is totally incompatible with the very nature of mythical systems. According to Vernant and Vidal-Naquet, no two myths have identical meanings (and, we might add, nor have any two variants of the same myth). It may be possible (by Proppian analysis) to postulate a universal narrative *structure* in myth, but it is impossible to postulate a universal narrative *signification*. As Jean-Pierre Vernant remarks:

> If all myths . . . repeat one another, if synonymy is the law of the genre, mythology, in its diversity, can no longer constitute a signifying system. Impotent to say anything else than Oedipus, Oedipus over and over again, it no longer means anything.
>
> (1972: 84)

The same may be said of what I have called personal myths, recurring phantasms which constitute individual systems of belief. While personalised by the signature in individual cases, these seemingly phantasmic narratives which recur with compulsive frequency in both life and text, may also be seen as moments of re-presentation in a larger synchronic system. The compulsive recurrence, in condensed or displaced form, of elements of such a system in personal dreams and fantasies underpins the archetypal corpus in the same way as belief and ritual underpin the social and religious corpus, but this recurrence can only be interpreted in a specific context.

Freud and Leonardo

The example I intend to use to show that both personal phantasm and social myth can only be 'elucidated' and interpreted in a personal and gendered way, and in a historical and social context, is Freud's only major study of illegitimacy, *Leonardo da Vinci and a Memory of his Childhood* (1910) (SE XI: 59–138).[7] In this chapter I want to look at its relationship to narratives of illegitimacy and at the problems it encounters in applying the Oedipus complex to alternative family structures. In Chapter 10 I will look at the compulsive nature of the text (due only partly to the material on which it was based).[8] The later chapter will deal with the way in which Freud used a fictive Leonardo to cope with his personal desires and fears in what I call 'delegitimation by proxy', thus producing an example of almost pure mythopoesis.

However, it is still possible to read, behind the Freudian myth-making, and even more in the actual visual and verbal texts of Leonardo with which he is concerned, the traces of other myths and other ideological positions. I, for instance, studying the

26

mythology of illegitimacy, am struck by the amazing fit between Leonardo's story and that of the hero of tradition. Freud took no account of this, in spite of the fact that Otto Rank's *Myth of the Birth of the Hero* had appeared in 1909, under his aegis. Leonardo's illegitimate birth, his adoption into his grandfather's house and fostering in a wealthy environment from which his father was mostly absent, his ousting from his position as heir presumptive by late-born legitimate siblings, his indictment for sodomy, his accession to fame, his posthumous apotheosis and lack of progeny present us with a remarkably familiar pattern.

What makes Freud's study so interesting to me is not just his choice of material, as well as the contrast between his romanticising of bastardy on the one hand and his homophobia on the other, but the fact that so much of his compelling narrative has been factually invalidated that it becomes clear that we are dealing as much with self-analysis as with an analysis of Leonardo. Its very factual inaccuracy enables us to see, in this 1910 work, a critical fishing in troubled waters which has its roots as much in the unconscious need to identify with genius as one's other as it does in the process of 'scientific research'. *Leonardo da Vinci and a Memory of his Childhood* is revealing in this way, because subsequent research has shown that three of the major premises in this 'case study' are based on misinformation, mistranslation and inadequate checking of sources. These will be discussed at greater length in Chapter 10. The ones that mainly concern us here relate to naming and to parental relations.

On the only evidence available at the time, Freud postulates that Leonardo, after his illegitimate birth, remained with his natural mother, Caterina, for several years before being taken into the household of his father, Ser Pietro da Vinci, to be fostered by his father's wife, Donna Albiera, and his father's mother, Monna Lucia da Vinci. He is therefore able to paint a remarkably moving picture of an intense sensual attachment between the single mother and her child, a bond which lasted several years. This is now proved to be a phantasmatic construction, telling us little about Leonardo but a great deal about the role of fantasy in Freudian wish-fulfilment and his intense personal desire for that imagined sexual union with the mother, a desire which underlies his development of the

Oedipus theory. Subsequent research has shown that Leonardo was taken into his *grandfather's* household very early, probably fulfilling the 80-year-old's need for a male grandchild, but also as a proof of his father's virility, since there had already been one childless marriage. The child was removed from his mother when a few months old,[9] and she soon married and had a legitimate child (P: 28).

Tales, tails and taboos

It was pointed out as early as 1923 (P: 30) that a large part of Freud's elaborate analysis of the childhood memory is based on a mistranslation. The English translation of the passage from the notebooks as it reads in SE XI: 82 is:

> It seems that I was always destined to be so deeply concerned with vultures [should be hawks or kites]; for I recall as one of my very earliest memories that while I was in my cradle a vulture [hawk] came down to me, and opened my mouth with its tail, and struck me many times with the tail against [should be within] my lips.

The German text he used gave *Geier* or 'vulture', as the translation of *nibio*, 'hawk' or 'kite', which was the name of the bird in the original Italian. Now Freud sees two phantasmatic layers in this memory. The first is homosexual in nature, seeing the *coda* or 'tail' as an accepted symbolic substitute for the penis; and the tail fluttering against the lips as a suggestion of *fellatio* – 'within my lips', makes this even stronger, as Freud notes himself (SE XI: 86). The homosexual nature of this memory/fantasy is, of course, even more strongly supported by the fact that the bird concerned is the hawk, an emblem of virility, or the kite with its 'long, forked tail' (ed. note; ibid.: 86).

It is Freud's second phantasmatic layer that is completely undermined by the mistranslation. Building on the fact that the vulture was an Egyptian mother-goddess, Mut, he constructs an elaborate narrative edifice whereby the bird's tail, while essentially phallic, also represents the lost nipple and the overlong breast-feeding which introduced the child to a paradise he was unable to forget.[10] As we have seen, this fantasy too has been disproved. It is rather a pity in a way, since it leads Freud to an interesting hypothesis concerning the way in which Leonardo's illegitimacy worked on his imagination:

> We can now reconstruct the origin of Leonardo's vulture phantasy. He once happened to read in one of the Fathers or in a book on natural history the statement that all vultures were females and could reproduce their kind without any assistance from a male: and at that point a memory sprang to his mind, which was transformed into the phantasy we have been discussing, but which meant to signify that he also had been such a vulture-child – he had had a mother, but no father. With this memory was associated, in the only way in which impressions of so great an age can find expression, an echo of the pleasure he had had at his mother's breast. The allusion made by the Fathers of the Church to the idea of the Blessed Virgin and her child – an idea cherished by every artist – must have played its part in helping the phantasy to appear valuable and important to him. Indeed in this way he was able to identify himself with the child Christ, the comforter and saviour not of this one woman alone.
>
> (SE XI: 90)

It is not clear to me why the fantasy of the vulture is needed to introduce the other (far more common) fantasy of identification with the divine child, but of course Freud was treading on very dangerous ground in 1910. At that time, and especially in Vienna, not only the position and hieratic narratives of the Church but also the great figures of art were considered sacrosanct. As if it were not shocking enough to discuss Leonardo's sexual tendencies, Freud then goes on to suggest a subversive, if repressed, identification with the divine child as a factor in paintings which were, and are, regarded as the most perfect representations of maternal love. One needs only to recall that, many years later, in 1934, Lord Raglan does not dare to mention Christ in his account of the multiple versions of the birth of the divine child who becomes the 'hero of tradition', although the omission leaves a hole in his argument which positively demands to be filled. It then becomes apparent that Freud's outspokenness must have caused real consternation in his own time, as must Rank's inclusion of Jesus in his list of mythical heroes.[11]

The rights and wrongs of the father

It seems that certain narratives of illegitimacy impose themselves on Freud, in spite of the efforts he makes to have Leonardo's story conform to the Oedipal pattern. His efforts lead him into some notable internal contradictions, but also some penetrating insights. However, there are some very pertinent questions about the nature of Oedipal structures which are not even mentioned by Freud. They are raised by Leonardo's relationship not to a single, neglectful father, but to no fewer than three father figures: the aged grandfather at Vinci, the absent father in Florence, and the ambiguous figure of his uncle Francesco, only sixteen years older, with whom he was brought up, and who loved him enough to insist on leaving Leonardo his property, in the teeth of family opposition (Eissler, 1961: 95). One might equally well ask whether this very positive relationship, rather than the lack of a father figure, as Freud suggests, was at the root of Leonardo's homosexuality.

In the same way, an Oedipal rivalry is evoked to account for Leonardo's love of display and extravagance, the need 'to out-herod Herod',[12] while at the same time Leonardo's reluctance to finish his works, or even to paint at all, is seen as a neurotic result of paternal absence: 'He created them [his works] and then cared no more about them, just as his father had not cared about him' (SE XI: 121). In view of this reading, it is all the more remarkable when, a few pages further on, Freud makes an unusual statement in regard to the positive benefits a lack of a father may bring:[13]

> In most other human beings – no less today than in primaeval times – the need for support from an authority of some sort is so compelling that the world begins to totter if that authority is threatened. Only Leonardo could dispense with that support; he would not have been able to do so had he not learnt in the first years of his life to do without his father. His later scientific research, with all its boldness and independence, presupposed the existence of infantile sexual researches uninhibited by his father, and was a prolongation of them with the sexual element excluded.
>
> (SE XI: 122–3)

This rare admission, which raises yet more questions since it discounts any form of *maternal* or grandparental authority, leads into the even more tendentious remark that Leonardo's refusal of all religion was also a consequence of this lack of a need to rely on paternal authority, and on the absence of 'paternal intimidation'.

In fact, only the Freudian postulate that Leonardo is unique of his kind can prevent some very awkward questions being asked about the universal nature of the Oedipus complex and, more particularly, about its applicability in social and historical contexts quite unlike that in which Freud lived and wrote. As Eissler shows (1961: 94–103), Leonardo's main source of resentment was not paternal neglect. It had two bases, both due to the strict social adherence in Florentine society to the conventions of the legitimate name of the father. One of these, fortunately enough, prevented his adopting his father's profession. When Ser Piero apprenticed him to Verrocchio, it was partly because the poor status of the guild of artists opened it to the illegitimate, as witness the bastardy of Alberti, Ghiberti, Giorgione and Filippino Lippi. Leonardo went to great lengths to endeavour to improve that image of his profession. The other, the source of great bitterness, prevented the natural child from inheriting and handed the patrimony over to his late-born siblings. This is the 'concealed and suppressed' element behind the notebook entry of his father's death:

> On July 9, 1504, Wednesday at 7 o'clock died Ser Piero da Vinci, notary at the palace of the Podestà, my father, at 7 o'clock. He was 80 years old, and left 10 sons and 2 daughters.
>
> (SE XI: 119)

Freud's remarkable statement that Leonardo might have written 'my poor father' but for 'affective inhibition' (ibid.: 120) is a wonderful example of ignoring both the social and the familial context and substituting an agenda of his own. It is as though Freud were capable of recognising the psychological effects of bastardy but incapable of relating them to the wide variations of cultural expectations and family structures.

Depicting the mother

Freud's personal expectations of mothering also governed his story, and, just as in so many of Freud's Oedipal narratives, the

familial and social situation of the nineteenth-century bourgeoisie is seen to impose itself on a quite different context.
Given the few facts we have, it is just as easy to postulate an
equally plausible narrative of a resentful and embittered girl,
sexually active and only too happy to give up an unwanted
child,[14] as it is to believe in the maternal symbiosis of the
Freudian dream (SE XI: 107). Such a hypothesis would also
bring into question some more general fantasies about mothers
and motherhood.

Freud's assumption that the foster-mother was good and
tender bears even less relation to the facts, since Leonardo was
brought up at Vinci while his father and stepmother lived in
Florence (see Eissler, 1961: 94ff.).[15] As for the grandmother
who did bring him up, the belief that she was 'no less good
and tender towards him than grandmothers usually are' (SE XI:
140–1)[16] is pure wishful thinking. It is just as naive as the belief
that these two women cared for him personally, when, in a
wealthy household of that period, the task would have been
delegated to a nurse. This is especially likely because the child
was taken in not long after the second marriage, when Donna
Albiera had not yet proved to be sterile. Freud's hypothesis is
that the son was only adopted because of that sterility, yet
Donna Albiera died in childbirth.

However wrong his facts are, Freud's intuitions are right in
stressing the importance, at both mythic and psychological levels,
of a childhood divided between natural and adoptive parents.
Certainly a theme of double mothering is present in the two
versions of *Santa Anna Metterza* (St Anne, the Virgin and Child)
as well as in the *Virgin of the Rocks*, and the relative age of the
two figures of St Anne and the Virgin would support Freud's
claim that Leonardo was consciously or unconsciously representing the pair of his natural mother and his father's young bride
rather than the conventional maternal trinity of grandmother,
mother and child.[17] We may ask, however, what this representation of double mothering tells us about Leonardo's relationship
with his grandmother. With our present knowledge, it is apparent
that his dream of tenderness and beauty was triggered by maternal
absence rather than maternal presence. The really startling and
significant thing about both versions of the *Santa Anna Metterza*
(in Paris and in London) is the *absence* of the very figure who is
obligatory in the genre, the dominating older woman. Why, we

may wonder, are the absent mothers present, and the presence of the grandmother absent, from such a central icon?

In fact, the tracing of the 'Mona Lisa smile' back to an infatuation with the over-cherished and cherishing single mother, Caterina, is a pure figment of the Freudian imagination. On the evidence, it is equally likely to have come from one of Leonardo's beautiful boys.[18] Yet, whatever my reservations, Freud's study is important for my purposes because it does highlight the name of the mother, and the fact that this is one of the few female names to recur in Leonardo's notebooks. Of the several mentions of a Caterina, the most telling is the detailed enumeration of her funeral expenses (SE XI: 104). Whether this was a result of love or hate, of reverence or guilt, we will never know, and, as Eissler remarks, it is really irrelevant whether this Caterina were the mother herself or a servant of the same name and age (1961: 88–93). The name itself bears the trace of an important relationship, as Freud rightly saw, and as he was the first to stress.

The mother in her own right

The essay also raises the question of the relationship of the child to maternal authority, to the single mother and, indeed, to the mother as woman, a whole person and not just a sexual and sensual love object. Yet one must realise that the image of the Freudian mother passively engrossed in her child and separated from *him* only by the patriarchal demands of the father is too limited to fit the patterns of other epochs and classes. In the numerous families where a child is brought up without a father, there remains a series of divisions, each necessary to the formation of the self. Each of these moments is experienced as a maternal rejection. Some of these forms of rejection may appear not only as the betrayal of the son on which Freud insists, but as a role model to the daughter.

1 The ejection of the child from uterine security. There is no need to add to the vast literature on this subject.
2 The possible removal of the child from the care of its natural mother, temporarily, as in fostering or wet-nursing; permanently, as in adoption. This is very common in the case of illegitimate birth.
3 Weaning by the mother or her substitute, which is always accompanied by the application of maternal authority in two

more basic fields, toilet-training and education in language, the mother tongue.

4 The reassertion by the mother of her own sexuality. This necessary rejection is not merely a function of paternal dominance, nor does the absence of the natural father ensure that the child is spared this 'trauma'. Young mothers, from Leonardo's mother Caterina through to Berthe Leduc in our case studies, have needs and demands which are not exclusively fulfilled through their children.

This trauma is often accompanied for the boy by another as he becomes aware of the answer to the question: 'Where do children come from?', which Freud sees as a key moment in sexual development. The male realisation of being unable to give birth is experienced as such a severe 'castration' that it is almost completely repressed, notably by Freud himself.[19] The girl, on the other hand, may experience her own potential as an empowerment, which compensates for the maternal rejection.[20]

5 The mother's need to return to her work. This is not merely some twentieth-century result of women's liberation, but the female condition for many peasants working in the fields, women returning to industry or domestic work, wives returning to their role as partner and shopkeeper. Often it meant complete separation from the child, who had to be entrusted to another. Complementary to this was the widespread custom in the Middle Ages, a practice continued much later in peasant societies, of sending the 7- or 8-year-old child away to another clan or family to be trained (see Ariès, 1973 and Sand, 1958).

These stages represent a progressive series of 'cuttings of the umbilical cord', each of which can engender myths, and most of which must be undergone by all children, whatever their family situation. In considering the widely applicable and influential Freudian myths of the 'lost paradise', the 'Oedipal situation' and the 'family romance', we will also try to take this series, and the mother's existence as woman and card-carrying member of the human race, into account.

Non-Oedipal models

The perception of the Oedipal story as a narrative variant rather than a universal model leads one to question whether there are, as Freud claims, underlying psychic 'truths' from which spring narratives, such as myths, or whether, rather, psychoanalysis convinces because it is a form of story-telling. Donald Spence (1982) and François Roustang (1983) have examined this relationship of psychoanalytic narratives to 'truth'. If the narrative produced by the psychoanalytic *mise en scène* (Leclaire, 1968: 174) contrives a satisfying 'fit' between the narratives of the analysee and the analyst, then perhaps the emotional value of the final 'fitting' story is more important than its role in establishing 'facts', which, being in the realm of the unconscious, are unavailable in the last resort. It is possible that the undeniable emotional relevance of Freud's Oedipus narrative to so many nineteenth-and twentieth-century men has produced a willingness to make it an emotional shoe to fit every foot.

Nevertheless, the overview of the different myths, archetypes and fictional narratives associated with the name of the mother shows that it is limiting and ideologically reductive to endeavour to present family experience in the light of the single myth of Oedipus. The stereotype of the legitimate bourgeois family, consisting of active father, passive mother and two or more sibling children, is a relatively recent creation. In certain epochs and social groups, for instance, the presence of two parents has been the exception rather than the norm. Bastards, orphans, foster-children, multiple family groupings, all require variable archetypes and live and dream different phantasms. This is not to detract from the seminal role of Freud's perceptions of sexual mythology and of those of Freudian *epigonen* such as Lacan and Kristeva. A major problem for psychoanalysis, however, has been a lack of historical and anthropological contextualisation. A danger in many analysts' synchronic world-view is the assumption that one's own patterns and those of one's class and gender, even of one's particular family, are universal.

I am inclined to believe, along with a substantial body of anthropologists and psychoanalysts, including Malinowski, Roheim, Reich, Deleuze and Guattari (see Anzieu, 1977) that the nuclear family is 'a functional formation depending on the structure and the culture of a given society' (Malinowski, cit. Anzieu, 1977: 86). To take one example, one must go back to earlier cultures to find a myth applicable to the situation, commonplace among the upper classes in a great part of Europe for centuries, where the newborn baby was taken from its mother and given to a wet-nurse (or, in an era of bottle-feeding, to child-minder or servant).[21] This child, like Oedipus himelf, often had little or no contact with its real/natural mother or father precisely in those formative years on which the Freudian hypothesis is based. A variety of different narratives resulted. Margaret Miles's 'The Virgin's One Bare Breast: Female Nudity and Religious Meaning in Tuscan Early Renaissance Culture' (in Suleiman, 1986) is one of the few works even to consider these problems and relate them to a body of art. In religious iconography, the faithful reflection of popularly accepted mythical patterns, but also, as Miles points out, of ideological attempts to influence those patterns, we can see the reflection of other familial myths. The historical role of the myth of St Anne, which we examine in Chapter 3, provides a similar approach to the extended family, the most common form until quite recent eras.

The discourse of psychoanalysis itself is conditioned by shifting ideologies of class, of gender and of religion. The danger is always that the observer or the analyst will assume the universality of their own experience. Medieval assumptions of rampant and uncontrollable wifely sexuality, for example, contrast quaintly with the Freudian picture of the passive or frigid wife. The social context which gave birth to stories like 'Hansel and Gretel', and in which peasant families were forced to abandon children in times of famine (see Grimmer, 1983: 213–39), would provide a very different reading of the tale from the frisson of the secure bourgeois child with a little Oedipal resentment to get out of his system. It is notable that even a very necessary corrective to the Oedipal scenario like Christiane Olivier's *Les Enfants de Jocaste* (Jocasta's Children) (1980) still tends to universalise from the experience of a limited and fairly homogeneous social group. Olivier's discussion of womb envy[22] as the complementary myth to the notorious penis envy finds ample textual evidence to support it (see Chapter 7). However her assumptions about the animosity of mother–daughter relations and the sexuality of mother–son relations seem posited on a heterosexual stereotype which would not be confirmed by the psychoanalytic experience of, for example, Luce Irigaray (1974).

THE PRIVATE USES OF MYTHOLOGY

The family romance

The same limitations apply to Freud's other major contribution to the discussion of bastardy, the 1909 essay on 'The Family Romance of the Neurotic' (SE IX: 236–41), and to the considerable literature it has generated. The first stage of the family romance occurs when the very young child, still unaware of sexual differentiation, becomes resentful of parental domination. He (or she – though, according to Freud, girls are less prone to aggressive daydreams) creates a fantasy of being a foundling or adopted child, born of parents of far higher social status than those he resents. In fact this daydream would appear, from anecdotal evidence, to be as common among girls as among boys. I would also dispute Freud's contention that the basis of the 'family romance' is mainly sexual. It occurs precisely at the age (a very early one) at which the child becomes aware of the advantages of wealth and social status.

The second stage is reached when the child becomes aware of sexual difference, *and* of the fact that 'he realizes that "*pater semper incertus est*", while the mother is "*certissima*"' (SE IX: 239). While this may be a traumatic moment for the 'he' who grasps the principle of the uncertainty of paternity for the first time, there is no mention of the effect on 'his' female equivalent. We may see the pairing of male and female desires and fears associated with the 'certainty' of parentage in that other homology of the phantasm or archetype, the folksong. The satisfaction of free-ranging male sexuality appears to be stated in each stanza of an old English song in which a father appeals to the incest taboo to forbid his daughter's marriage with every boy she mentions, because:

> I hate to tell you, daughter,
> What your mother never knew,
> But Johnny (etc. etc.) is a son of mine
> And so he's kin to you.

The triumphant and comic reversal at the end is not only the female's revenge, but also the revelation of female desire. The daughter goes to her mother with her troubles, only to be reassured:

He's not the one who sired you
So marry whom you will.

This popular narrative provides a needed corrective to Freud's male-centred perspective. It also makes his omissions more remarkable. There is no discussion in this essay of the trauma and feelings of inadequacy that the uncertainty about fathering might induce in the male child, the argument simply moves straight on to the bastard fantasy. In this, the child delegitimates himself by imagining his mother unfaithful in order to provide himself with a father of princely status. We may add, in view of the sort of textual evidence discussed in later chapters, the question of whether a child, reared not only on fairy tales but on regular church attendance, might not also fantasise a father of divine status.

Finally, in a reversal of this delegitimatory pattern, the child may relegitimate himself by fantasising the delegitimation of his siblings, whom he imagines born of adulterine unions, while he alone is his father's rightful heir.

We may well speculate, as with the Oedipus story, how far this model is generally applicable, and how gender, family structure and illegitimacy affect it. It raises the same problems. We must ask whether narrative itself, here based on the early dissemination and influence of Grimms' tales, may be seen as a founding metaphor in Freud's thought, or whether it is the founding metaphor, the phantasm, that produces narrative. Freud's assumption is that a deep-seated desire to improve the status of one's parents, and especially one's father, or better still to dispose of him, gives rise to wish-fulfilment fantasies in the mould of the narrative of the 'Hero of Tradition'. Another possibility, however, is that the diet of simplified mythology and bowdlerised wonder tales, on which bourgeois children (like myself many years later) were brought up, was in itself the source of the fantasies.

A similar problem is raised by Marthe Robert's excellent and influential work *Roman des origines et origines du roman* (The Novel of Origins and the Origins of the Novel) (1976) and of Otto Rank's *Der Mythus von der Geburt des Helden* (The Myth of the Birth of the Hero) (1909), on which it is based. In these works myths of illegitimacy are seen only as phantasmatic by-products of the male bourgeois child's experience of a stable and

hence emprisoning family situation. The recurrence of the structures of desire which lead a male child to fantasise himself as a
foundling free of both unwanted siblings and parental limitations is certainly incontrovertible. Robert's equation of the
dream of the mysterious birth of the foundling with the impulse
to create a world which retreats to the maternal sphere, a lost
paradise from which sexuality is excluded, fits with a certain
historical period and a certain ideology of female passivity. It
suits novels such as *Le Grand Meaulnes* (1913) to perfection.[23]
However, it takes no account of the child involved in active
matriarchal structures or of the quite different fantasies of
female children even in a patriarchy. Indeed it elides another
possible Freudian interpretation, which equates the fantastic
not with an asexual paradise (Robert, 1976: 128), but with the
highly sexualised domain of polymorphous perversion and of
multiple and mutable shapes and desires (see Jackson, 1981).

Even more debatable is Robert's identification of the source of
realist fiction with fantasies of maternal guilt and of an unknown, all-powerful father. Her version of the phantasm of the
Bastard is worth quoting, if only because it exemplifies mythology in action. The myth common to both Greek and Judaeo-
Christian ideology whereby creative power is virile paternal
power, and woman only 'the chosen vessel', and in which that
creative power can only be acquired by the son overcoming the
father, becomes in this version the founding narrative of realism:

> The *mysterious* birth of the Foundling was of no use to him
> [the realist writer] in this situation, but as soon as he
> exchanges it for the *shameful* and *glorious* birth of the
> Bastard – glory and shame here are identical – one con-
> firms the other – he takes a personal role in the intimate
> process of engendering, he is the one who changes the
> bonds of blood, creates family relationships, 'competes
> with legitimacy', in short participates actively in the secret
> fabrication of life, like his father he peoples the world, but
> without the limitations of the flesh, like God.
>
> (Robert, 1976: 57–8)

This remarkable piece of mythologisation is, of course, only one
fiction, one possible narrative among others. We find ambivalent
and complementary scenarios for realist writers even in the
classic case of Balzac, who, on the one hand, indulges in

positively Strangelovian fantasies of the retention and accumulation of his virile powers and, on the other, seeks metaphoric access to the female realm of gestation and reproduction.[24]

At about the same time as Robert is universalising the mythological scenarios of Freud and Rank, Charles Mauron is producing an equally valid but opposite psychoanalytic supposition, whereby the individual childhood trauma is turned by creative writers into a recurring mythic scenario. His *Des Métaphores obsédants au mythe personnel* (From Obsessive Metaphors to Personal Myth) (1972) sees phantasms as individual rather than archetypal. The truth is somewhere between the two. Personal scenarios are multiple, ever-changing and polysemous, but they tend, as I have tried to show, to cannibalise mythical and archetypal elements which are useful to the personal scenario and which enable an ongoing autography. One must also take into account the relation between personal experience, ideological discourse and mythical discourse in different periods.

Gender and matricide

Difference in gender and gendering is another obvious change in contextualisation which must be taken into account when extending the possibilities of both the Oedipal pattern and the family romance. There is a very useful discussion in Marianne Hirsch, *The Mother Daughter Plot*, which questions the acceptance of Freudian patterns in such recent works on narrative as Peter Brooks's *Reading for the Plot* (1984). Most of her work is understandably devoted to the matricide in effigy common in the fiction of nineteenth- and early twentieth-century women writers who needed to achieve personal liberation from the law of the Father, and to the well-known problem of maternal reinforcement of that law. Only briefly, at the end of her work, does she consider what new myths and models the children of already liberated women or of strong single mothers might adopt. As she says: 'But for the suppressed mother–daughter connection to make its way into fiction, either the Oedipal patterns of plot would have to be reimagined and transformed or Oedipal paradigms abandoned altogether' (1989: 67). In particular, when discussing the Freudian family romance pattern, she sees its nineteenth-century female equivalent as a sort of reversed Oedipus: 'The Freudian family romance pattern clearly implies that women need to kill or eliminate their mothers from their lives, if they are not to resign themselves to a weak imagination' (ibid.: 56). The evidence to support this contention includes the fact that the Brontës, George Eliot, Elizabeth Gaskell and Elizabeth Barrett Browning were all motherless. I find the list interesting, although I am not sure that Mary Shelley, dominated by and devoted to her dead mother, makes a good addition. It does seem clear, however, that the mother a daughter needs to kill in effigy is the one who has been conditioned into rigid enforcement of patriarchal conventions. Feminists also need to admit that matriarchy can breed tyrants, and that any form of power can lead to excess. However, one needs to look at the contrasting list of the women I deal with in some of my case studies to see that the matricidal pattern is not universal, even in the nineteenth century. All the women writers I deal with were devoted to their mothers, who were alive during their daughters' maturity – although George Sand may be said to have burned what she adored. It is at least interesting to speculate how far this very different pattern is due to the father's absence.

However, all these women had to live through and outgrow their first attachment to a form of family romance, which, in the case of the bastard or of the socially ex-centric, is invariably one of *relegitimation*. To provide an example of mythological proportions of the relegitimation not only of a proclaimed bastard, but of a female to boot, one has only to look at the example of Queen Elizabeth I of England,[25] which will be used as an important case study in the following chapter on myth in history. She was able not only to assume the name but to use the law of the Father.

The bastard does not need to fantasise a missing father: he already exists. Particularly if that father is already known to be of higher social status, he is mythologised, and, when his rejection or death is found to be irretrievable, other male mentors may be called on to take his place. The final delegitimation and assumption of the name and of the way of the mother is the last and most difficult stage, which only certain bastards achieve and fewer still put into writing. We will be examining this sequence in detail in the case studies which follow.

The way of the mother

If, for both men and women, the mastering of patriarchal power and the law of the Father is a means of relegitimation, there exists in the last resort that other entry into creative power by delegitimation which I have called the way of the mother. Instead of the schizoid divisions and rigid gendering of conventional social codes, delegitimation involves a conscious exploitation of difference and multiplicity. My argument runs something like this: one can look at naming, and hence at genealogy, in two ways, either as the conventional male genealogy: a direct line, the male name, law, the arbitrary, convention; or one can look at it in terms of a female genealogy: a line of flight, in which the name of the mother, because it constantly shifts sideways, and can never be grasped, is the ground of *différance* and not merely of absence.

What illegitimacy does, by making the line of flight tangible and by breaking the continuity, is to actualise transgression, but also to point to a way of using drift for one's own purposes. So one can argue that matriarchy merely substitutes another form of the symbolic order in its law, whereas illegitimacy, especially when not socially integrated, offers a genuine discontinuity. This is why the first impulse of the bastard is always towards relegitimation, since the advantages of transgression are seldom immediately perceptible.

As we have seen, examples of both tendencies may be found in the stories universal to humankind but also particular to our own individual upbringing. Early listening to often-repeated oral tales is but the first step in the assimilation of a long line of mythical texts, historical, religious and political as well as literary, on which we base our own 'indirect' mythical discourse. Myths of ex-centricity, of boundaries and extremes, of inclusion and exclusion, encourage the enactment, in discourse or in life, of the belief that the exception can always overcome the rule.

3

Mythical histories, historical myths

If myth can be seen as one of the structures of desire, as when the ancient mythical accounts of exclusion are adapted to the new faiths of psychoanalysis, myth is equally, and necessarily, both a social orientation and a social justification.[1] Now we move on from the would-be synchronic to the more diachronic dimension of mythopoesis. To each his or her myth. Each *mise en scène* in the performance of life or the performance of death requires different key narratives. What is important to remember is that the choice of narrative and the uses to which it is put depend not just on personal experience but on the social and historical context which determines and mediates the discourse of both addressor and addressee. Different historical periods breed new myths, but there is also a stock of archetypal stories which resurface with changes in social and cultural conditions. Attitudes to culture are reflected not just in the growth but in the revival of myth. For example, the myth of the divine child, which has just been examined in detail, occurs all over the world and in different historical epochs. We will find it recurring in different forms in the case studies which follow. But, as we have seen, early variants, which have been considered as mere literature, can gain new shape and new credence and come into fashion again, as cultural changes take place, or when they are reshaped in a powerful conceptual system such as the Freudian.

I want to look now at the social and personal exploitation of a series of myths and beliefs, some of which have persisted over centuries, while others have arisen or mutated in response to specific social pressures. The chapter follows a shift in social values and hence in the ideological uses of myths of bastardy.

In the earlier hierarchical order dominated by royal and noble lines, illegitimacy could either be positively valorised as proof of the father's wealth and virility or negatively valorised as the contamination of the patriarchal line. The suggestion of miraculous birth linked with illegitimacy, for example, maintains its aura of potency and lingers long after its ideological function of bolstering the usurpation of the structures of power has ceased to operate. However, as the egalitarian bourgeois order takes over after the French Revolution, there is a shift to a purely negative valorisation of illegitimacy as proof of the mother's shame. While the extreme polarisation characteristic of myths of the bastard continues to influence both social attitudes and the autographies of the illegitimate, it easily tips over into that other binary opposition which evaluates the masculine as positive and the feminine as negative. The very use of the patronym marks positive inclusion and that of the matronym negation and difference. An egalitarian order fears difference and endeavours to exclude it. Yet the very condemnation and exclusion of difference in the form of the illegitimate, and the mothers who give birth to them, creates a new maternal identity as a site for a critique of the order itself.

Particularly important for this study, and directly linked to questions of nomination, is the fact that representations of gender, reproduction and legitimacy change with changing power relations. As these representations change, so myths arise, are recycled or are modified to justify the resignifications which naturalise the cultural. For example, even in systems which are fundamentally patriarchal and in which all actual power belongs to the males, the relationship of gender to descent varies according to their adherence to the principle of *mater certa, pater semper incertus*, or 'maternity is the only certainty'. In Roman law, both males and females had the right to pass citizen status on to their children, whereas a law of Pericles made Athenian citizenship dependent on the mother;[2] and in Jewish law female blood and female line are what determines Jewishness. In Western medieval Europe, on the other hand, and up to the seventeenth century, it is only the father's blood which confers nobility, whether of the bar dexter or of the bar sinister, except perhaps in the case of royalty. Class privilege descends through the male line.

The family romance as history

Perhaps the most startling example, both of relegitimation by reintegration with the male line and of the ideological recycling of myth, occurs in the historical activities of Queen Elizabeth I of England. Her story, as I mentioned earlier, is also the example *par excellence* of the family romance of the bastard. Elizabeth and her older sister Mary carried the impulse towards relegitimation to its furthest possible limits. Whereas Mary chose the conventional path of relegitimation which made her delegate her authority to a husband, Prince Philip of Spain, and to that even greater representative of the law of the Father, the Catholic Church, Elizabeth put the family romance into action by recreating herself in the image of her father. Henry VIII never really considered his daughters as heirs. Mary, the daughter of his first wife, Catherine of Aragon, 'had been bastardized by the divorce that allowed him to marry Anne [Boleyn]' (Marcus, 1989: 401), and Elizabeth was declared illegitimate at the age of two and a half, when her mother was beheaded for adultery. While Mary and Elizabeth were named as heirs to the throne in Henry's will, this was not signed, and they were never officially relegitimated (ibid.: 403).

When Mary succeeded to the throne, her submission to the law of the Father, in the form of Pope and husband, involved a hysterical piety and, sadly, no fewer than two equally hysterical pregnancies as she tried to assume the female role and produce an heir. Elizabeth, while successfully retaining her head on her shoulders throughout Mary's reign, seems to have prudently determined on a quite different and far more difficult course of conduct. Building on her family resemblance to Henry VIII, her English blood and her Tudor inheritance, she embarked on the complicated manoeuvres which turned her from her father's illegitimate daughter into his legitimate heir and made her at once monarch, or father, *and* Virgin Mother to her country:

At the age of twenty-five Elizabeth was crowned queen. Her coronation pageant underscored what for years had been a major element of her self-presentation and the public's perception of her: she was her father's daughter. The first show was a three-tiered arch displaying Unity and Concord. On the bottom tier were represented Henry VIII and his queen; on the next, Henry VIII and Anne Boleyn (redeemed after so many years of obloquy); and on the top, Elizabeth I.

(ibid.: 407)

This is a successful plagiarism of the medieval popularity of the iconic Tree of Jesse, which showed in branch form the genealogy of David, with Mary and her child as its ultimate flower. The introduction of a representation of the female into the male line formed part of the medieval development of the myth of Mary from the apocryphal texts. The coronation 'tree' and Elizabeth's enactment of the role of 'Virgin Queen' are therefore an early example of the use of anti-myths based on the story of the virgin birth.

What interests me particularly is the use that Elizabeth makes of language in order to re-gender and relegitimate herself, since it provides an antithetical and complementary discourse to that which we shall see certain male writers using in their process of delegitimation. A certain feminisation of discourse is seen by these writers to give access to the way of the mother (see Chapter 8), whereas, for Elizabeth, it is a masculinisation of discourse that gives access to the law of the Father.

Elizabeth as queen had the task of making the language of monarchy her own as a woman, but without creating the subversion that appropriation of male discourse could easily imply (Marcus, 1989: 408). Marcus gives as her clearest example the time when Elizabeth offered herself as 'a model of kingly courage', using on this unique occasion, when England needed to rally against the Armada, not only manly discourse but the male vestimentary code in the form of a silver cuirass. This was the moment of her famous declaration: 'I have the body of a weak and feeble woman, but I have the heart and stomach of a king, and of a king of England too' (ibid.: 409). This assertion of the 'male prerogative through language' was intensified as her refusal of marriage made it essential that she embody the name of the Father in herself. She named herself 'Monarch and prince sovereign' rather than the earlier 'sovereign lady' (ibid.: 411). Gradually she assumed the full title of king:

> To be a King and wear a crown is a thing more glorious to them that see it, than it is pleasant to them that bear it. For myself, I was never so much enticed with the glorious name of a King or a royal authority of a Queen, as delighted that

46

God hath made me His instrument to maintain His truth
and glory.

(ibid.: 412)

The double gendering of the female hero of tradition

The assumption that as monarch she could assume both the
divine right of the king and the equally transcendent role of virgin
mother and queen meant that she actually embodied and foreshadowed the Saint-Simonian myth of a representative godhead
in which the two sexes were combined. By the end of her reign:

> She no longer needed to present herself symbolically as her
> father's son, but had grown to political 'manhood' in her
> own right, eclipsing Henry VIII's glory in her own life and
> rule. Like the emblematic phoenix, a device closely associ-
> ated with the queen, she embodied her own succession –
> she was queen, king, and prince – encompassing within her
> own nature the separate beings required for an actual
> generational transfer of the crown.
>
> (Marcus, 1989: 414)

In her ambivalence and double gendering Elizabeth finally
transcended the family romance and mere relegitimation. It is
no longer a simple case of the search for official recognition or
even of the affirmation of paternity. In her final mythologisation,
it is she who confers legitimacy and public recognition on
others, 'her mysterious containment of opposites seeming to
exempt her from the impermanence of ordinary life' (ibid.: 415).

In the story of Elizabeth, which then becomes a myth in its own
right, we see one of the very rare instances of a female 'hero of
tradition'. The declaration of her illegitimacy, her exile and
upbringing by ladies-in-waiting, her precocious learning, her
persecution by Mary, her return to claim her father's throne, her
resistance to calumny and the demands that she produce an heir,
together with her apparent belief in her own immortality, tell a
familiar tale. Like other such heroes, she had no heir to succeed
her. It is important to note, however, that she would have had
less success in adapting the archetype to her own purposes if the
myth of the Virgin Queen of Heaven had not already existed as a
narrative validated by passionate faith. The two narratives were
needed to complement each other in the popular imagination.

Patriarchal myths

Most of the following case studies will examine the texts of French writers who, after the end of the *ancien régime* and the 1789 Revolution, used matronyms and maternal pseudonyms. These will illustrate the shifts in mythology which accompanied the attempted denial of the right to claim paternity. Perhaps we should look first at some of the myths of paternity and maternity that characterised earlier epochs. Claude Grimmer has been active in documenting the shifts in the representation of illegitimacy in France, and I will mainly use his documentation. Some of his case studies remind one of the argument about bastardy of Isidore of Seville in the sixth century, who made the ancient claim, when he wanted to emphasise the consanguinity of fathers and sons, that only the father's 'blood' was operative in the making of a child (cf. Apollo at the end of the *Oresteia*: see p.179). However, when Isidore, the Church Father, is talking about illegitimate children 'who do not take the name of the father', the biology changes completely and such children are said to be 'from the seed of the mother's genitals', as if the father had no input at all. At other times, Isidore argues that both father and mother are involved (Laqueur, 1990: 56).[3]

In the fifteenth and sixteenth centuries the clan had to be strengthened and the virility of its head ritually confirmed. Births were frequently registered as 'mother unknown', a really remarkable feat (which reversed for ideological reasons the *mater certa, pater incertus* principle), and the patronym was often used for both legitimate and illegitimate children (Meyer, 1980: 249). This use of the Roman code whereby *pater est quem nuptiae demonstrant* – or, if you are married, he is the father – remained in use until quite recent times. In France, before 1970, if a married woman had a child by someone not her husband, there were three possibilities:

1 The husband disavowed paternity (myths of the chastisement of adultery).
2 The husband was considered the father (myth of St Joseph; see below).
3 The wife gave birth anonymously, and her lover (the true father) declared the child of 'unknown mother' (this procedure was known as a declaration *sous X*).[4]

Thanks to the ritual affirmation of virility by both right-handed and left-handed procreation, 30 per cent of noble births in parts of France at the time of the Renaissance were illegitimate against only 1 per cent of births among the lower classes (Grimmer, 1983: 169). The prevalence of similar customs among the English nobility can be seen in the figures of Gloucester and his sons in Shakespeare's *King Lear*.[5] History does not relate the incidence of abortion and infanticide in France at the time, although the promulgation of a royal decree in 1556, making declaration of pregnancy obligatory for all unmarried women, tells its own story (ibid.: 200). By the seventeenth century the need to contain the nobility and to limit the proliferation of non-taxpayers (ibid.: 191) was reshaping social attitudes, and only the king and those of royal blood still performed the *public* rituals of virility in the production and legitimation of royal bastards.

The myth behind these manifestations harks back to the legendary fertility of the king of the gods, such as Zeus. The cult of myths of miraculous birth and divine fertility, like other myths, follows the patterns of cultural mutations. For example, the models of the Arthurian cycle, with its plethora of royal/divine bastards, starting with Arthur himself, and especially interesting in the ambivalent figure of Merlin, both 'child of the devil' and wise guardian of king and country, were the most prevalent in the Middle Ages. With the resurgence of classical myths in the Renaissance the emphasis shifted from the models of the Arthurian cycle back to those of Olympus. Hercules, the adulterine child of Alcmene and Zeus/Amphitryon and a rather ambiguous figure of hyper-virility (see Loraux, 1989), then renewed his role as the authorising figure of bastardy (Paul-Lévy, 1981: 208).

The myth of the absent royal or divine father and the natural son's relegitimation by extraordinary valour was adopted as inspiration for their life story by such royal bastards as William the Conqueror, Don Juan of Austria (who used the figure of Hercules as his bowsprit at the battle of Lepanto) and the Maréchal Maurice de Saxe.[6] Such figures then went on to acquire mythical dimensions for future generations. This to and fro between myth as a system of faith, myth as fantasy, and myth as ideology is particularly marked in the history of bastardy. A variant, which might be given the name of the Abraham myth (see pp.23–4), consists in the proof of paternal fertility which sees the bastard brought in to maintain the line in spite of an infertile wife. One well-known literary example is that of Boccaccio, who was born in Paris of mother unknown and was taken back to Italy by his father, but the *locus classicus* is that of Leonardo da Vinci, which we have already examined in looking at the psychoanalytic use of myth. This pattern may still be found among the aristocracy in the early nineteenth century, as the case of the Duke of Gordon attests. One of his acknowledged and illegitimate family, Georgina, relegitimated by being wed with great pomp from the family home, became a pioneer settler of Melbourne.

Another not uncommon paternal phenomenon, in cultures which see paternity as a proof of virility, manifests itself in what we may call the myth of the Holy Family or the myth of St Joseph. It occurs in the case where a woman's husband, for reasons of convenience, such as acquiring an heir, for reasons of hypocrisy, such as not losing face, or, it must be emphasised, for reasons of love, accepts as his own the 'cuckoo in the nest', a child fathered by another. The importance of these cases for my study is in the resulting ambivalence of the name. The classic case is that of the artist Eugène Delacroix, who was born in 1798 to what was essentially still a family of the *ancien régime*. Since Delacroix's father had a serious operation on the prostate only seven months before his presumed son's birth, the paternity was generally attributed to Talleyrand.[7] However, Delacroix senior went to great pains to acknowledge him as his son. In situations like this, the patronym becomes the matronym, since the child bears the name not of his or her biological father, but of the mother's husband. The double paternity, acknowledged and unacknowledged, produces, as I have said, both an awareness of one's identity as fiction and, of course, an ambivalence of the signature. The redoubled father figure or, in cases such as that of Leonardo, the double mother, becomes a figurative extension of the divided self which incorporates the shadowy figure of the other (see Chapter 4 on double maternity). Delacroix's *Dante and Virgil*, for instance, may be seen as the complementary paternal text to Leonardo's maternal text of *The Virgin and St Anne*.

Matriarchal myths

Another myth, closely linked to the alternative structures of illegitimacy, glorifies the matriarchal system that can supplement or replace the patriarchal in times of war or family dissolution. A vital role was often played by the matriarch in late medieval culture in her economic and social control of the clan or extended family. Even although she was seen by Church and State as having no position of power but only one of delegation, her activities spanned a social range which went from the chatelaine left to control the feudal group in times of war or the merchant's wife managing the business during his journeys, to the farmer's wife controlling domestic production and sales. This matriarchal presence found a reflection in the cult of the maternal trinity at the end of the fifteenth century (Freud, 1987). In a series of paintings and statues, the matriarchal figure of St Anne dominated and contained that of her daughter Mary and grandson Jesus. We will see how this archetype resurfaces in other historical contexts and becomes a figurative equivalent of the family ruled by the mother.

Jean Pierre Maïdani-Gérard (in Freud, 1987: 183–90) has shown that, already at the end of the fifteenth century when Leonardo produced his *Santa Anna Metterza* (St Anne with Virgin and Child), there existed three strong parallel traditions in popular religious iconography of the family:

> 1. The Holy Family (*Sainte Famille, Santa Famiglia, Heilige Familie* . . .) 'This is the most common theme. It represents the traditional group . . . of the Christ Child, the Virgin Mary and Saint Joseph. It is also the *humanissima trinitas* as opposed to the Divine Trinity (*divinissima trinitas*)' (ibid.: 187).

This tradition, at first glance canonising the nuclear family, presents the problem of the ambiguity of the paternal position. The human father is only a stand-in for the absent divine father, necessary to the myth of the divine child. The ubiquity of this ambiguous message in popular culture must be taken into account when considering the different forms of the 'family romance'.

> 2. St Anne with Virgin and Child (*Sainte Anne en tierce, Heilige Anna Selbdritt, Santa Anna Metterza* . . .) This is the theme which Leonardo adopted. As we have seen: 'It has no canonical basis and is inspired by the apocryphal Gospels. These, in spite of the non-recognition by the official ecclesiastical authorities, spread, through trends in

popular piety, in devotion as well as in iconography. So much so that they were – at least in the West – officially recognised and experienced a remarkable flowering among Catholic christian communities, precisely and mainly at the end of the 15th century and up to 1520' (ibid.: 187). In 1584, the feast-day of St Anne was officially consecrated.

The popular faith in the maternal trinity canonises a matriarchal tradition, from which the father is temporarily or permanently absent (transcendent but unrepresentable). In this tradition St Anne is shown as older, 'but also taller, more majestic, sovereign: all caring, all powerful, predominant' (ibid.: 186). The importance of the various versions of the myth of St Anne may be seen in the sculptures and stained glass of Chartres cathedral, to take only the best-known example. In this flowering of a matriarchal myth lies the representation of a different distribution of power, a reality in many women's lives (wives of soldiers, of labourers moving in search of work, of traders). It has a particular significance for families 'of the left hand'. We will see several examples of this family structure, with its emphasis on grandmaternal power, love and education (St Anne is traditionally shown instructing the Virgin), in families we study, from George Sand to Violette Leduc.

3. The Holy Clan (*Die Heilige Sippe, Santa Parantela, la Sainte Parenté* . . .)

'Strictly speaking, this designation applies only to the whole of the extended family descended from Anne – to which are frequently added the descendants of Esmeria, sister of Anne, mother of Elisabeth and grandmother of John the Baptist.[8] The Holy Clan also has no basis in canonical texts. Like the theme of Santa Anna Metterza, it is inspired by the apocryphal Gospels and *The Golden Legend* of Jacques de Voragine, a text of the Middle Ages which nourished the piety and art of the Christian West for centuries' (ibid.: 187).

This iconography of the extended family, which is supported by the attribution of miraculous births to Anne and Elisabeth, as well as Mary, again provides the myth desperately needed by social reality, and a fit between the needs of popular piety and a religious tradition born in a quite different culture. The extended families becoming common today, with the partners and children of first, second and third marriages forming a new type of clan, will also need to find an ideological base in new forms of myth.

Illegitimacy with a place in the social structure

The ex-centric, left-handed social structure[9] to which those with even a trace of royal blood proudly belonged makes interesting use of both the matronym and the name or title created *ex nihilo*. We see in effect the operation of a matriarchal structure authorised by regal or semi-regal paternity. Charles de Morny is quoted as claiming: 'In my family we have been bastards from mother to son for three generations' (Grimmer, 1983: 290), and we will follow such a structure, both ideological and fictional, in the work of George Sand.[10] Her important family patrimony, first in terms of royal benefits to her grandmother, then as a means to military preferment to her father, and finally as a selling point for her own works to a suitably impressed bourgeois public, was the left-handed descent from Augustus of Saxony and the Maréchal de Saxe. Yet the family structure over several generations was a matriarchal one, the 'female genealogy' studied in Chapter 4, and we will find that the myth of St Anne is as dominant as that of Hercules in her account of her predecessors, in her life and her works.

There existed a system of social 'sub-sets' (see Laslett, 1980), by which, in France up till the seventeenth century (and even the eighteenth at the highest social level), parallel matriarchal systems were accepted and ritualised in society as a whole. The rule of the mother was seen in many social formats as complementary to the law of the Father, but the notion of male blood and the male line was dominant. The patronym generally prevailed over the matronym, and some forms of illegitimacy had a prescribed place in the social structure. One clear example of a 'bastardy-prone sub-set', to use Laslett's formulation, is to be found in the world of the theatre. The exclusion of actors, like gypsies and vagrants, from the rites of legitimation (marriage, baptism, burial in consecrated ground) had early been formalised by the Church, following in the ancient Roman tradition. This rule of exclusion was applied very strictly during the Middle Ages and Renaissance, less strictly up to the end of the *ancien régime*.

The most complete charting that I have found of the history of one theatrical family, complete with meticulous record and archive searches, is in Francis Ambrière's history of two famous nineteenth-century actresses, *Mademoiselle Mars et Marie Dorval* (1992).[11] He points out that the theatre itself had been from the first an intensely exclusive profession, which was passed down from father to son and from mother to daughter over many generations. It was a way of life from which outsiders, except for a few monied camp-followers who worked their way in, were rigorously barred (A: 67). In spite of this almost domestic flavour, some churches were still refusing to marry actors as late as 1785 (A: 685).

The upheaval of the French Revolution meant both a flowering of the now deregulated theatre, and a break-up of tight local family structures. Actresses, in particular, were even more exposed than actors to two problems: employment via the 'casting couch' and the need for a 'protector' to make ends meet. Since, even after the Revolution, and no matter how famous, they were excluded from polite society and equated with courtesans, there was very little incentive not to be kept women. Many of them were also depressingly prolific, though not all so prolific as Mrs Jordan, the eighteenth-century star, who, apart from her first 'casting couch' pregnancy, bore the Duke of Clarence ten children while continuing with her career. The fact that women continued to act until quite an advanced stage of pregnancy (the expression 'born in a trunk' comes from solid social fact) makes one realise how different were social standards, and audience expectations, as recently as a century ago.

The two main subjects of Ambrière's research, the two most famous actresses of the early nineteenth century, both belonged to bastardy-prone sub-sets and were actually related by marriage thanks to the intense clannishness of the theatre world. In Mademoiselle Mars' case her entire family, siblings and children, were illegitimate. See Figure 1, which also shows the variation in naming possible in such families. However, thanks to her wealth, the third generation was triumphantly relegitimated when her bastard son Alphonse married his bastard cousin Eugénie. One can compare the English example of Mrs Jordan, the illegitimate daughter of a small-time actress, Grace Phillips, and 'the stage struck son of a family of Irish gentry, Francis Bland' (Kelly, 1980: 54). She used neither matronym nor

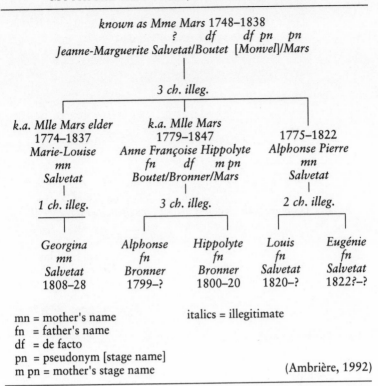

Figure 1 Three generations of an illegitimate family

patronym, but first the name Dorothy Francis, and then that of Mrs Jordan. A friend suggested: 'she had crossed the water and should take the name of Jordan' (ibid.: 56). Her numerous illegitimate children were relegitimated in the eyes of society by the royal blood of their father, the Duke of Clarence. The children were Fitzclarences, the Fitz signifying noble bastardy.

The case of that other celebrated actress, Marie Dorval, was rather like that of her friend George Sand, who admired her independent career and her self-reliance (to compare their family structure, see Figure 3 in Chapter 4). There were wide variations between legitimacy and illegitimacy in Dorval's immediate family and even in her children, who were divided fifty-fifty between those who had a right to the patronym and those who merely appropriated it. I give Marie Dorval's genealogy not in

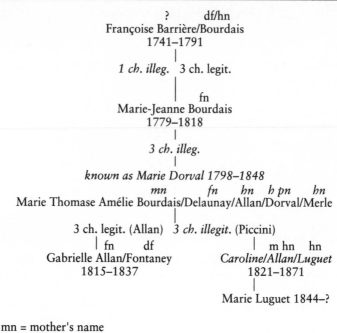

```
              ?        df/hn
        Françoise Barrière/Bourdais
              1741–1791
                  |
        1 ch. illeg.   3 ch. legit.
                  |
                        fn
           Marie-Jeanne Bourdais
              1779–1818
                  |
              3 ch. illeg.
                  |
       known as Marie Dorval 1798–1848
              mn      fn    hn   h pn   hn
  Marie Thomase Amélie Bourdais/Delaunay/Allan/Dorval/Merle
                  |
       3 ch. legit. (Allan)  3 ch. illegit. (Piccini)
         | fn     df              | m hn   hn
    Gabrielle Allan/Fontaney      Caroline/Allan/Luguet
         1815–1837                   1821–1871
                                        |
                                Marie Luguet 1844–?
```

mn = mother's name
fn = father's name
hn = husband's name
pn = pseudonym or stage name
m hn = mother's husband's name
h pn = husband's pseudonym
df = de facto husband
italics = illegitimate

Figure 2 A female genealogy: Marie Dorval

its entirety (for the immense ramifications, see Ambrière), but as a female genealogy. That is, I show a mother–daughter lineage over five generations. (Ambrière follows the male line back another three generations.) It is considered here because the habits of the theatrical family are still closer to the *ancien régime* than to the ideologies of the nineteenth century. I mark the different types of name used so as to show the wide diversity and possible variations, but I do not give the details of all surviving children in all generations.

A genealogical tree is a picture of what a family *should* look like, according to an agreed set of criteria. Its very bias represents an ideological position. In contrast to the ideological bias of the traditional tree, the most striking thing in these female genealogies is the fluidity of the name. Matronyms, patronyms, married and *de facto* names are complicated by the use of stage names. Actresses tended to sign their name in different ways according to whether they wished to be recognised or not. Thus their real name often served as a mask (to avoid prosecution, for instance), while it was their stage name that carried with it a greater conviction and air of reality. A look at the implications of Dorval's names shows the protean transformations. Is the result instability or diversity, a fragmented or a multiple self? She had a right to the name Delaunay because her father acknowledged paternity; however, she used the name Bourdais because it was on her mother's theatrical clan that her livelihood at first depended. She privately used her first (actor) husband's true name, Allan, but publicly his stage name Dorval. Dorval is a common stage name, and also the name of the protagonist in several famous plays, the first of which is Diderot's *Le Fils naturel* (The Natural Son) (1757), which, as we shall see, was a major factor in the positive image of bastardy. When her husband left her she became La Dorval, the star, but kept the private use of the name Allan for the children she bore to a lover. The name of her second husband, Merle, was used privately, not just as legitimation in the increasingly censorious atmosphere of the nineteenth century, but as a shield for various dubious financial dealings. It is perhaps interesting to note that several of Marie's lovers, of whom the best-known is the poet Vigny, belonged to that other bastardy-prone sub-set, playwrights. One, Alexandre Dumas, himself the son of a Napoleonic general who was illegitimate and half black into the bargain, did his best to reproduce his genealogy as often as possible, most notably in his son, the novelist. And times were changing: society was in flux and illegitimacy no longer socially sanctioned.

Revalorisation and devalorisation

Important lessons about narratives and mythologies of alterity and exclusion, about the relation of the exception to the norm, and of the dexter and the sinister, can be drawn from the ideological shift which resulted in the revalorisation of the name of the mother. In the late eighteenth century, with the renewed emphasis on maternal shame and guilt and with censure and interdiction descending on both illegitimacy and divorce, both a devalorisation and a revalorisation of the name of the mother occurred. With this shift in ideologies of legitimacy and the gradual move into the modern world there is a corresponding shift in mythology.

The growing use of the matronym reflects an important transformation of the notion of responsibility. By the late seventeenth century 'the name of the father may no longer be given or pronounced outside the bounds of conjugal legitimacy' (Paul-Lévy, 1981: 192) unless with the father's permission, and, of course, fathers do continue to allow the use of the patronym in many birth certificates of the illegitimate. However, by the eighteenth century, as Grimmer notes, 'The bastard is no longer an element of prestige, a necessary link in the survival of the line, but in every case the evidence of a fault, a fault for which the woman is primarily responsible' (ibid.: 231). A series of eighteenth-century laws forbidding 'recherche de paternité' and denying access to the patronym, unless sanctioned by the father, were finally enshrined in clause 340 of the Code Napoléon (ibid.: 196). There are interesting ideological implications accompanying this shift in prevalence from 'mother unknown' to 'father unknown'. It begins as a phenomenon of the need to limit inheritance, since the mother cannot establish a line, but is also a symptom of increasing urbanisation, since illegitimacy becomes as endemic in the fluid proletarian relationships of the big city as it was earlier in the noble clan (see Grogan, 1992: 6–7). As we have seen, other factors, such as the approval or disapproval in different social groups like that of the theatre, are at work too. However, the woman, now considered solely responsible for giving birth to her shame, is also thereby rendered solely responsible as provider and genetrix.[12] There is an important social resignification of the name and the way of the mother.

The noise in the system

It is no accident that the first major figure, chronologically, in the case histories that follow is Olympe de Gouges. She makes telling use of a major discursive shift, whereby the cult of nature in the eighteenth century has a surprising semantic spin-off.

This is a period when religious and social censure of even noble illegitimacy is becoming more intense. Yet, mainly thanks to Diderot, in works such as *Le Fils naturel* (1757), and to Rousseau's glorification of the 'natural man', the term 'natural child' acquires by osmosis a positive valorisation, and a series of literary works exploit the notion of the 'natural' as right and good. Even the highly conservative Chateaubriand gives a starring role, in *Atala* (1801), to a natural child who is also a child of nature. This association lingers on in France from Diderot well into the nineteenth century,[13] and we will find the reflections of the myth of the natural in a number of the works we study in detail. It is really startling to compare the totally exaggerated virtue of Diderot's hero with the equally incredible satanic villainy of the bastard Wringim in James Hogg's *Memoirs of a Justified Sinner* (1823),[14] which leaves that of Shakespeare's archetypal Edmund (*King Lear*) in the shade. Even their names represent extremes. Dorval is respectably upper-class and *un coeur d'or*, whereas Wringim, like all adulterine children, is a 'ring-in', a cheat, a fraud and a 'parasite'.[15] We are also looking at two different national traditions, the Scottish harking back to an older and darker one, as yet untouched by the Enlightenment, while some 'enlightened' French are endeavouring to change a deep-seated prejudice, without much effect except on the intelligentsia.

Olympe de Gouges, as we will see in Chapter 5, asserted her own right to 'natural' aristocracy. Mainly, however, she attempted to revalorise women. Her delegitimation and her choice of the matronym went hand in hand with her assertion of women's rights to divorce, to maintenance, to the vote and to free contractual union. Authority immediately attempted to silence this noise in the system, and the law of the Father was violently reimposed. Yet our study of the workings of the signature in the nineteenth and twentieth centuries shows that the name of the mother acquires a force proportionally linked to the vehemence of its repression. It is a constantly recurring factor in both the history and the mythology of revolution, where the figure of Marianne has rather more subversive force than she has been credited with (see Chapter 7). One of the findings of this study which has imposed itself more and more is the suprising variety of spin-offs from the cult of the name of the Mother *par excellence*, that of the Virgin Mary. The more intense the cult, the greater the spread of the name, and the greater the possibilities of the creation of anti-myths. The first of these was the use of the name Marianne as a figure of the Revolution, and the irony is that it was right-wing satirists who first used the common name of the most humble of peasants to deride the people's dream (Agulhon, 1981: 9, 32). We will be following the permutations of the anti-myths of Mary over one hundred years or more.

It seems strange to link such an apparently negative phenomenon as a full-blown revival of the myth of Eve (Grogan, 1992: 10), which raises the cry of 'the woman tempted me' and promises that hers shall be the retribution of giving birth in pain, with anything potentially positive; yet, as we have surmised, the devalorisation of illegitimacy by attributing it to woman alone may have permitted new forms of delegitimation and new subversive myths of female responsibility. In the early nineteenth century, the 'masculine feminists' (the term is Benoîte Groult's (1977)) establish what we will call the myth of Sophia. In the doctrines of Condorcet, Saint-Simon, Lamennais, Fourier and their disciples woman is not only equal to man, but potentially better, purer and wiser.[16] At both ends of the religious and political spectrum there is an amazing recrudescence of emphasis on parthenogenesis. The two eccentric figures of the Abbé Constant and the Père Enfantin and their cults of the God Mother exploit the hidden kinship between the myth of Sophia and the myth of Mary:

> The New Mary, the woman we await, is called to complete the work of God; but in partnership with man, not as a submissive slave. She too will save the world and crush the serpent's head; but the redeemer who must do so with her will not say to her with an authoritative air: Woman, what is there in common between you and me? He calls her to his side to share authority, to bring her face of light, of grace, of modesty and wisdom to the work which he has so nobly begun and which he is completing with such courage.
>
> (Enfantin, cit. Grogan, 1992: 144)[17]

It is in the co-temporaneous work of Flora Tristan that we will find the twin mythologies of Sophie and Marie (and the semantic possibilities of the names) used with their full potential as anti-myths. She also envisages the worship of a paternal–maternal trinity, composed of man, woman and child yet to be born, which is to be the symbol of the combined rule of the law of the Father and the law of the Mother.

This revalorisation was also a polarisation produced by the nineteenth-century bourgeois vindictiveness against illegitimacy. The change in attitudes was partly a factor of the class shift, which saw a 30 per cent rate of ex-nuptial births become a proletarian, rather than a noble, phenomenon (see Grogan, 1992: 7). Single mothers, ex-nuptial births and wives who refused their husband's name bore the burden of the curse of Eve, but also the burden of identity and responsibility. Grogan gives several examples of Saint-Simonian feminists who insisted on maternal independence. She quotes Madame Casaubon:

> WOMAN IS THE FAMILY
> *The child must bear her name.*
> *Certitude LIES where no doubt exists,* and the fruit must bear the name of the tree which gave it life, not that of the gardener who grafted the bud.
>
> (cit. ibid.: 135)

Flora Tristan may also stand as an example of the most common form of female delegitimation in the modern era, the woman who establishes her signature by refusing her husband's name and with it the law of the Father. Tristan and her like were a scandal but in some cases a paying scandal. And it is precisely because the name of the mother became a scandal that it became sought after as an expression of otherness. Female multiplicity, female irreducibility, female sexuality became necessary factors of disruption, of interference, of noise in the system. As soon as this noise was seen to produce mutation in the system, as soon as it became a factor in the signature, it was recuperated into the creative network. It was then that delegitimation became not only the assumption of illegitimacy or of marital rebellion but the symbol of a wider rejection of the law of the Father. The matronym and the maternal pseudonym acquired a symbolic value, representing as they do the 'parasite' which produces a gradual mutation of the patriarchal system.

It must be remembered that delegitimation not only enabled female writers to establish a signature, but maintained that signature by producing the ex-centric as a saleable commodity.

The pariah's claim to the name of the mother became not only a public scandal but a paying business. Exploiting her very exclusion became a way of establishing the right and the capacity of the woman alone to earn her own living and opened the possibility for twentieth-century woman to enact one last myth of her revolutionary forebears, the myth of the new man or woman. The archetype here (another case of history become myth) could be seen as the symbolically self-named Desiderius Erasmus, the son of a priest and a doctor's daughter. The 'new man', a product of the free union of superior physical and intellectual stock (the contamination of other ideologies of the period may be perceived here), was to be the standard-bearer of the new age of equality, emancipation and, presumably, eugenics. A dangerously utopian vision. Flora Tristan's version of the new woman who is also natural child and love child is unsurprisingly called Marie. Indeed the novel in which she appears, *Méphis* (1838), is a veritable compendium of the mythologies of illegitimacy, past, present and future. Naturally, when planned parenthood and single motherhood become social realities rather than utopian dreams, the strains which the myth of the 'new man' and the aspiration to perfection impose upon both mother and child become apparent (see Paul-Lévy, 1981).

Exclusion and desire

In other words, one of the advantages of the autographic and autothanatographic narratives of illegitimacy and delegitimation is that they offer an entry into a polymorphous and ex-centric experience which shapes both life and fiction. The limitation of experience to the legitimate and socially sanctioned, even in their phantasms of escape, would never allow us to reach a subversive potential equal to that of the alternative mythologies of the excluded. The structures of desire are as variable as the ideologies and the gendering which shape them. We will see, for instance, that the spread of literacy, which in the twentieth century permits proletarian bastards access for the first time to literary expression, also permits writers such as Genet and Leduc, like their great nineteenth-century forerunner Louise Michel, to give voice to personal fictions which are not only socially and sexually, but also linguistically and structurally, subversive.

Access to the name and the way of the mother becomes a focus of desire in a parallel series of creative revolutions. In the twentieth century this noise in the system not only produces mutations at the overt political level but helps to force the literary recognition of the polysemy of gender, pioneered so long before by Olympe de Gouges. The voices of illegitimacy form a heteroglossia with those of the proletariat, of the homosexual, of the dispossessed. Otherness permeates and re-shapes social identity and mythology. The name of the mother is the factor which recurs to link a series of such phenomena together over 200 years. By tracing the narratives associated with it we become spectators to the performances of the *mises en scène* of the ex-centric.

4

A female genealogy: the en-gendering of George Sand

George Sand's *Histoire de ma vie* is of special interest in any study of systematised alterity, since it provides a view, perhaps unique, of the interactions of six generations of matriarchy and thus gives us a rare example of what Irigaray (1987) calls a female genealogy. This genealogy runs from the forceful and tempestuous Aurora of Koenigsmark (1662–1728), who gives a royal bastard to the house of Saxony, through to Maurice Dudevant (1823–89), almost unique among male writers in choosing to sign his works not only with the name of the mother, Sand, but with a name and a signature that his mother had chosen and created almost *ex nihilo*. The genealogy comes to an end in the seventh generation, with the childless death of the fourth Aurore in 1961. It features a wild profusion of surnames, which contrasts with a quite deliberate and chosen sequence of given names, Aurore–Maurice–Aurore–Maurice–Aurore–Maurice–Aurore, which marks the importance of the female line. The only father in the group who was present at his child's upbringing was the last, Maurice Sand. Every generation, even the sixth – if Sand's daughter, Solange Dudevant/Sand/Clésinger was, as is generally believed, an adulterine child – had illegitimate half-siblings, whether or not they were themselves bastards.[1] If this modified family tree is compared to that of the Pléiade edition, from which it is taken, it will be seen how distorting 'normal' genealogies can be. The Pléiade version admits, necessarily, two bastards, Maurice de Saxe and Marie-Aurore de Saxe, yet omits Sand's half-brother and -sister, who are equally vital to her story.

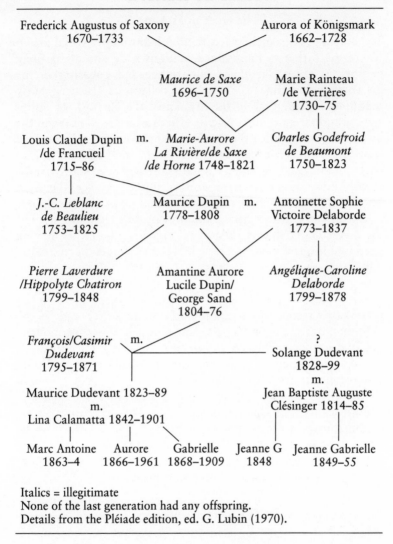

Italics = illegitimate
None of the last generation had any offspring.
Details from the Pléiade edition, ed. G. Lubin (1970).

Figure 3 Seven generations of George Sand's immediate family

The myth of St Anne

The matriarchal social structure, dominant in any social group where the father is uninvolved, unknown or absent for long periods, is given particular importance and cohesion in the instance of illegitimacy. The maternal figure is also frequently redoubled, in the case of the orphan or the bastard, by adoption, grandparental nurturing or other fostering. We saw, in the instance of Leonardo, the doubling of the mother represented iconically in the two figures of the Virgin and St Anne. In that particular case, the grandmaternal figure has been subtly transformed into a much younger woman, but, in essence, the myth of St Anne is a celebration of matriarchal power, in the figures of the maternal trinity, the grandmother, the virgin mother and the divine child. In this version of the myth, the father, having exercised his godly prerogative, leaves the women in control of the child's upbringing; St Anne's traditional role is an educational one.

Sand's autobiography in a sense incarnates the myth, in its remarkable testament to grandmotherly authority and to the moulding of the unconscious by the tensions of double mothering. In the process of describing an amazing web of relegitimation and delegitimation, it highlights the fact that the oppositional force of illegitimacy always has active potential, but that this can be cancelled out by a patriarchal structure which channels and neutralises its reproductive possibilities. The drive towards relegitimation, always the first impulse, the 'family romance' of the bastard, remains at war with the equally pressing call for justice and the desire for revolution, which, as we will see, require specific social conditions to come to fruition.

The female genealogy

Whatever the legal status of the women involved, a female genealogy provides interesting tensions for two reasons. First, it is as Irigaray (1987: 174) says, necessarily bisexual, since each matronym is also a patronym. Endeavouring to follow the maternal line to its roots, however, is a constant digression, a line of flight, since each step backwards finds, instead of the renewable sameness of the patronym, the infinite difference of the name of the mother. (I will refer to Figure 3, a genealogy of Sand's family, modelled on information from OA I: lviii–lvix, but modified to include some of the more important illegitimate relations, in order to show the remarkable possibilities of difference and digression if one follows the maternal, rather than the paternal, connections.) When one adds to the already protean scenario of legitimate patriarchy the infinite possibilities of bastardy, where the name of the father, that of the mother, pseudonyms, *noms de guerre*, and place-names or toponyms jostle one another in wild profusion, the potential of multiple identity is always present, either as a threat or as a promise. Sand's family history is a perfect example. Each member of Sand's family lived potential multiplicity in different ways, since, even if, like Sand herself, they were officially legitimate, they remained linked to the family complex, whose notoriety Sand exploits, both professionally and personally, in the resolution of the double binds which are both her strength and her weakness. She must always be both inside and outside social boundaries, both landowner and pariah, both good mother and whore. Hers is not a revolutionary stance; rather than change society she wants to infiltrate and exploit it. The delegitimatory movement in her life and work is always accompanied by a compensatory relegitimation.

In considering the autobiographical writing of George Sand as paradigmatic of a certain form of the representation of illegitimacy which mediates a constant swing between relegitimation and delegitimation, between opposition and conformity, and between the conservatism of the country and the socialism prevalent in the Paris of the 1830s, one must see her as the creature of a very particular social context. Her critics have accepted rather too easily her own version of her upbringing, the mythologised struggle which features in *Histoire de ma vie* (Story of my Life) (1854–5), and which enables the child Aurore to play such a saintly role as she passionately rejects money in the name of love. They have seen it as a simple matter of black and white, aristocracy versus the plebs.

Patronyms, matronyms and toponyms

We should, rather, be aware that we are dealing with the after-effects of a parallel society, one sanctioned by custom in the *ancien régime*, an example of a 'bastardy-prone sub-set'. This particular sub-set allowed noble illegitimates a certain social status, while rigorously excluding them from property and inheritance and permitting marriage only within the same caste or with the rising middle classes. Royal bastards were, of course, the exception. If acknowledged, the divinity which shapes a king, not to mention the gift of a title and lands, ensured the acceptance of royal offspring into the ranks of the nobility. This was the case for Maurice de Saxe, the son of Augustus the Strong of Saxony, king of Poland, who was Sand's great-grandfather, as she hastens to inform us. Maurice de Saxe was the perfect incarnation of the myth of Hercules, the divine/royal bastard whose exploits as Marshal of France made a name for him in his own right.

The mistresses of the nobility, like the Maréchal de Saxe, had their marginalised place in the social order, recognised but not received, more *demi-monde* than *monde*. Their children, however, varied in status, a status marked by three grades of naming. Those who received the patronym, like Maurice de Saxe or, among the *hobereaux* or country landowners, Sand's husband François (Casimir) Dudevant, had some hope of assimilation into society, though, as we shall see in Casimir's case, this was far from automatic. Those who were named by the use of a toponym, like Sand's great-uncle, the Abbé de Beaumont, were given a certain status but usually no inheritance. Finally, those who were forced to use the matronym, like Sand's half-brother Hippolyte Chatiron, had no status socially, although their claim to financial support was often recognised. Now these offspring were neither of the *monde* nor of the *demi-monde* but a curious hybrid group which renewed itself from generation to generation, and one where the patterns of marginalisation gave a shifting nature to the desperate attempts at stability of this society of the left hand.

On the one hand, then, among the bastards of the nobility, you have a group frantically exhibiting, in their attempts at re-legitimation, the signs of their 'aristocracy', and producing such exaggerations as the apparent inability of Sand's grandmother, Mme Dupin, to use her legs, even to climb one flight of stairs,[2] or her outdated insistence that she be addressed in the third person. On the other, you have an existential instability which marks the identity itself and which is most clearly seen in the extraordinary metamorphoses of the name, particularly but not only the names of women.

The name as line of flight

Once again, the example of Sand's grandmother shows the remarkable vagaries to which a name could be subject. She was not registered as Aurore de Saxe at her birth in 1748, although Maurice de Saxe, in inseminating his mistress Marie Rainteau, was reproducing the pattern of his own procreation, by Augustus of Saxony on Aurora of Koenigsmark. The main difference was that this first Aurora, in the long and rather confusing line of women so called, was herself of the highest nobility, and the first Maurice had the advantage of royal upbringing as well as royal parentage, though apparently the latter was rather thinly spread, since Augustus sired some hundred bastards. However, Maurice de Saxe and Marie Rainteau's child, Marie-Aurore, was originally given the name of a fictitious father, one La Rivière, an encoded procedure also adopted, as we shall see, in naming her grandson. Marie Rainteau (also spelt Rinteau), in her career as a high-class courtesan, had, moreover, adopted the *nom de guerre* of De Verrières, by which she was known until her death, although she occasionally added De Furcy to the list. It is not clear by which name the little Marie-Aurore was known for the first fifteen years of her life, but these years set a pattern of double mothering which she later repeated for her grand-daughter, since she was removed from all contact with her *demimondaine* mother by her aunt, the Dauphine of France, and sent to the fashionable convent education of Saint-Cyr.

Before her marriage in 1766, she petitioned to have her birth certificate changed, and was officially, and most unusually, recognised as the natural daughter of Maurice de Saxe by special act of parliament. This raised her status from that of a user of the matronym to that of one permitted the patronym, an unusual privilege for females. Marie-Aurore de Saxe then assumed yet another name by becoming Aurore de Horne (or Horn). Even her title was problematic, since her husband may or may not have been a count. Her marital status was equally strange. The marriage was probably never consummated, and De Horne died conveniently in a duel (or was he murdered?) shortly after. Marie-Aurore, bereft of her protectress, was forced to return to her mother's roof and its 'moral danger'. A remarkably level-headed girl, she used her situation to the best advantage, not only making a hit with her aunt Geneviève de

Verrières' protector, one of the richest men in France, but, after her mother's death and her own retreat to a convent, persuading him to marry her into the bargain. She thus acquired two more names, and became Mme Dupin de Francueil. The marriage of a 29-year-old woman to a 61-year-old man was surprisingly successful (indeed, it turned out to be a love match), and its offspring was Sand's father, Maurice.

I have gone into some detail over this involved bit of family history in order to show a number of important things about Sand's grandmother, and her shaping influence. Sand was educated by her *bonne maman*, Marie-Aurore Dupin, as she became, but it must be clear by now that this strong-willed lady was no mere conservative relic of the *ancien régime*, but a woman who had lived through an amazing variety of names and experiences, who had fought tooth and nail for her rights, and who incarnated a process of successful relegitimation. She was not, as Deutelbaum and Huff (1985) suggest, simply a feudal hangover; nor was her only motivation in her fight for her granddaughter a jealous passion to supplant her son's plebeian wife. Both these factors were involved, but one must also remember that she knew the price of being socially marginalised, just as she knew the stigma of being illegitimate. In her eyes, and in society's, there was a world of difference between her granddaughter, who had, after all, only made it to the right side of the blanket by the skin of her teeth,[3] being raised with an illegitimate half-sister in a back street in Paris, and being raised with an unacknowledged half-brother as the potential chatelaine of Nohant. The mere fact that this was, in fact, the choice, and that Sand did spend most of her childhood with one illegitimate sibling or the other, shows the social transgression on both sides of the family and makes it clear that the potential for de-legitimation was as real an issue to Aurore Dupin (Sand) as the drive for relegitimation had been in her namesake.

Mediating the double mothers

To understand Sand's self-mythologisation, one must appreciate her strange position as mediator and bone of contention between her grandmother and her mother, and the way in which both women, their idiosyncratic and independent minds and their complementary obsessions, shaped the to and fro between conservatism and opposition which was Sand's way of creating herself in writing. Almost the only thing they had in common was the name Dupin, and a passionate love for the charming and irresponsible Maurice, the son of one and the husband of the other. Sand participated in this disculpation and adoration of her father, who died in a riding accident when she was 6.

Sand's mother, as her daughter tartly observed, was at least legitimate (OA I: 16), unlike her mother-in-law. Antoinette Sophie Victoire Delaborde was a plebeian, a beautiful, hard-working and intelligent girl, forced by hard circumstances into near-prostitution at the age of 14, who acquired through her vivacity and beauty a series of protectors, the last of whom was the dashing aide-de-camp Maurice Dupin. They both already had illegitimate children. In accordance with the customs of the time, *her* daughter was a scandal, *his* son a mere peccadillo. When, after a string of miscarriages, Sophie was finally about to produce a full-term child, Maurice succumbed to his better impulses, committed the ultimate social sin, and married her. Her mother-in-law, the ex Marie-Aurore de Saxe, whose history we know, was scandalised as well as jealous, and did her best to have the marriage annulled, but in the end was forced to receive the daughter she did not want and the granddaughter she did.

Everything conspired to set the two women at loggerheads. Sophie was young, poor, ill-educated, artistic, intuitive, physically active, sexually passionate and manic-depressive. She was subject to wild swings in mood, and paranoia helped on by feelings of inferiority. Marie-Aurore was old, rigidly self-disciplined, authoritarian, matriarchal, sexually and physically inactive, unimaginative, a believer in reason and a disciple of Rousseau and Voltaire. One had the power of the body, and the other the power of the mind. One, to the child, represented life and the other death. She was to learn the hard way that one also represented insanity and the other sanity.[4]

The spoken and the unspoken

There is a strange shadow behind Sand's story, about which one can only speculate, but which may help to explain the older woman's determination to separate mother and daughter. One must remember that the threat of syphilis hung over the nineteenth century, as AIDS does over ours. Indeed it probably provided the explanation for the non-consummation of Marie-Aurore's first marriage back in 1766. The medical advice that she should on no account sleep with her husband is difficult to explain in any other way.[5] Sophie and Maurice, in the next generation, had had a string of partners each, and there is something very suggestive about the succession of miscarriages and the fact that the baby which followed the little Aurore was born blind and only lived a short time. Sophie's ever-increasing mental instability must also be taken into account. Thus, when Marie-Aurore Dupin signed a contract with Sophie exchanging a respectable annuity for the possession of her granddaughter, there may have been other factors beside sheer pride of possession at work. It also is easy to forget, in sympathising with little Aurore's passionate determination not to be separated from her mother, that it was probably more normal for a child of the period to be brought up by servants in the upper class, and grandparents in the lower class, than by her actual mother. The close physical bond between Sophie and her child, even the fact that Aurore had been breast-fed, were part of an extraordinary set of circumstances. Sand's own romanticisation of her life tends to obscure factors which she prefers not to mention, but I think there has also been a trend in feminist criticism to read her work and life in terms of our own ideologies and expectations, rather than in the context of the period and that of her belonging from the outset in a subtly marginalised parallel world.

We have seen that Marie-Aurore Dupin, as is so often the case in families, faithfully reproduced, in the upbringing of her granddaughter and namesake, the pattern of double mothering which had been her own. Indeed, in her eyes the situation *was* the same and Sophie was no more and no less a courtesan than Marie de Verrières, in spite of her tardy marriage. Association with Sophie was social suicide (OA I: 1125), as Sand discovered, to her cost, after her grandmother's death, when her choice of living with her mother not only led to bitter unhappiness caused by her mother's unstable personality, but to the necessity of marriage into the parallel, marginalised world, represented by the illegitimate François (Casimir) Dudevant. Casimir, in spite of bearing the patronym, had a long struggle with his own second mother, the Baronne Dudevant, before he was able to claim his father's inheritance.

As I have said, *Histoire de ma vie* is the story of a double mothering, of a child torn between the 'good' mother, *bonne maman*, and the 'bad' mother, represented to the child as the fallen woman, in a last desperate attempt by her grandmother to speak the unspoken, and force the child to face reality (OA I: 855–7). As has been frequently observed, perhaps the most revealing fictional representation of this dilemma (and, I would add, of a kind of negative version of the myth of St Anne) probably occurs in *La Petite Fadette* (1849). Naomi Schor (1986) rightly emphasises the vital importance of doubling in this book, particularly the pseudo-doubling of gender in the twin protagonists, but I would wish to stress the importance of the maternal duplication. The strange claim has been made that Fadette has no adequate female role-model, because she has been abandoned by her camp-follower mother.[6] This completely ignores the source of Fadette's power, not to mention wealth, which comes, of course, from the lessons she has learned from her grandmother. It is witch lore that provides her veterinary and herbal skills, as well as her extraordinary gifts of healing and therapy. Sand redistributes for fictional purposes the qualities and faults of her own two mothers. The healing powers and empathy with animals of Fadette are traits of Sophie, as is the sexuality of Fadette's absent mother, while the use of money and knowledge as power comes from her grandmother.[7] The important point is that, for the marginalised to succeed, they need to master the codes of two quite different groups, those of the excluded and those of the establishment, and this requires the exercise of considerable intelligence; but their success is also quite cynically related to controlling wealth. In this fairy tale of relegitimation, both wealth and intelligence are shown as the prerogatives of a woman who is mediatrix between worlds, and eventually mistress of farm, husband and her own destiny.

Mother tongue, master tongue

The child Aurore learned to mediate between two conflicting maternal obsessions by acquiring the mastery of language, and the internalisation of narratives which permit a to and fro between disparate worlds and codes.[8] Sand's recreation of her childhood shows this shift between the oral mother tongue and

73

the written master tongue, and is possibly the best thing she ever wrote. To quote her worst enemy, Baudelaire,[9] 'But genius is only *childhood retrieved* at will, childhood now endowed with virile [!] organs to express itself, and with the analytic mind which permits it to give order to the sum of materials involuntarily acquired.'[10] At times she attains this genius, though it is always endangered by over-facility, moralising and self-justification. The code-shifting necessary for the voluntary return to childhood is first seen at work in the manuscript of *Voyage en Espagne* (Travels in Spain) (OA II: 471–4), an early and very conscious effort to retrieve the language and mind-set of a very small girl. The simple recovery of these experiences and sensations lays the foundation for the more artfully composed and elaborated version of the same events in the autobiography. However, the heteroglossia which makes those chapters (OA I: 553–85) so convincing would not have been possible without the preliminary experiments in *énonciation* and multiple voicing which characterise *Voyage en Espagne* and the later companion piece *Voyage en Auvergne* (Travels in Auvergne), where not one, but many different, voices intermingle. The *mise en abyme* of this multiplication of language and identity is beautifully suggested, in the text of the stay in Madrid, by the 4-year-old Aurore's discovery of an echo:

> I came back on to the terrace and I called my mother; the voice repeated the word in a very soft but very clear voice, and that gave me a lot to think about. I raised my voice, I called my own name, which was returned to me immediately, but more indistinctly . . . . The strangest impression for me was to hear my own name repeated in my own voice. Then a queer explanation occurred to me. It was that I was double, and that there was around me another *me* which I couldn't see, but which saw me all the time, since it replied to me all the time . . . . I concluded that everything and everybody had their reflection, their double, their other *me*, and I eagerly desired to see mine.[11]

Thus language enables mediation between two selves (and one may note that one of these selves is masculine), two worlds and two mothers. Aurore's first recorded adventure, at the age of 6 months, is one of mediation, symbolised by the ring which she carries in token of reconciliation from her grandmother to her mother. Didier shows how the very first 'room of her own', her grandmother's dressing-room, is itself a mediatory space:

> It is in this refuge that writing is born: a doubly uterine refuge, since the grandmother's boudoir is visited by the cricket, a substitute for the maternal bird: thus the two mothers are finally reconciled, and the recovered identity permits creation.[12]

But mediatory experience is also what permits her to develop multiple identities and eventually leads to her own fictionalisation. Her redoubling in language also permits that other form of mediation, the ironic stance whereby one becomes the eavesdropper or 'reader' of the communication between oneself and others. Indeed, it is this power of reading that permits her to be both self and other, the first step towards literature. As Chambers remarks:

> literature can be described as *the discourse of power made readable*, that is, realized as the mediated phenomenon that it is, and so as subject to reading. And it is because it is subject to reading that it can be relativized through irony, or it can have its authority eroded through the melancholic 'fading' of autonomous identity into otherness, or finally it can be appropriated and turned to 'other' purposes, which are those of seduction as the deflection of desire.
>
> (1991: 18)

Both the ironic doubling of self and the sense of shifting identity seem to develop early in the marginalised. The capacity of participating in one world while 'reading' it in another is a faculty Aurore shares with her brother Hippolyte (OA I: 673,777). Only she, however, makes the further move into literature, grasping the discourse of power without, it must be said, really further cultivating her very considerable powers of irony.

Another major form of dialogism in Sand's life she owes partly to the forces of circumstance and partly to family tradition. It is seldom remarked that Aurore's cross-dressing dates back to her childhood, well before she became George. When Hippolyte decided to teach her to ride, she probably took to breeches because there was no side-saddle in the stables, since neither her mother nor her grandmother was a horsewoman. In her passionate affair with the horse, comfort and safety remained the criteria. This came as no shock to Sophie, who had herself worn boy's clothes for safety in the troubled times of the Terror. Mme Dupin probably also felt it added an element of security to her granddaughter's excursions.

However, it permitted as well the experience of what Louise Michel (see pp. 137–8) calls 'masculine invisibility'. This is why I call this early cross-dressing a training in dialogism, in the experience of a different body language and a different reception of the codes of behaviour. Her later adoption of masculine attire was equally practical in origin, to save money and avoid harassment. It also, of course, at first provided a wonderful mantle of invisibility. It was only as the new name and signature took shape that Sand was able to exploit the scandal of cross-dressing as a myth in its own right, which inevitably then acquired a certain control over her life.

Aurore, even as a child, also necessarily mediated in her discourse the implications of her two mothers being double in themselves, a mass of paradoxes. The conventional Mme Dupin braved public opinion among her country neighbours in maintaining her Voltairean agnosticism. On the other hand, this overpoweringly authoritarian figure was, in many respects, ruled by her servants. She seems to us rigid, static and entropic, and yet it is she who encourages the all-important development of the power of written expression, which the mother, acutely conscious of her own purely oral and popular culture, violently rejects. Most importantly, Mme Dupin is the proprietor of Nohant, and life at Nohant, formal in many respects, still enables the child's identification with the land and with nature, alien to Sophie, who is city-born and bred. On the mother's side, Sophie's passionate physicality and scorn for the idle rich are tempered by the practicality of the working woman. She will make many sacrifices and weave seductive dreams, but never endanger the steady income which her contract with Mme Dupin ensures.

Contracts and the law of the Father

The dominance of the law of the Father in relegitimation is marked at each stage in the family history by a written, officially sanctioned document such as this contract. Sand records these events and shows how clearly she is aware of the power of the written word in the master discourse. She describes in great detail, for instance, how Aurore de Saxe's relegitimation is marked by a series of documents. First there is the act of parliament which gives her the right to the patronym. There follow her two marriage certificates, the birth certificate of her son, her husband's will and the title to Nohant. She keeps complete control over her son through her title to the land and money, which then enables her to enforce the contract that gives her power over Sophie and her child.

Sophie, too, knows the value of documents. After all, where would she be without her marriage certificate and Aurore's birth certificate, all that stand between her family and abject poverty? It is not just paranoia that makes her insist that her daughter be married under the *régime dotal*, which preserves her right to control her own property. Sand learns her lesson well, and sees to it that her very delegitimation is contractually ensured. The documents of the official separation which permits her not only to revert to her maiden name but to keep the custody of her children, which in effect delegitimates them too, are acquired at great expense and difficulty. Equally vital to her are the publisher's contracts which are her proof of financial and personal independence, fame and power.[13] It is revealing that she actually thinks of the establishment of her new name and signature in the same contractual terms as marriage:

> I was baptised, obscure and carefree, between the manuscript of *Indiana*, which was then my whole future, and a thousand-franc note which was at that moment my whole fortune. It was a contract, a new marriage between the apprentice poet that I was and the humble muse who had consoled me in my troubles. Heaven preserve me from upsetting what I left fate to accomplish. What is a name in our revolutionised and revolutionary world? A number for those who do nothing, an ensign or a motto for those who work or fight. The one I was given, I, and I alone, made after the event, by my hard work.[14]

In other words, apart from the external contract for payment, there are two internal contracts which must be honoured in *Histoire de ma vie*: the contract between author and readership which produces the signature, and the autobiographical 'pact', described by Lejeune (1975), a pact between author and reader which postulates the identity of author, narrator and character in any work which claims to be autobiographical. The first contract is immeasurably the more important, particularly for an author who has, in both senses of the word, made a name for herself. The second, as Béatrice Didier (1984) has shown, is also subject to the important distinction between narratee (I would add narrative audience (see Maclean, 1988)) and reader. According to Didier, Sand establishes as her narratee an 'ideal reader', a friend and confidante, with whom she can play a maternal role, and on whose sympathy she can depend (1984: 255). While this narratee is posited as female, Sand, ever conscious of sales, is careful not to create any category of excluded male readers.

Model or portrait?

Sand's immense reading public in the 1850s read her life through the expectations engendered by her own fiction and the fiction others created about her, and she tailors her account of that life and that of her forebears to suit those expectations. In other words she is writing the life of George Sand, rather than that of Aurore Dupin, and, as she rightly says, George Sand is completely her own creation. What, then, is the autobiographical pact? The double self of Aurore Dupin and George Sand (she signs her publisher's contracts with both names) ensures that the pact itself is double. The author is both male and female, both Parisian bohemian (Sand) and a child of the Berry (George) (OA II: 139), both chatelaine of Nohant and delegitimated wife.

What we are dealing with is rather the narrative contract, in which the reader and author are often partners in *mauvaise foi* (Didier, 1984: 247). The author keeps faith not only with the audience expectations engendered by her signature, but with her own view of what the author–reader relation should be, and what will ensure the fidelity of her audience. These considerations, in their turn, engender the author. Nancy Miller (1980) makes the excellent *rapprochement* with Colette's famous epigraph to *La Naissance du jour* (Break of Day) (1928): 'Do you imagine, when reading my books, that I am drawing my portrait? Patience: it's only my model.'[15]

One must remember too the extent to which Sand's writing was governed by the written contract with her publishers, which was not only a source of income, but a vital source of self-esteem. Whatever the circumstances of her tempestuous private life, she wrote for hours every night, often turning out a book in a few weeks, as well as producing an endless stream of correspondence. She certainly needed money, but even more she needed the stream of narrative which mediated her relation to the world and satisfied her need for constant communication. Unfortunately this compulsive productivity was frequently at the expense of revision. Even her closest friends, like Delacroix, deplored this excessive facility:

> These writers are all alike. Even poor Aurore shares the same faults among her other valuable qualities. [Not one] of them works, but this is not because they are idle. They do not know how to work, that is to say, they cannot prune, condense, summarize, and pull their work into shape. The need to write for so much a line will be fatal to stronger talents than theirs. They accumulate capital from the volumes they pile up; it is impossible to make master-pieces today.
>
> (Delacroix, 1979: 198)

Her autography suffers from this prolixity, but performs a neat balancing act between editing and exploiting the royal scandal of her origins, while at the same time drawing on the sympathy evoked by her republican identification with the working class. I call it an *autography* because it creates a *model*, not a portrait, the double model of the passionate mother and the good mother, which Sand always sought to combine in the myth she endeavoured to live. One leads, at times, to her romanticisation of herself and of her family; the other, we might as well face the fact, quite often contributes to her capacity for long-winded sententiousness.

Wishful thinking and the natural child

As we have already seen, in the eighteenth and nineteenth centuries there was an enormous gulf between the romanticisation of the natural child in literature, where nature had been enshrined by Rousseau as the highest value, and his or her marginalisation in life. Sand romanticises the natural child in the manner of a Diderot or of a Dumas (see Fellows, 1981). Such literary effusions as Diderot's *Le Fils naturel*, whose protagonist is called Dorval, are linked in her mind to her friend Marie Dorval, whose bastardy-prone sub-set we have already examined (Figure 2, Chapter 3). Sand sees her as belonging to that network of 'noble bastards' (OA I: 229–30), the theatre world, and Dorval had played a lead in Dumas's *Antony*, to which Sand often refers (see OA II: 225,432). She often emulates the Rousseauesque flights of Diderot and the Romantics in her fiction, like *François le Champi* (1847). This is the story, as critics have pointed out (Busine, 1984), of a Freudian paradise where a bastard child, born without the name of the father and without the Oedipus complex, can successfully overcome the incest taboo, finally marrying his foster-mother and inheriting from his natural mother, an unusual double header. The book, to compensate for the massive unconscious transgression, is almost nauseatingly moral and sentimental at the conscious level.

The romanticisation of the natural child is not limited to her fiction, however, but is also present in her autobiography and related writings, like *Mon Grand-oncle* (1875). This story of her great-uncle, the Abbé de Beaumont, illegitimate son of Marie de Verrières and the Duc de Bouillon, and half-brother to Marie-Aurore de Saxe (Dupin), is an amazing concoction of fact and fiction, of family and oral history, of anecdotal and mythical elements. The narrative combines personal reminiscence with stories handed down to the niece of the Abbé's housekeeper. The whole relies heavily on the myth of the good bastard, the noble love child more handsome, more intelligent, and more virtuous than his legitimate brothers. It is laced with other tried and true motifs of popular fiction, such as the ducal father, jealous of his son's success with his own mistress, who runs his sword through the pile of clothes where the offender is hiding. The son, of course, never makes a sound. Folkloric, too, is the scene where the good de Beaumont confronts the Committee of Public Safety and wins the release of his abject crippled brother, the Duke, by his upright demeanour and folksy humour. The true story of de Beaumont is hard to disentangle from the myth. He may even have done all these things; we are by now well aware of the tendency to actualise in one's life the pattern of myth, whether of one's own or another's making. When we meet him in *Histoire de ma vie*, he is an aged and courtly cynic, a neutralised annuitant, unable to pass on his name, which was that of a property owned by his father, and honest enough not to spurn the lowly Sophie because of a past which was also that of his mother. He is a natural mediator, a refreshing source of good advice and good food among the female vendettas, but as prone as his sister to the entropic effects of his situation, cocooned in the décor and the mind set of the *ancien régime*.

A more insidious mythologisation, because linked to the writer's own self-esteem, is the one in which Sand envelops her half-brother, Hippolyte Chatiron. Born in 1799, five years before Sand, to her father Maurice and a carpenter's daughter, Anne-Catherine Chatiron, Hippolyte has an extraordinary birth certificate on which he is given the name of Pierre Laverdure, a pure fiction and name of convenience (see above), and is also called 'fils naturel de La Patrie' (OA I: 1304). Apparently a common euphemism in those revolutionary days, I regard this as one of the more startling manifestations of, and variations on, the use of the name of the mother. It shows an allegory of the motherland as actual womb, the natural mother of her children, just as the earth was the genetrix of Antaeus and the source of his strength.

Now Hippolyte was actually always called not by the name of convenience given on his birth certificate, but by the name of his real mother, which put him pretty low in the pecking order. However, in the tradition of the family, and like his illegitimate half-uncle, the archbishop Leblanc de Beaulieu,[16] Hippolyte was completely brought up by the servants of his grandmother, who, in spite of this, never openly acknowledged him. Sand was never told the straight truth, and he was merely introduced to her by the words: 'This is Hippolyte', although, as she says herself, there is no such thing as a secret in a house full of servants. The children loved one another, in spite of the boy's hyperactivity and propensity to violent mischief. They shared the cynical solidarity of unhappy childhood. Yet at Hippolyte's death Sand wrote:

He was the companion of my early years; he was the bastard born to be happy, in other words the spoilt child at home . . . . In certain circles, the love child arouses so much

81

interest that he ends up becoming, if not the king of the family, the one who dares everything and who is forgiven everything, because our heart needs to make up to him for being abandoned by society. In fact, being nothing officially, and unable to make any legal claims on my household, Hippolyte had always imposed on it his turbulent character, his good heart and his hot head.[17]

Even putting oneself into the context of the time, one cannot help feeling aghast at the sheer *mauvaise foi* of this obituary to her half-brother, who died of alcoholism at the age of 49. To call him lucky or even happy seems a cruel self-delusion. Certainly, she had repeatedly excused the violent and irrational behaviour of his last years, but he had, from his childhood, displayed equal affection for the sister who had, after all, displaced him and shattered any hopes he might have had of inheriting Nohant. Both children were to some extent scapegoats, subjected to quite extraordinary violence by sexually and socially frustrated tutors and servants.[18] But Hippolyte was also in a way the death's-head at Sand's feast, the figure of institutionalised illegitimacy. He had a specific place within a closed social structure, the place assigned by the patriarchy. Indeed, Mme Dupin, by giving him his 'rights', was encoding the very social structure which produced her. In it the positions of both legal and 'natural' children were strictly enforced. Sand was always conscious that, had she been one month premature, she would have been excluded from the benefits of the patriarchy but ruled by its laws, on exactly the same terms as Hippolyte, who was always a reminder that there, but for the grace of God, went Aurore herself.[19] In her account, she stresses the slimness of the margin, just as she stresses the ex-centric social status of grandmother, husband and half her relations, in order to maintain her oppositionality. Hippolyte is a necessary figure by his very lack of self-discipline, which is contrasted with his sister's force of character, just as his illegitimacy is contrasted with her self-conscious delegitimation. She exploits from the first her inheritance of marginality. Yet at the same time this is always offset by her position as proprietor of Nohant, which is also enhanced by her calm acceptance of the presence of Hippolyte in the country and his complementary double, her half-sister Caroline, in Paris. By romanticising this pair as 'nature's gentlefolk', Sand is able to enjoy both her delegitimation as free spirit and her relegitimation as good mother and eventual mistress of the art of being a grandmother.

The art of being a grandmother

Indeed, *Histoire de ma vie* is a document which looks forward as much as it looks back, on the knife edge between two phases of Sand's life and of her autography. It tells the story of a spectacularly successful delegitimation, which, as has often been pointed out, coincided exactly with the period between the revolution of 1830 (Sand left her husband and came to Paris in December of that year) and the revolution of 1848, whose failure saw her retreat to Nohant. However, it also lays the foundations of a shift from opposition to authority, and, by desexualising and depoliticising that turbulent period, creates the mythical foundations for a relegitimation, consolidated from about 1855, when *Histoire de ma vie* finished appearing, to Sand's death in 1876. The first period is associated with the figure of her mother, solidarity with the working class and with the excluded, sexual freedom, passion and intuition. The second reasserts the dominant figure of the maternal trinity, that of the grandmother, of wealth and reason, of infiltration of the patriarchy, and of mastery of the symbolic code. This is associated with the name Aurore, that of the cynical matriarch who 'masters' the system from within. The first Aurora (of Koenigsmark) occupied the two greatest positions of female power possible in the seventeenth century, first as royal mistress and then as Abbess of the convent of Quedlinburg. Sand makes the portrait of Aurora of Koenigsmark, which she keeps in her bedroom and both dislikes and admires, address her in these terms:

> 'With what nonsense are you addling your poor brain, degenerate offspring of my proud race? With what chimera of equality do you fill your dreams? Love is not what you think; men will never be what you hope. They are only made to be deceived, by kings, by women and by themselves.'[20]

Marie-Aurore de Saxe taught by example the same lesson of matriarchal power and the same secret scorn of men. Both these women, in fact, used traditional female tactics, those so despised by Olympe de Gouges (see pp. 91–2), to manipulate patriarchy from within. The whole correspondence between the second Aurore and her son, which fills so many pages of *Histoire de ma vie* – abusively, many have argued – may be seen, in fact, to have the function of reinforcing an acquired pattern of behaviour and to have its place in the history of a matriarchy. Maurice Dupin is manipulated by his mother, in the name of devotion, exactly as he is manipulated by his daughter, since Sand alters his correspondence and polishes his image for her own purposes. As George Sand, she scorned 'feminine' wiles, but remained a matriarch. The difference was that she was a matriarch who openly asserted her equality with her masculine counterparts.

Sand's devotion to her son, the next Maurice, was quite the dominant passion in her life. As she says herself, all her liaisons were in essence maternal, but any would have been sacrificed without compunction to Maurice. When she uses the term 'maternal', one must remember that her bond to *her* mother, Sophie, was, for many years, an all-consuming physical and sexual passion. In a mirror effect, her relationship to her daughter, Solange, turned into a devouring sexual hatred.[21] The first maternal trinity she endeavoured to form, based on herself, her daughter, and her daughter's daughter, ended in tragedy with the deaths of two successive granddaughters and an inter-necine war with Solange. Although the end of her life was dedicated to setting up yet another maternal trinity, this time completely in the name of the mother, the name Sand which she had made for herself and which was also taken by her son, the pattern she was following was that of the family tradition, of the female genealogy. The only surprise is that, when Maurice married, late in life, she approved of his wife. One cannot help feeling that the death of Maurice's first child, a son, was more than compensated for by the birth of another little Aurore, who brought the wheel full circle.

It is fitting that Sand's last book should have been *Contes de ma grand-mère* (Tales of My Grandmother), a title displaying an inherent ambivalence. In whose name does it tell its tales? Does the author assume the role of grandmother or does she speak for *her* grandmother? The position of *énonciation* and that of the narrator are basically unstable. Ambivalent to the last, the book contains, in 'Le chêne parlant' [The Talking Oak], yet another piece of mythologising of Nature, who takes the shape of the oak tree, as the second mother of an outcast child. Present in the same story is the last evocation of the negative myth of St Anne, in which an old witch figure gives the child dubious knowledge and tainted wealth but also love. Yet the collection of stories combines this compulsive replay of a personal myth with other tales which are mere saleable exotica and pastiches of Mme de Ségur. The oral tradition is coupled with the literary exercise, as Sand remains double to the end.

Patterns of alterity

I think we can see, in the female genealogy of *Histoire de ma vie*, the possibilities of lines of flight, of divergence and infiltration of the patriarchal model. The protean character of the name of the mother is abundantly visible. The possibilities of freedom it provides are greatly enhanced by the inherent instability of illegitimacy, but this also provokes existential anxiety and the initial 'family romance', the dream of relegitimation. In Sand's case, this pattern is reversed, and, victim as she is to her grandmother's successful implementation of this dream, her first impulse is to glory in the role of pariah, and to seek exclusion from her social class, from the name of the father, and from the taboos on female sexuality.

I have concentrated on the maternal mythologisation, with its inherent doubleness, rather than on the other doubleness which appears to take the form of androgyny and 'virilisation'. I made this limitation, first because the subject is so abundantly covered in Sand criticism, where, however, she is often presented as either a ball-breaking castrator or, equally falsely, as a proto-feminist, and second because, as I have suggested, I believe that a great deal of her cross-dressing was, as she says, a practical step to bodily freedom and saving money. It was also a fantastic publicity stunt, *un scandale qui rapporte*, in itself a myth which took control of its creator. The male–female ambiguity is only part of a larger pattern of double binds, such as mother–mistress or bohemian–landowner, inherent in the texts.

I also hope that this family study has supported the conclusions I came to in Chapter 2, that the single model of the Oedipus is inadequate and does not account for deep-seated complexes and patterns of familial behaviour generated by traditional structures other than that of the bourgeois family. The myth of St Anne and the maternal trinity is but one of the models of alterity *in potentia*. Whether such a matriarchal model is ultimately but a mirror image of the law of the Father, a manifestation of otherness that merely reinforces tradition, is a moot point. In the end, I think the answer depends on our context and our reading. Like Freud, we find the message we are conditioned to find. I, for instance, have always read *La Petite Fadette*, even at the age of 9, as an oppositional text. But this was because I was already reading from a position of alterity. Perhaps the greatest interest of the alternative family history is that it makes such shifts in position possible, just as following a female genealogy opens on to the difference of our en-gendering and not its sameness.

5

Opposition and revolution: Olympe de Gouges and the rights of the dispossessed

... alone, looking out of the dining-room window, I saw an old woman who, holding her worn shoes in her hand, was yelling as hard as she could: 'I'm revorting! I'm revorting!' ... The ridiculousness of this revolt struck me greatly. An old woman against a regiment!

(Stendhal, 1973: 74–5)

The distinction which I want to explore in this chapter is that between opposition and revolution.[1] My interest is in the way in which they differ in their manipulation of the rules of exclusion, and their relation to legitimation and delegitimation. Social structures are always founded upon relationships of exclusion. Exclusion works by establishing sets, defined, like all sets, by relationships of difference, and displaying the shifting boundaries that characterise all paradigmatic sets. Thus the rules of birth will establish insider–outsider relationships different from those of education, and the heterosexual–homosexual divide will create shifting groups within other normative sets of sex or wealth. In earlier chapters, we have begun to formulate theories dealing extensively with the insider–outsider relationship formed by the legitimate–illegitimate divide. The drive to control by setting up closed insider circles admitting only those who correspond to the 'norm' is always strong. Those within the circle can thus define themselves by their relation of 'otherness' to those excluded. The notions of limits, of boundaries, of distinctions thus generated are frequently codified into actual written law.

Starting with the situation in France at the end of the eighteenth century, we have seen that those excluded from the dominant social groups frequently have a form of power and of voice. Except in the case of the nobility, however, it is a power that tends to rely on practice rather than on law, and a voice which tends to be oral rather than written. The power, for instance, of servants was a very real one, but it was an oppositional power, whose undermining of authority ranged from outright theft to manipulation by the production of subtle discomfort. The master controlled the written records, the servant's voice with rare exceptions was heard only in the spaces of exclusion, such as the kitchen and servants' hall. Whatever the form of exclusion in different social contexts, the 'other voice' has always existed, the question being rather where and in what company it may be heard. As we saw in Chapter 4, in the acceptance of noble bastardy, oppositional practice may even become an implicit cultural code, but one denied an official voice. Thus it is characteristic of the oppositional that the servants' hall should institute a hierarchy equivalent to that of the masters.

Opposition and oppositional practice constitute a recognition and acceptance of exclusion, by the very fact that the ground for manoeuvre is chosen with the laws of exclusion in mind. Sometimes it works by ritualised inversion. A characteristic oppositional practice would be the inversions of the three days of carnival when servants become 'masters', the wise become 'fools', and men become 'women' (see Bakhtin, 1968). But these inversions are themselves recognitions of the norms of the *status quo*, though they may eventually involve a gradual erosion of values, more productive of social evolution than revolution itself (see Bloch, 1962). Still, in the short run, the other voice knows it must revert to being the hidden voice. Revolution, on the other hand, questions the processes and relationships of exclusion themselves and seeks to overthrow the norms, only, of course, to replace them with other norms. The old woman Stendhal saw, about 1788, had probably used oppositional practices all her life. She had survived, after all. Why did a short-lived workers' uprising trigger her sudden revolt?

The dead-letter office

We must remember, too, that revolution in its turn may become the ground work for a whole new attempt at legitimation. In this chapter and Chapter 7, I choose the very different writings of two women revolutionaries, Olympe de Gouges (1748–93) and Louise Michel (1830–1905) as my main examples, but the model is much more widely applicable. My belief is that the collection of documents of 'forgotten female production', such as those used here, is not much more useful than the reverential collection of used baby clothes, unless one can also theorise both their production and their consumption, or non-consumption. In that theorisation Derrida's allegory of the postal service (1980) can be a useful tool. It posits that communication is not transparent: just because you produce a message – post a letter – does not mean that the letter necessarily arrives or that it is read. All sorts of factors intervene: the writing, the postman, the stamping or non-stamping, the envelope, and so on. We must theorise why women's texts mostly ended up in the dead-letter office. What made them inaudible, their message unreadable? To find out we have to go beyond the conspiracy theory of misogyny. These texts were generally as inaudible to women as to men.

If we read today the passionate outbursts of Olympe de Gouges, demanding that both the 'natural' child and the thinking woman should be truly accepted as natural, that is, equal, or Louise Michel's refusal of all hierarchy, including textual hierarchy, in the name of anarchy, *we* can, if we wish, hear their message. Yet, although they were read when they appeared, their message was so scandalous, so incongruous in its context, that it was not heard. Thereafter, for nearly 200 years in the one case, and 100 in the other, they were consigned to the dead-letter office. I want to look at the factors involved in the production of these texts, including that of gender, and particularly at the loosening of social shibboleths in the onset of revolution. The problem of their consumption will also be raised, though it really demands a separate study informed by cultural theories of reception.

A question which must be asked is not just how language is used, but what authorises it and how it is heard. Control consists in the setting of boundaries, especially in language, and what is beyond a codified boundary becomes invisible and inaudible, just as what is beyond a nutritional boundary becomes inedible. Messages which do not fit the frame of expectation of a given culture – for example, scientific experiments and findings which contradict the received ideas of the scientific establishment – are simply *totgeschwiegen*.[2] It is important to realise that this is usually not a conscious conspiracy of silence, but in most cases the well-known unwillingness of the human mind to absorb or to remember anything which lies outside its habitual trajectories. Robert de Beaugrande (1988) has shown us recently how texts are immediately subject not only to the limitations of the producer's discourse, but also to the distortions of the consumer's fields of perception and memory. The other factor he has clearly demonstrated in action is the one I intend to discuss now, the mechanism of exclusion.

Women's oppositional practice

Although the systems of exclusion were many, varied, and deeply enforced in pre-revolutionary France, yet, as Olympe de Gouges pointed out, the most general and most deeply normative relationship of exclusion was that between men and women.[3] That exclusion, constant through all ranks of society, produced, as exclusion must, a complex set of oppositional practices and an extensive counter-culture. I wish to suggest that the startling modernity, the almost prophetic nature of Olympe de Gouges's revolutionary claims, springs in part from the fact that she was excluded, or excluded herself, as much from *women's* oppositional practices as from the norms of masculine society. She was forced to demand a society which would accept her on her own terms, a genuinely revolutionary project. Of course, in the 1790s, as Benoîte Groult, to whose work I owe an enormous debt, says: 'To attempt a second revolution within the revolution seemed mad and totally fanciful' (G: 42).[4]

Women at this period indulged in very different forms of oppositional practice according to their place in society. Peasant female counter-culture, for instance, was purely oral, based on song, story-telling, and gossip, by women speaking in the different dialects, the mother tongues of their regions (see Maclean, 1987). We will see how Louise Michel gives written expression to these hidden discourses. This sub-culture was strongly centred on productive and reproductive values and the *rites de passage* of childbirth and death. Even here, in the career of Olympe de Gouges, we can see the double exclusion operating. She was born Marie Gouze, the love child of a noble father and a bourgeois mother, who was hastily married off to a (bought?) husband. Olympe herself was forcibly married at 16, a mother at 17, a widow at 18, but found a 'protector' who allowed her to escape from her southern village. Yet, when she moved to Paris she excluded herself from the Languedoc of her birth, and spoke French as a second language retaining the accent and emphases of the south.

The bourgeois women of the *tiers-état* in the towns varied enormously in wealth and education. But, generally speaking, their oppositional force had a strong economic base in the household and in the power of domestic management, in spite of the fact that a husband had complete legal control over his wife's money as well as her person. When Olympe, widowed at 18, refused not only to remarry but even to call herself by her husband's name, and chose to live as a single mother under a name of her own devising, refusing the norms of patriarchy, she excluded herself from any solidarity with the respectable women, *femmes honnêtes*, who manoeuvred within those norms, in a regularised complicity with the society which constituted them as other.

Her very beauty presented a series of dilemmas, and raises interesting questions of opposition and exclusion. Beauty is an extreme form of otherness, a dangerous object of desire and obsession, only to be contained by known rituals and reified by male fetishisation. A beautiful woman is traditionally accept-able only as saint or harlot, angel or devil. Olympe was quickly categorised as harlot (G: 18). Yet, once again, she refused all categorisation. On the one hand, she excluded herself from the counter-culture and oppositional practices of the courtesans; at the same time, on the other hand, she refused to marry her protector. The tradition of the kept woman encouraged the men of the period to connive at oppositional practice. Treating woman as a fetish, it was possible to say, without losing face, 'I can deny her nothing', and admit one's mistress to a very great degree of real power, as adviser, as manipulator, as blackmailer. Yet it would have been totally impossible for the same man to say: 'She is my equal.'[5] Olympe de Gouges sums up this female assumption of power:

Women have done more evil than good. Constraint and

dissimulation have been their lot. What strength snatched from them, trickery gave back; they resorted to all the resources of their charms, and the most irreproachable man could not resist them. Poison, steel, everything was in their power; they were in command of crime as of virtue. The French government, especially, has been dependent, for centuries, on the nocturnal administration of women; the cabinet had no secrets from their indiscretion; embassy, command, ministry, presidency, pontificate, cardinalate, in short everything which stands for masculine stupidity, profane and sacred, has all been subject to the greed and ambition of this sex, formerly despicable and respected, and since the revolution, respectable and despised.[6]

Writing as woman

The area of counter-culture which was the most developed, and to which Olympe should naturally have belonged, was that of the salons, the closed and influential world of intelligent upper-class women. It was a circle, or series of eccentric circles, 'other' to the rituals of male power in court and Church, and yet playing off them and playing with them. Olympe was excluded from this world by her illegitimacy (her noble literary father only acknowledged her privately); hence her defiant assumption of the *particule* in her *nom de plume*, which was constructed from the name of the mother,[7] not that of the father which was denied her. Her rejection of her Christian (in both senses of the word) name, Marie, in favour of Olympe, also substituted fashionable pantheism for patriarchal Catholicism. Even more remarkably, and from her first publications onwards, she uses the Enlightenment cult of Nature to validate and indeed give special worth to her own status as a 'natural' child. Her first plays carry the same message as her 1792 letter to Bernadin de Saint-Pierre:

> The man of genius, the enlightened man, never disdains the literary fruit produced by the workings of Nature alone. I can even call myself one of her favorite children. She has done everything for me. . . .[8]

Her attempt at autography, *Mémoire de Madame de Valmont*

(1788), which makes the same claims, was published thinly veiled by yet another aristocratic pseudonym, probably for fear of reprisals from the Le Franc de Pompignan (her father's) family. Written in the popular form of an exchange of letters, its substratum of truth, including extracts from what is probably a genuine correspondence with her father, is heavily fictionalised and mythologised. Although the heroine emerges as definitely too good to be true, her account does show the mechanisms of exclusion in action, those of social and religious prejudice in particular. There is also a wonderful (and probably apocryphal) letter from her father, attempting to dissuade her from a literary career:

> If persons of your sex become rational and profound in their works, what will become of us, us men, today so light and superficial? Farewell the superiority of which we were so proud. The ladies will dictate to us . . . . This revolution will be dangerous . . . . Women may write but they are forbidden, for the good of the world, to indulge in it pretentiously.[9]

This seems more like Olympe's own voice, but it would be impossible even to parody some of the male reactions to her work, in their extreme misogyny. Her first play, for instance, which questioned the slave trade, *L'Esclavage des nègres* (The Enslavement of the Negroes) (1788), provoked a storm of attacks on her person, her morals, and her literary ability from outraged colonists. The reaction was unsurprising, since thus early in her career she equated her literary (and gendered) revolution with the political climate of the time, and made her slave hero appeal to 'the sweet laws of Nature' (Gouges, 1989: 34). As the play's most recent editor, Eléni Varikas, says:

> Her *Zamore et Mirza* [original title] constitutes one of the hidden traces that help us to reconstitute the genealogy of the dissenting tradition which, in spite of its vaguenesses, its contradictions, its reversals, did, in a way, resist the ploys of instrumental reason to preserve the subversive elements in the universalising promises of natural law.
>
> (ibid.: 26)

What also put her beyond the pale as a playwright was her lack of education.[10] Not only was she near-illiterate when she came to Paris but, even more damning to her career as literary lady, she conspicuously lacked social education. As she says:

> I must obtain a plenary indulgence for all my faults, which are heavy rather than light: faults in French, faults in construction, faults in style, faults in knowledge, faults in creating interest, faults in wit, faults in genius . . . . In fact, I was taught nothing. Brought up in a district where French is badly spoken, I don't know the principles, I don't know anything. I display my ignorance proudly, I dictate with my soul, never with my mind.[11]

She always had to dictate her work, a very important factor in her written production, and she never did learn to behave like a lady.[12] The anarchy of revolution was her natural element, the 'oral' immediacy of pamphlets and wall posters suited both her rhetorical verve and her impetuous temperament, better in fact than her chosen *métier* of playwright. Her writing is marked by a constant heteroglossia in which different discourses mingle: the varied discourses of class, the contrived language of literature, the impetuousness of oral rhetoric, and the partially grasped 'masculine' discourses of politics and philosophy. Coming from a different context, one which would have given her the heritage of culture of which she felt she had been cheated, she might have been another Madame de Staël, but her production would then have been oppositional rather than revolutionary. And it is the making of the revolutionary that interests me here. My research points to the presence of similar backgrounds for other revolutionary women,[13] as we will see in the examples of Louise Michel and Flora Tristan. All three were, of course, dismissed as women of bad reputation, hysteric and possibly insane, and were excluded from 'respectable' female society. All found it difficult to suffer fools gladly, and remained unshaken in the conviction of their own genius. Males with similar profiles, while also starting on the revolutionary path, have more easily been assimilated into the oppositional, and institutionalised, structures of society, as the twentieth-century careers of Ernest Bevan and Willy Brandt bear witness. Their very great achievements as reformers are more easily recognised.

Tactics and solidarity

One of the interesting features of institutionalised exclusion is that it will sooner admit and even encourage oppositional practice than come to terms with the demands of the excluded to be included in the structures of power.[14] From the eighteenth to the twentieth century a typical formalisation of opposition is seen in the constant admonition to women in France: 'You already have power, why do you want rights?' This may have been particularly strong in France because of the semi-institutionalisation of the 'power behind the throne' and the tradition of female manipulation of those in positions of authority. Women who achieved position and respect by these means used tactics rather than strategy, as de Certeau defines them:

> Tactics has no place except in that of the other. Also it must play with the terrain imposed on it, organised by the law of a strange force . . . . It operates blow by blow . . . . What it gains cannot be held . . . . It must vigilantly utilise the gaps which the particular combination of circumstances opens in the control of the proprietary power. It poaches there. It creates surprises. It is possible for it to be where no one expects it. It is wile. In sum it is an art of the weak.
>
> (1980: 6)

Skilled in use of tactics, they had good reason to reassure men that they accepted the *status quo*. Benoîte Groult quotes Madame de Staël as saying: 'Women are rightly excluded from civil and public matters. Nothing is more opposed to their natural vocation' (G: 37).[15] And that other heroine of the revolution, Madame Roland, who in 1792 wielded very real power for a while, as the strong head behind her husband, reassured men: 'We want no rule but through your hearts and no throne but in your hearts' (G: 38).[16] Not that it did her much good. The myth of protection was accepted by women and men alike; a protector seems more beneficent than a master. The Jacobin editors of *Révolutions de Paris* merely echoed the conservative position and foreshadowed that of the public prosecutor when they pontificated:

> The honour of women consists in cultivating in silence all the virtues of their sex, under the veil of modesty and in the

shadow of retreat. It is not incumbent on women to show the way to me. . . .

(Blanc, 1989: 128)

Olympe de Gouges, from her social and literary position outside the pale, correctly identified in her 'Préface pour les dames' (1791), the problem of women as being one of solidarity. For a revolution of any kind to be successful a group of people needs to forge common bonds and a feeling of group identity. As a result of their socialisation and the construction of their gender, women tended to forge a singular identity, each for herself. There was a certain counter-culture which achieved momentary solidarity by mocking men for the ease with which they could be manipulated, and a group solidarity in events such as childbirth. But by and large, women were comfortable only with established oppositional practice, and so ideologically conditioned that the thought of openly claiming equality with men was not only shocking but frightening. A woman differently socialised, in rebellion against the law of the Father because it was first represented by a man she knew *not* to be her true father, and then by a marriage forced on her at 16, Olympe succeeded in escaping from the system. As she says: 'I cleared a new way for myself'(G: 124). But such a woman had necessarily to encounter extreme difficulty in finding unity with other women, and, without it, there was no hope of starting her revolution within the revolution. The necessary pride and egocentricity which sustained her in her quest, first for literary and then for political fame, made the possibility of group cohesion unlikely.

From 1790 to 1792, documentation like that in *Les Femmes dans la révolution française* (Women in the French Revolution) reveals that other voices, such as those of Etta Palm and Théroigne de Méricourt,[17] were raised to demand justice for women. In the patriotic frenzy of the women's march on Versailles, there seemed to be some hope of a feminist ground swell, but the main demands of women, voiced in many pamphlets and *affiches*,[18] were for marital justice and rights to inheritance and divorce. Even here the voices of women were generally oppositional rather than revolutionary. They demanded more fair play for women, but *within* the existing system. Questioning the very nature of the system was the true scandal.

96

Exclusion and the rights of man

Now, similarly, the scandal of the *Declaration of the Rights of Man and of the Citizen* was precisely that it denied the traditional patterns of exclusion. If all men were born free and equal, what became of the distinctions between the three estates and the complicated traditions of rank? If all citizens had equal rights and responsibilities, what became of the myths of protection associated with the first and second estates? The seventeen articles, by key words of exclusion such as 'distinction' and 'limits', and key words of inclusion such as 'equal', 'admissible', question the legal and judicial bases of social exclusion. However, they must, as Lyotard (1983: 209–12) points out, set up a new and complicated mechanism of legitimation for their claims. This never resolves any basic contradiction between the rights of humanity on the one hand and those of a member of the French nation on the other, since 'the legitimation of communities by their names and traditional stories resists legitimation by an Idea' (ibid.: 212). An attempt at resolution is made only by an appeal to a 'meta-authority', the Supreme Being. However, even when they speak of humanity, they still only mean the male half, and they never question the customary biological bases of exclusion. As Cobban says: 'Privilege was the enemy, equality the aim, though it must be remembered that the equality desired by the Third Estate was an equality not of property but of status' (Cobban, 1963: 263). And status, of course, is what is maintained by the strategies of power. Status is precisely what women were denied by sex and custom.

The *Declaration of the Rights of Man* was just what it said, 'man' here excluding foreigners, most Jews, slaves (until the rewrite in 1793) and, of course, women. The *Cahiers de doléances* (Records of Grievances) of 1789, at least in the version I have read, in a collection of documents rightly called *1789 les Français* [not *françaises*] *ont la parole* (Goubert and Denis, 1964), scarcely mentions women at all, apart from one reference to rape by billeted soldiers, one to childbirth, and a couple to the need for convent schools. The *Cahiers* sent to the King did not, of course, include the separately published *Remontrances, plaintes et doléances des dames françoises, à l'occasion de l'Assemblée des Etats-Généraux* (Remonstrances, Complaints and Grievances of the Ladies of France, on the

Occasion of the Assembly of the Estates-General) (1789).[19] That word *dames* (ladies) is revealing; here, as in the writings of Mary Wollstonecraft, education and social status still operate a form of exclusion: only certain women's rights are being vindicated. Even Olympe, in her 1789 petition for a desperately needed maternity hospital, demands one only for well-brought-up women, who should not have to mix with the common people (G: 82).

The Rights of Woman

In order to see how Olympe uses and subverts the master tongue to write of that other revolution she desires both as woman and as bastard, I want to examine the full text of *Les Droits de la femme* (The Rights of Woman) (1791), which is seldom if ever reproduced, partly because, in the 'objective' terms of traditional debate, the first and fourth parts seem to undermine its authority. The four sections each have a different form and different addressees, and each shows us a different facet of its authorial thought and rhetoric. The first part is an extraordinary dedication in epistolary form: TO THE QUEEN. The second, a feminist rewriting of the *Declaration* itself, is addressed to Man and, more particularly, to the members of the National Assembly. The third is a *Postambule* addressed to Woman, admonitory to bourgeois women in tone but also proposing a complete revolution in marriage, or, rather, family relationships. The fourth, a postscript called a joke (though it is no laughing matter) and addressed to the friendly reader, is the purely personal account of an altercation with a cheating cab-driver and a surly *commissaire de paix*, in which, most emphatically, the personal is also political. The postscript (in a different font) even has its own untidy P.S. (in an even smaller font), telling us something about the extraordinary spontaneity with which these pamphlets were rushed into print.

The dedication

The dedication to the Queen, which seems fairly mind-boggling when viewed in the sole context of women's rights, actually represents its author's most deep-seated and most recurrent fantasy. Such fantasies seem to provide an essential prop to the ego. This fantasy, an obvious response to her situation of social exclusion, recurs obsessively in her works, and involves a series of situations in which she sees herself as equal to the Queen. It begins fairly meekly in the *Remarques patriotiques* of 1788, and assumes quite extraordinary proportions after the Revolution of 1789 permits authorial liberties which would previously have meant incarceration in the Bastille. In 1790 she allows herself a person-to-person chat with the queen, with an amazing tone of intimacy, in her *Adresse à la Reine* (Address to the Queen). There she says:

> Everything convinces me, Madam, that, isolated from any pernicious advice, alone, at peace with yourself, you feel in your heart everything which goes on in mine, everything that an individual without reproach can experience.[20]

The sentiments are repeated in the preface to the play *Mirabeau aux Champs-Elisées* (1791), and in the woman-to-woman advice of the dedication of *Les Droits de la femme*: 'Madam, support such a noble cause; defend this unhappy sex, and you will soon get one half of the kingdom on your side, and at least a third of the other half.'[21] Their most outrageous manifestation comes in 1792, in another address to the Queen prefacing the *Description de la fête du 3 juin* (Description of the Festival of 3 June), and, most blatantly, when Olympe puts herself on stage in a play entitled *La France sauvée, ou Le Tyran détrôné* (France Saved, or The Tyrant Dethroned),[22] in which she penetrates to the Queen's own apartments, lectures the lady-in-waiting while Marie Antoinette listens from behind a curtain, and, most symbolically, dares to take a seat in the virtual presence of royalty. This fantasy of regal equality may be seen as the guiding myth of Olympe's destiny and came to an end only on the scaffold, where she was indeed equal to the Queen.

The dedication to the Queen, and its amazing vision of Marie Antoinette as head of a women's movement, is also an interesting demonstration of the revolutionary quest for status. Just as the *tiers-état* from 1789 to 1792 could not really feel included in the apparatus of power unless its new status was given legitimation by the consent of a constitutional monarch, so women in their demands for equal status needed to drag the coach of monarchy behind them, as they had literally done on 6 October 1789. The sanctioning of status by symbolic means was still seen as necessary, just as the appeal to Nature in the second section was a retrieval of the philosophical territory needed as legitimation.

The declaration

The second part begins with an appeal to Man to return to Nature and accede to the 'natural' course of justice, and is a typical manifestation of that deification of the natural which springs from the teachings of Rousseau in particular. This view, as we have seen, is particularly attractive to the natural child. Already, in the *Mémoire de Madame de Valmont*, the connection is clearly stated:

> I do not know if Religion and if God himself ordered the stifling of the cries of illegitimate blood, but the voice of Nature speaks in me, she tells me that her law is that which God himself prescribed for man.
>
> (Gouges, 1788: 120)[23]

An important feature of the 'Declaration of the rights of woman and of the citizeness' that follows the appeal to Nature is that it copies exactly the structure of the *Declaration of the Rights of Man*. It thus avoids, at least in the seventeen articles, the rhetorical excesses of the letter to the Queen, but, much more importantly, it undermines men's discourse from within. It is an early and most telling demonstration of the feminist axiom that no discourse is neutral. A close comparison of the two texts shows that, simply by changing the gender of key nouns and pronouns in many of the articles, the text is delegitimated, allowing a space for the revolution within the revolution. To adapt Nancy Miller's quotation from Peggy Kamuf, Olympe's rewriting:

> refusing the [language] of a hegemonic paternity . . . allows for the emergence of a less stable rhetoric of maternity; 'reading a text . . . *as if*, in other words, it were illegitimate, recognized by its mother who can only give it a borrowed name'.
>
> (1990: 71–2)

The revolutionary egalitarianism and self-evident justice of the famous declaration are shown, by a semiotic *tour de force*, to conceal another more deeply rooted ideology. If 'man', as women were assured, then as now, subsumed the category of woman, how was it possible that, in some clauses, the mere substitution of 'women' for 'men' and 'citizeness' for 'citizen' was enough to produce a 'scandalous' and 'ridiculous' text? It was a text immediately repressed or rubbished by *ad hominem* (or *ad feminam*) attacks on the writer's sanity.[24] The master tongue in all ages claims to speak in the voice of sanity and reason, both ideological constructs as Foucault (1961) has clearly demonstrated. To this the Revolution added the claim to speak in the voice of Nature, a claim which could also be subverted to the use of minorities, as when the Black hero of *L'Esclavage des nègres* said: 'I like his Nature more than I do him [the white man]. She has set in my soul the laws of humanity and of a wise equality'(Gouges, 1989: 36).

The preamble to the 'Declaration of the rights of woman' immediately raises the problem of the exclusion of woman. Speaking of sexual subordination, which is seen as an exception to the laws of Nature, it claims: 'Man alone worked this exception up into a principle' (DF: 5).[25] The extraordinary feature of the following seventeen articles is that, merely by making the same claims for women as had been established for men, she sets in place all the major demands of feminism, a breathtakingly modern perspective, which France, at least, had to wait nearly 150 years to see fulfilled.

Article One states the principle of sexual equality.

Article Two not only states the right to own property (one denied to all married women) but also, by the use of the term 'security', the right to protection from rape and assault, vital not only to married women but also to domestic servants and working women generally.

Article Three demands citizenship for both sexes.

Article Four defines the boundaries which exclude woman as those set by the tyranny of man: 'Liberty and justice consist in giving back everything that belongs to others' (DF: 8)[26] – in this case woman's natural rights.

Article Five appeals to the laws of nature and reason, not custom, thereby admitting the possibility of divorce.

Article Six transforms the famous 'career open to all talents' into the first statement of equal opportunity.

Article Seven reinforces the principle of inclusion by

demanding equal punishment (the only right immediately granted!).

Article Eight demands that punishment be limited to that laid down by law, thereby denying the customary right of husbands to assault their wives.

Article Nine demands punishment by the forces of the law alone.

Article Ten demands freedom of opinion and the right of women to public office, and contains the famous statement: 'woman has the right to mount the scaffold; she should also have the right to mount the Tribune' (DF: 10).[27]

Article Eleven demands, as a result of free speech, the right to file paternity suits, forbidden to women at the time. (Revealingly, this is the only demand which is added, and not merely re-gendered.)

Article Twelve is notable by omission, it speaks of the need for 'a major utility' to guarantee women's rights rather than for 'a public force' (an army), as was demanded for men.

Article Thirteen extends to women the principle of no taxation without representation.

Article Fourteen demands equality not only of taxation, but of representation on the board which determines it.

Article Fifteen demands government accountability to both sexes.

Article Sixteen demands truly universal suffrage: 'the constitution is null and void, if the *majority* of individuals who make up the Nation has not co-operated in drawing it up' (DF: 11; my emphasis).[28]

Article Seventeen demands the right to own property: *none*, including thereby married women, may be deprived of it.

Postambule

This document is truly revolutionary in that it is based on principles of inclusion, of equality of status before the law, not on women's age-old tactics of opposition. In the third section, addressed to women, the 'Postambule', Olympe actually contrasts oppositional practice with revolutionary practice: 'In the

centuries of corruption you only ruled over men's weakness . . . .
Whatever may be the barriers that are opposed to you, it is in
your power to set yourselves free; you have only to set your
minds to it' (DF: 12–13).[29] Such a view of revolutionary practice
was – then and later – particularly likely to prove anathema to
male revolutionaries.

This section demands not only equal education for women,
and the legalisation of prostitution, but makes a frontal attack
on marriage, unchanged by the new regime:

> Marriage is the tomb of confidence and love. A married
> woman may, with impunity, give bastards to her husband,
> and the fortune which does not belong to them. She who is
> unmarried has but a feeble right: ancient and inhuman
> laws refused her, for her children, this right to the name
> and the property of their father, and new laws have not
> been made in this regard.[30]

She then goes on to suggest that, in a proposed *Contrat social de
l'homme et de la femme* (Social Contract of Man and Woman),
unions may be freely entered into and freely dissolved, while the
children of all the mother's partnerships, or all the father's,
would inherit equally. We have not quite got there, with our
concepts of guiltless divorce and *de facto* inheritance, but we are
working on it! An addition, quite out of step with the beliefs of
the time, was the demand that white colonists should treat their
half-caste bastards equally with their other offspring.[31]

Postscript

The last section, a disaster in practical terms, if she expected the
whole document to be taken seriously, since it switches to the
discourse of women's gossip, is still quite relevant, since it
shows how a woman alone is really treated in everyday dealings.
Cheated by a cab-driver and her demand for redress despised by
officials, she is finally jokingly asked by an uninterested magis-
trate whether she proposes to take her complaint to the National
Assembly, to which she replies that she might just do that. And
that, of course, is what she is doing.

The authorities might have forgotten, if not forgiven, the
aberration of the 'Declaration of the rights of woman and of the
citizeness', since neither men nor women took it seriously. It

could be regarded as belonging to the realm of the unheard. But Olympe's fate was sealed when she attempted a move into the male revolutionary arena and publicly denounced the tyranny of Robespierre. In July 1793 she was arrested. The ultimate irony was that on 28 June 1793 the Convention had passed a law helping single mothers and giving abandoned children the same rights as other citizens. In fact, on the very day she appeared before the Revolutionary Tribunal a law was passed giving natural children the right to bear their father's name, and, in some cases, to inherit from him (Blanc, 1989: 194). How right Mirabeau had been in paying tribute to the debt owed to this *ignorante* (ibid.: 97). No acknowledgement was made in the Convention of debts owed to her or any other revolutionary woman. Rather, in October 1793 women's clubs were banned and any gathering of more than five women forbidden, thus putting an end to the revolution of the second sex.

The final exclusion

There is one form of undeniably permanent exclusion, one boundary most sharply defined, and one right to which the revolution admitted women: the guillotine. Within a space of twenty-one days at the end of 1793 three participants in the 'monstrous regiment' – 'brawling and contentious women', in the eyes of the Committee of Public Safety – were executed: Marie Antoinette, political puppet of Austria and debauched wife; Olympe de Gouges, whose madness led her to think herself a statesman; and Madame Roland, part-time *philosophe* and queen for a day, in the words of the *Moniteur universel* (G: 60). In Olympe's Golgotha she was refused her chosen name, and tried as Marie Gouze, Veuve Aubry. Just as she had been denied at the time of her birth by her father, so too she was repudiated at the time of her death by her son, an officer in the Republican army (G: 52–6).

Benoîte Groult also quotes the words of the *procureur* Charmette, the day after Olympe's execution. Firmly dismissing a delegation of Republican women in red bonnets, he admonished them:

Remember that haughty woman, la Roland, who thought herself fit to rule the Republic and sped to her own destruction . . . . Remember that virago, that man–woman, the impudent Olympe de Gouges, who forsook all her household duties, wished to play politics and committed crimes . . . . This forgetfulness of the virtues of her sex led her to the scaffold.

All these immoral beings have been obliterated by the vengeful blade of the law. And you would wish to imitate them? No! You should feel that you are only truly interesting and worthy of respect when you are once again what Nature wanted you to be. We want women to be respected, that is why we will force them to respect themselves.[32]

This silencing of the 'other voice' of the Revolution bitterly recalls Olympe's remark about 'the ambition of this sex formerly despicable and respected, and since the revolution, respectable and despised'. It also shows that 'Nature' is a goddess to whom any ideology may make appeal.

At the beginning of the *Postambule* to the 'Declaration of the rights of woman' Olympe de Gouges says that the legislators of France may wish to repeat the excluding words of the Legislator of the Wedding at Cana: 'Woman, what have I to do with thee?' Perhaps, as a farewell to her as the 'other voice' of revolutionary woman, we may recall the other half of the quotation from John 11: 4: 'Mine hour is not yet come.'

6

The male/female Messiah:
Flora Tristan

If autobiography is a sort of *mise en scène*, in which the personal myth ultimately created depends as much on the ideologies current in society as on the 'facts' experienced, then the early nineteenth century in France produced one of the most fertile breeding-grounds for such myths. The utopian writings of Saint-Simon and his followers led as much to a quest for a mythical experience, in time, in space and in personal interaction, as to a demand for the betterment of society. One area where the lived event is readily transmuted into 'fiction' by the very process of its representation is that of the journey. Every journey may be seen as potential allegory, just as lived experience may be allegorised as journey. We will explore this exchange between life and archetype in the writings of Flora Tristan (1803–44), but it must be remembered that she is paradigmatic of a whole group of writers for whom the voyage was as much a mystical as a physical rite of passage. The traveller's tale was a literary staple of the times, and the destination might be as close and as real as Spain or Italy, or as fantastic as the Icaria of Cabet's *Voyage en Icarie* (1840). The voyage readily becomes the quest and lends itself as much to autography, which I have characterised as a self-portrait to live by, as to autothanatography, which I have suggested is rather a self-portrait to die by, a way of guiding reception and perception.

Another rich source for the creation of both public and personal myths – again closely, but not exclusively, bound to the utopian thinkers – was the divinisation of woman: not any woman, but that strange hybrid who has always been the stuff of myth and religion, and who combines the magical potency of virginity with the wisdom and sacrificial reputation of mother-

106

hood. We have already studied the role of the Virgin Mary as the best-known representative of this paradigm. In the early nineteenth century, the mass revival of the cult of the Mother of God was a feature of extreme right-wing thought, but also, in an inverted form, as one more anti-myth, a feature of oppositional 'socialist' literature and practices. For example: 'Saint-Simon's ex-secretary, Auguste Comte, gets rid of any suggestion of equality by doffing his hat religiously to the Virgin-Mother Clotilde de Vaux, his platonic mistress' (Desanti, 1972: 182). The cult culminated among the orthodox in the proclamation of the extremely dubious doctrine of the Immaculate Conception of the Virgin Mary herself, enshrined by Pius IX in 1854. Among the heretical, if not lunatic, fringe which preyed on women as effectively as the black-coated 'crows' anathematised by novelists from Stendhal to Zola, the search for the divine Mother by the Père Enfantin in the early 1830s (which also permitted Enfantin to eulogise bastardy), and the publication of Abbé Constant's *Assomption de la femme* in 1841, and his *La Mère de Dieu* in 1844, are just the best-known and more eccentric manifestations.[1]

Less notorious, but widespread among writers and philosophers, was that cult of a female idealisation as source of wisdom and spiritual guidance, which I have called the myth of Sophia. The very prevalence of the name Sophie in Europe at the time bears witness to its pervasiveness. While Novalis displays possibly the purest form of the cult in his confusion between the real woman and the mythical figure, Sophia recurs syncretically in disparate forms from Goethe's *Iphigenia in Tauris* (1787) to Nerval's *Aurelia* (1855).[2] Sophia may, on the one hand, be represented as an idealised but passive figure or, on the other, as a source of prophecy, advice and even actual leadership. Her prestige is important in the growing quest for recognition and equality by women. It is, or may be seen as, incompatible to worship a female divine principle while treating actual women as retarded children according to Napoleonic precept. The fact that the Saint-Simonians and the Fourierists accorded an important part to women in their utopian plans and societies is not unrelated to the Sophia phenomenon. Enfantin's words at his trial give this its most extreme expression:

I affirm that he amongst you who shall commune in hope and love with our God, who is not only good as a Father,

but who is also tender as a Mother, I affirm that *he*
amongst you who shall communicate with Him and Her
will have taken on, by that alone, a new life . . . . He is and
She is the Father and the Mother of all men and all women.
(cit. Desanti, 1972: 65)

Now all these myths may be taken to represent a divinisation
of the excluded, of the social other. It is always much easier to
equate the excluded other with the divine or the satanic than to
accept it. The quest story (one version of which was outlined in
Chapter 2), especially in various religious manifestations, con-
sistently deifies the outcast and the bastard, while the heretical
versions of Mariolatry could be seen as having similar implications for the mothering of a miraculous child. Finally, the
manifestations of Sophia allow a possible perception of woman
as leader and fuse with the still living tradition of Joan of Arc,
(also revived at this time: cf. Schiller's *Die Jungfrau von Orleans*
(The Maid of Orleans) (1801)). All these archetypes are woven
into the writings of the period, but nowhere so paradigmatically
as in the autographic writings of the woman who made the title
of Pariah her signature.

Flora Tristan, as soon as she acquired the skills of writing,
became an assiduous creator of both autography and autothanatography. Her life had from the start a certain mythical
flavour which positively encouraged her towards the quest. It
also bore all the marks of a curious doubleness, in nationality,
in sexuality and in attitudes towards the law of the Father. She
was the illegitimate child of a wealthy Peruvian career officer,
who died when she was 4, and a French girl of beauty but
undistinguished family background. On the father's side, the
'marriage', religious but unregistered, and subsequent birth
fitted into the multi-family patriarchal system of the privileged,
dating back to feudal days. It was a normal marriage of the left
hand, setting up a loved household which was still not recognised, and excluded in terms of family structures or inheritance.
It belonged to the patterns of noble illegitimacy which characterised the *ancien régime*, in which the child could take the
name of the father and assume a fixed place in the family
hierarchy, and which we observed in the case of George Sand's
genealogy. Symptomatically, when Flora finally reached Peru,
her uncle accepted without too much difficulty that she should

receive one-fifth of her father's inheritance, since that was the bastard's due. On the French side, however, once the father was dead, Flora and her mother belonged to the new post-revolutionary regime, in which the fault and the responsibility were the woman's. The adult Flora was torn in her imagination between two possibilities: a return to the old ways and a relegitimation through the name of the father, and a more radical and more modern performance of exclusion in a delegitimation whereby she assumed the prerogatives of the outcast.

Left poor and ill-educated, she discovered the penalties of her position early when a young lover was prevented from marrying her. The importance of this early humiliation, to which she refers obsessively, cannot be overestimated. The injury was compounded when she was forced into marriage with her employer at the age of 18. After four years of unremitting drudgery and pregnancy, she got the chance at 21 to escape her husband and wasted no time in taking it. Her first act of social defiance was to abandon her married name, and the first result of the years of abject poverty and social humiliation which followed was a burning desire for relegitimation by recognition as her father's child. This resumption of the father's name, Tristan, became so important that she even seems to identify with the semantic *trace* (sorrow) contained in it. Suffering became something she courted and rejoiced in.

No room at the inn

It should be remembered that Tristan could never have brought her dreams to fruition if it had not been for the unremitting support of her mother, Anne-Pierre Laisnay (known as Thérèse), who must have had considerable strength of character to find the means to nurture children dumped on her for long periods, and to withstand the threats of physical violence from the discarded husband. Flora was so concerned with her paternal inheritance that she did less than justice to her mother.[3] Yet the myth of St Anne and the trinity of grandmother, mother and daughter is once again to be discerned in the background to Tristan's story. We have little record of the years between 1825, when she took refuge with her mother, and 1832, when she managed to organise the trip to Peru. One merely finds a kind of palimpsestic record of their humiliations in her first published work, *Nécessité de faire bon accueil aux femmes étrangères* (Necessity of Welcoming Foreign Women) (1835), which was not and could not be written until after her return from Peru. The work already bears the marks of the myths developed there, that were to shape her life and writings. The archetypes of the descent to Hell and the temptations in the desert are already quite fully developed in it.

Since the later narratives, as I will show, were heavily influenced by biblical precedent, I am suggesting another narrative parallel from the Gospels for the exclusion that was formative in those early years. The scarifying experiences of a woman who must journey alone with little or no money, exposed to the petty persecutions and innuendo of landladies and servants, are shatteringly portrayed in the *mise en scène* that I call 'No Room at the Inn':

> For a long time we travelled as a woman *alone*, a foreigner, and we know, as a result, all the misery of that cruel situation. We found ourselves a foreigner in Paris, in provincial towns, in villages, at watering places. We also traversed several counties of England and its immense capital. We visited much of America, and our words will only be the echo of our soul; for we only know how to speak of things we have ourself experienced.[4]

A feature which does not seem to have changed much, in spite of the passing of decades, is the quality of insult which can infuse the words 'Madame est seule?' ('Madam is on her own?'). The evil intentions attributed to any and every male visitor received by a woman alone evoke one of her rare sparks of humour: 'The landlady will fear it, her tenants will be sure of it, and finally the servants will swear to it.'[5] All that is known of Flora's movements in this period is that she worked for some English women and made several trips to England. She is so morbidly determined to cover her tracks that one can deduce menial employment, probably as a lady's-maid, although her husband suggested prostitution as a more disobliging alternative. This seems highly unlikely in view of the fears I will discuss in what follows. *Nécessité* already shows another result of Tristan's grimly acquired self-sufficiency, the pronounced and 'un-feminine' capacity for organisation. It takes the form of a vindication of the rights of women travellers in the shape of a proposed association of support. One can see *en herbe* some of the exasperation at the incapacity of the dispossessed to stand up for themselves which was to inform *Union ouvrière* (The Workers' Union) (1843). According to Desanti, Tristan became acquainted with the writings of Mary Wollstonecraft at this time, but she gives no evidence to support her claim.

On the one hand, Tristan suffered from the fact that, as biological woman, she was cursed with an excessive fertility which threatened her with mental extinction and physical exhaustion in unremitting pregnancy. She refused this as desperately as she refused the legal enslavement of a wife to her husband.[6] On the other hand, one of the few weapons she had in her determined battle against social odds was precisely that of her physical beauty. Her gendered construction as feminine was vital to her oppositional practices, yet she had at all costs to prevent it leading to actual sexual intercourse, since that threatened the nightmare of pregnancy. One result, of which we shall see the consequences, was the reassumption of a kind of false virginity, as first her sons were jettisoned and later even her daughter became increasingly irrelevant. She became, to use Sartre's term (see p. 159), a 'maculate' virgin. Indeed, when she met Captain Chabrié and enlisted his support in 1829 she preferred to suggest that her daughter was born out of wedlock rather than accept her married status. This showed considerable courage, but also a burgeoning mythopoesis. Her other main asset, beside her courage and beauty, was a remarkable capacity for verbal expression and persuasion.

One can reconstruct from *Pérégrinations d'une paria* (Peregrinations of a Pariah) (1838)[7] the palimpsestic narrative stages by which she performed her exclusion and structured her future. Her autographies are always geared towards an image of what is to come as much as of what has been, and they shape the events of her life in the past to conform with the desired outcome in the future. Nearly all these archetypal narratives take the form of journeys. The first stage, prompted by her meeting with the ship's captain who knew Peru, but also by the remarkable fit between her story and that of 'the hero with a thousand faces', to use Campbell's term (1968), was the most traditional quest story of all. In it, the bastard outcast travels over water to a far land, overcomes enormous difficulties, is eventually recognised as the lord's son or daughter, and wins fortune and recognition.

The odd thing is not that she dreamed this dream, but that in 1833 she set about turning it into reality. She was eventually to exploit her six-month ordeal on a sailing ship and her adventures in Peru in a way totally different from her original hopes.

At another level the quest story is much more subtle. This second stage involves the clever outcast learning to exploit the gift of speech which has always been hers (and this is traditionally a women's story) by turning it into the gift of tongues. If the folktale heroine speaks to animals, the real traveller speaks to foreigners. Flora had already acquired some English, but, as we have seen, the earlier travels, which did nothing for the myth, were almost completely repressed in her memory and her writings. This new journey across the water brought with it not just a knowledge of Spanish, but a more general acquisition of power through the word. Thus her search brought, eventually, *not* relegitimation, since the name of the father eluded her and she could bear it only with the bar sinister, but an entry into the full powers of the symbolic. Ironically, this was to permit the delegitimation which permanently alienated her both from her father's family and from the law of the Father.

Literate only with difficulty before that period, as her letters bear witness, she set out to find her inheritance but instead found a different treasure, the authority of the word. In *Pérégrinations* she called it a *tombeau*, because the Peruvian equivalent of winning a lottery was unearthing a tomb which contained the buried treasure of the Incas. Copying the moral of the folktale, she pointed out that the real *tombeau* is the treasure amassed through assiduous cultivation of one's own capacities. The hidden quest of Tristan which underlies the surface exotica is the story of self-education.

The journey on the ship *Méxicain* encouraged long hours of the reading aloud common at the time, and a remarkable variety of classics, from Voltaire to Hugo, were read and re-read (P: 72). The journal she kept is the other side of this education, the apprenticeship into written language, which we can trace if we read *Pérégrinations* as a *Bildungsroman*. As well as learning to write and read Spanish, she taught herself a command of educated French. The gift of persuasive speech which gave her mastery over the traditional oppositional female practices, such as the manipulation of men, would never have been enough in itself to allow her challenge *to* male domination and to the Law of the Father (see Deleuze and Guattari, 1975: 17). Only the full range of the symbolic, and of the master tongue, the written language, would permit that move, 'an appropriation to [her] own purposes of the alienating language of power' (Chambers, 1991: 105), to take place. A letter to Buloz (7 March 1837), after he had dared to criticise her style, bears witness to the strength of the challenge, and to the strength of her rejection of male conventions:

> As well, I don't see why you take an interest in style except in relation to the rules of grammar. I sign my articles, thenceforward I take responsibility for them. And if *know-alls* find faults in them, let them attack me. I'll be able to find a reply. All my work is sprinkled with what you call bold strokes which permit me to avoid the monotony of *academic taste*, it is they which will make me what God wished me to be, a special being.[8]

The journey into the desert

This brings us to the third and most important stage in the narrative progression. By the time Tristan actually comes to write *Pérégrinations* in 1836 and 1837, as distinct from the earlier living and recording of the experiences there related, her goals have changed, and a narrative which is to plot the future is superimposed on the earlier structures, retrospectively altering the whole emphasis:

> Into the bargain, before beginning this book, I carefully examined all the possible consequences of my narration, and, no matter how painful the duties my conscience imposed on me, my apostle's faith did not waver; I did not draw back from their fulfilment.[9]

A third quest narrative, the most potent of all, superseded and modified the quest of the bastard for relegitimation and that of the excluded for the master tongue. This was the archetype of the journey into the desert. The myth of the apotheosis of the divine bastard, whose passage through hardship, and resistance to temptation, reveal him with even more certainty as the Messiah, the chosen of God, has great power at any time through its religious imprimatur, but was particularly potent when Tristan was writing because of the utopian thinking of the Fourierists, and the Messianic excesses of Considérant, the Père Enfantin and the Abbé Constant.

Tristan chooses to open her text with a series of apostrophes, or rather fulminations, to the Peruvians and to the French, similar in tone to John the Baptist's address to the Pharisees – 'Oh generation of vipers' – which prefaces Jesus' temptation in the desert:

> 'Fools! I am sorry for you and do not hate you; your disdain wounds me, but does not trouble my conscience. The same laws and prejudices which victimise me also fill your lives with bitterness; lacking the courage to shake off their yoke, you make yourselves their servile instruments. Oh! if you treat in such a way those whose elevation of soul and generosity of heart would incline to devotion to your cause, I tell you, you will long remain in your period of unhappiness.'
>
> This outburst restored my courage, I felt more calm; God, all unknown to me, had come to dwell in me.[10]

John's outburst is of course followed by the baptism of Jesus and the voice from Heaven saying: 'This is my beloved Son, in whom I am well pleased.'[11] There follows the extraordinary account of Jesus' flight into the desert borne through the air by the Devil, and the three temptations, by hunger, by glory and by power, followed by an angelic resanctification (Matthew 4: 1–11, Luke 4: 1–13). One must also remember that the ministry of Christ which ensued was an essentially peripatetic affair. The Gospel story has always had the ambivalent power of using the patriarchy to subvert the patriarchy. The undermining comes from within. It is both sanctioned and unsanctioned, authoritative and oppositional. *Pérégrinations* consciously follows a similar pattern, and Tristan's choice to proclaim herself both pariah *and* chosen one is inscribed from the beginning.

This inscription is a necessary step in establishing her *signature*, which, as we have seen, is not only the name by which an author takes responsibility for the work, but also the seal of the relationship between addressor and addressee, and, more particularly, between writer and reader. Tristan's relationship to her readers is strangely ambivalent, in the tradition of the Gospels. She demands respect *and* opprobrium. This is prefigured in the ambiguous relation of narrator to narratee, which on the one hand presumes admiration and sympathy, and on the other glories in the very details most guaranteed not only to outrage her Peruvian relations and ensure the removal of the annuity which was her only means of support, but also to scandalise the Paris reader. Masochism becomes martyrdom:

> Blessed are they which are persecuted for righteousness' sake: for theirs is the kingdom of heaven.

> Blessed are ye, when men shall revile you, and persecute you, and shall say all manner of evil against you falsely, for my sake.
>
> (Matthew 5: 10–11)

The hellish journey of six months on a sailing ship round the Horn, crammed in a cabin fifteen feet by twelve with six men, on which not a day passed without vomiting, figures not just as an ordeal of initiation. She also shows it as a period of fasting and temptation, not *of* the besotted captain Chabrié but *by* him. Having deluded him with the belief that she was a single mother, she offered the captain the chance to play St Joseph to her Virgin Mary, a chance he greeted with enthusiasm. However, she had no intention of playing out the drama of the Holy Family; nor, in spite of certain protestations, was her chosen martyrdom that of the mother. The narratives she foregrounds and which can be seen to shape her life do not include a *pietà*. Hers is always a leading role, even if it leads to a crucifixion.

The most significant textual witness to this *mise en scène* is Chapter 7, entitled 'The desert'. The description of the ascension into the high wasteland between Islay and Arequipa is based on two models, Moses' ascension, at the behest of God, to the barren heights of Mount Sinai (P: 112), and Jesus' view of all the kingdoms of the earth from the exceeding high mountain. Her very real journey through the wilderness becomes fraught with allegory, as Flora suffers 'le tourment de l'ange déchu, banni du ciel' ('the torments of the fallen angel, banished from heaven') (P: 113). At the same time, like her two august predecessors, she is visited by the Almighty.

It is therefore a necessary development of the chosen myth, or the myth of the Chosen, that Don Pio, Flora's uncle, who made what seems in the circumstances the fair offer of a home and a small annuity, should be vilified as a monument of pride and avarice. When his offer was rejected with as much contumely as the temptations of Satan, his niece was merely acting out the scenario she had established for herself, the performance of martyrdom. The journey into the desert cannot achieve its full allegorical purpose unless the narrator, exposed to its torments and temptations, can emerge triumphantly as the new Messiah. The story is not yet complete in *Pérégrinations* but the outline is already there. This autography is as much a prefiguration as an account after the event.

Our Lady of Sorrows

The other prefiguration, which both competes with the journey into the desert and complements it, is the highly ambiguous shedding of Tristan's married name and identity, what I have called her role as false virgin, and which permits another apotheosis, that of the Virgin Mother as general and queen. The first *mise-en-abyme* is that of the procession of Our Lady, and the enactment by the crowd of the story in which the Queen of Heaven arrives to save the troops from defeat:

> The populace was intoxicated; it clapped its hands, jumped with joy and shouted at the top of its voice: Long live Jesus Christ! Long live the holy Virgin! Long live our lord *don Joseph*! Long live our most noble lord the pope! Viva! Viva! Viva![12]

It is as though *Pérégrinations* presents two competing apotheoses, that of the male Messiah and that of the Virgin Mother. These appear over and over in Tristan's life and work, until by the end of her life she has combined them, appearing as the fully developed female Messiah leading the workers into battle. In *Méphis*,[13] which we will examine more fully, the hero, a painter at the time, is offered '60 francs de ma *femme guide de l'humanité*, à condition que j'en ferais une *sainte vierge*' ('60 francs for my *woman guiding humanity*, on condition that I changed her into a *holy virgin*') (M I: 221). It is fairly clear that the reverse principle applies in Flora's own art, and that the holy virgin may be reworked to produce a representation of woman leading humanity. The role of female/male saviour was in harmony with both the more heretical forms of primitive Christianity prevalent at the time, and an incipient feminism that was to strengthen as Flora met other rebels against patriarchy. Prosper Enfantin, for instance, a pseudo-feminist who was leading many female believers to despair and even suicide at just this time (Tristan, 1980: 231), proclaimed that he was destined to discover the 'Père Suprême en quête éternelle d'une Mère Suprême pour fournir le couple saint-simonien' ('Supreme Father in eternal quest of a Supreme Mother to produce the Saint-Simonian couple') (Desanti, 1984: 214).

Female models different from any Flora had encountered in France abounded in Peru. They ranged from her disempowered and embittered female relations to the liberated women of Lima:

> The woman of Lima, in all the situations of life, is always *herself*; she never endures any constraint: as a girl she escapes from the control of her parents by the freedom her costume gives her; when she marries, she does not take her husband's name, keeps her own and always remains mistress of her home.[14]

The almost feudal world of the convents, that produced enclosed worlds such as are now only imagined in feminist utopias or, more usually, dystopias, revealed an extraordinary form of female domination. The power of abbesses in their enclosed empires, which turned them into beneficent queens or dreaded monsters, provided one example of woman as leader. At the other end of the scale of monstrosity, even the account of the *ravañas*, the camp followers who actually led the way for the soldiers so much less ferocious than they, revealed the same preoccupation.

The strongest role-model, however, both for the female general and for her other face, Our Lady of Sorrows, was Señora Gamarra, the president's wife, who was for a while virtual ruler of Peru in her own right. She displayed both the arrogance of royalty, even in defeat, and the stigmata of the martyr in her racking attacks of epilepsy. Flora makes sure her readers know that she herself was able to dominate this outstanding woman by the mere power of her gaze. However, the momentary dream of rivalling the Señora Presidente Gamarra, and the 'Temptation' (the chapter heading) of using Colonel Escudero as the means to power, encounter the sexual problem. Even with a partner worthy of her, but whom she feels capable of dominating, she can never rule through a man. Her way must lie outside marriage. Only by the mythopoesis of exclusion can she step away from her female body while at the same time exploiting the elements of the sacred associated with the feminine.

Méphis or bastardy 'with the lot'

Immediately after *Pérégrinations*, Tristan wrote her only novel *Méphis* (1838), in which she elaborated the myth of the double self, both male and female, both outcast and artist, both mother and virgin, both triumphant and crucified. As we have seen, Tristan said that she was only capable of writing herself. The novel, flawed to put it mildly, and bearing all the marks of hasty and undiscriminating production, is still a fascinating document, not only of the author's conscious and unconscious preoccupations, but also of the ideologies of her circle, by this time including serious social reformers like Considérant. At the conscious level, it deliberately exploits all the positive myths of illegitimacy, those of the divine child, of Sophia and Mary, of the matriarchal and the holy family, of the crucified outcast and of the new woman. At the unconscious level, it bears the traces of a dominant bisexuality that surfaces in the letters, though apparently remaining at the stage of words rather than deeds. In the more adaptable world of fiction, the problem is solved by incarnation in the double personas of the hero *and* the heroine. Perhaps the easiest way to relate the book to my central preoccupations is to examine the question of naming in *Méphis* and whether it is linked to the regime of the Father or to that of the Mother.

The novel divides into two halves. In the first, the hero, Jean Labarre, alias John Lysberry, alias Méphis, tells his own story in direct speech. In the second, the heroine, Maréquita, tells her story in the third person through a written document. Méphis is the name she bestows on Jean/John when they meet. It is of course short for Méphistopheles, which means 'he who hates the light, or lover of darkness'. Flora chooses the name because of the same inverted symbolism and worship of an anti-god that characterises Baudelaire's 'Litanies of Satan'.[15] Méphis is a revolutionary, a proletarian and a feminist. He spends his time moving between exclusion and inclusion, between his humble French family and the English aristocrats who adopt him, between the establishment of the art world and the netherworld of the prison system, and, above all, between the way of the mother and that of the father. The law of the Father and the dictates of the establishment are represented by the painter Girodet, who first encourages his protégé, then rejects him when he dares question his master's teachings.

The realm of the mother consists in a representation of the sort of maternal trinity we discussed earlier, but it is interesting to consider the names chosen for that trinity. The grandmother, the St Anne figure, is Méphis' own mother, who cares for her daughter Marie's illegitimate daughter. Marie has died a martyr's death, shattered by the shame of her rape, but her place in the trinity has been taken by her sister Sophie, whose devotion and wisdom keep the family together. I will not labour the symbolism, but one should be aware that Tristan is drawing on the codes and myths current at the time. Méphis, as lord of darkness, is seeking justice not only for his own family but for all the dispossessed, the 'Morlocks' or dwellers in darkness.[16]

Angelic androgyny or demonic hybridity

Maréquita, 'little Marie' in Spanish,[17] has a different but equally significant semiotic history, more closely linked to Flora's own. Our heroine first appears shrouded in mystery, proclaiming in song that no one knows whence she comes, and that her father was a black rock and her mother a wandering wave. This could be seen merely as a rush of romanticism to the head, but if we remember that Flora's mother was named Anne-Pierre and her father Mariano, a more interesting subtext begins to appear. We may ask *who* is the rock (Pierre) and who the bitter wave (Maria means bitter), and see the whole merging of male and female as one more enactment of the androgyny so essential to Tristan's thought.

In order to understand the intertextuality, it is important to note that the first chapter has an epigraph from Balzac's *Séraphita* (1833): 'Our instinct is precisely what makes us so perfect. What you others learn, *we* feel.'[18] Séraphita was an angel, androgynous like all angels. Maréquita, like her/him in name, will not attain like perfection until she is united with Méphis to complement her all too 'feminine' nature.

When we read the novel as writing illegitimacy, it is important to realise that it contains another, anti-Balzacian, agenda. In 1834 there appeared the powerful short story 'La fille aux yeux d'or' (The Girl with the Golden Eyes), in which Balzac exploited to the full the traditional demonisation of bastardy. In it a half-brother, Henri de Marsay, and sister, Margarita de San-Réal, also known as Mariquita, the natural children of a dissipated English aristocrat, indulge in what turns out to be a sort of incest by proxy. De Marsay, wily, degenerate and represented as feminised, attracts the sensual Pasquita, who is, unbeknown to him, the kept mistress of his sister Margarita, a passionate, beautiful lesbian, shown as masculinised. They have a brief exotic affair, in which Pasquita first dresses him in women's clothes and finally betrays herself by calling him Mariquita. Realising that he has been trapped in a bisexual masquerade, Henri goes to take his revenge on the girl, only to be forestalled by Mariquita herself. Having discovered the betrayal, she kills Pasquita with peculiar ferocity, and de Marsay is forced to see in this bloody tigress his identical image. While she seeks refuge in exile, her brother moves on to corrupt political power. Both bastards are portrayed as hybrids in every way: of impure blood, socially neither fish nor fowl, of mixed nationality, and, above all, sexually deviant.[19]

Now, Tristan's text sets out to reverse this scenario. Her hero, given the demonic name of Méphis, lives a life devoted to others and dies a Christ-like death. Her heroine, Maréquita, shares with Balzac's her name, her illegitimacy, her passionate disposition, her sexual liberation and her hybrid nationality. But she eventually treads the strait path, if not of virtue, then of political correctness, and of heterosexuality, while Balzac's Mariquita/Margarita treads the primrose path of lust, murder and, of course, homosexuality. The two extremes, both so characteristic of portrayals of bastardy, could not be better illustrated.

Marriage versus love

In her portrayal of Maréquita, Tristan is also violent in her condemnation of the shackles of femininity (of which she sees the corset as metonymic). She takes a very modern view of the gendering enforced by a patriarchal society, indeed one as modern as her narrative plotting is old-fashioned, and her heroine is, to some extent, her mouthpiece. Maréquita's Spanish name, as a diminutive, bears an obvious relationship to the Florita which was the name given to Flora in Peru. In case the reader should miss the point, Maréquita's incredibly villainous husband is called Hazcal, a transparent anagram of Flora's married name, Chazal.

The main division between the regime of the traditional name of the Father and that of the name of the Mother, which is seen as heralded by female emancipation, is marked by two different acts of begetting. In the first, Méphis is persuaded to enact the 'divine' role of inseminator in one more comedy of the Holy Family, engendering the heir his noble patron is impotent to produce, and leaving the child to take the ducal name. Far other is his ideal and brief union with Maréquita, which produces a true love child, who is cast in the unenviable role of new woman and future leader. The daughter is, unsurprisingly, called Marie, and the 'three in one' formed by Méphis and the pregnant Maréquita will have its phantasmatic development in the 'Dieux' Tristan later envisaged, a divine figure equally composed of mother, father and embryo.[20] It is Méphis, soon to suffer a martyr's death and leave the field to his daughter, who in fact preaches the reversal of the accepted codes of feminine behaviour. He expects a true woman to make her free choice of partner: 'Je serais ton époux lorsque tu me diras: viens, je te "choisis" parmi tous, tu es à moi' ('I will be your spouse when you say to me: come, I "choose" you among all, you are mine') (ME II: 144). Méphis dies after the impregnation, Maréquita after the birth, and Marie is left, at the end of this farrago, to be the standard-bearer for the myriads of pariahs and proletarians (ME II: 293).

The signature

The success of this extraordinary compilation of the bastard narrative, in all its conceivable and inconceivable forms, was ensured by the fidelity with which Tristan's life imitated her art. Just as *Pérégrinations* had appeared, and she was correcting the proofs of *Méphis*, she was shot and nearly killed by her husband, Chazal. The books promptly sold extremely well and she became a public figure. As she acquired an audience she also acquired a signature. To some extent she was 'written', after that, by her own notoriety. The *succès de scandale* of the books ensured two things: that Tristan was known, and that she was judged. The more she was judged, the more she was reviled, the more she attained that special power of the word which belonged to the female pariah.

I think it is worth considering the way in which the very name, Flora Tristan, had by now become the seal of the delegitimation that ensured both her repute and her disrepute. 'Flora' contained at this stage not only its usual connotations of beauty and divinity, but also the *trace* of Florita and the natural child's quest for recognition, of Maréquita and the transformation of the wronged wife into the divine mother, and, last but not least, of Séraphita and the angelic androgyne. Flora was also reinforced by the consonance with *paria*, just as this central term is itself reinforced by the string of alliterative manipulations of the signifier playing on the letter p (eg. *pérégrinations, paria, Pérou, promenades*) that runs through the paratextual apparatus of titles, prefaces and epigraphs. This apparatus is a vital factor in the constitution of the signature. To the protean variations of the given name, we may add the implications of the surname, Tristan. So conspicuously *not* her married name, but fought for and won in a court of law, not even the full name of her father (Tristan y Moscozo, of which the second name Moscozo, the indicator, by Spanish tradition, of the maternal line, is precisely the element of her father's name that is lost to Tristan by her illegitimacy), it contained the *trace* of a relationship twice distanced and made mythic, by illegitimacy and by death. It also contains a not inconsiderable group of phonemes – [r i s t] – which link it to the thematics of redemption and crucifixion. One scarcely needs to labour the point that Tristan was also the perfect name for Our Lady of Sorrows.

It was thus a subtle combination of the manipulated and the fortuitous, of the real and the imaginary, of the conscious and the unconscious, which enabled Tristan to perform her exclusion. Just as the narratees in her books are defiantly divided between those represented as only too ready to cast the first stone and those who identify with the outcast, so her actual readers divided, in her eyes at least, between the proletarians and the phalansterians[21] to whom she was a heroine, and the philistines and pharisees to whom she was a scandal and therefore a fascination.

The Way of the Cross

This very notoriety set up the last journey, the *via dolorosa*, a myth that had already appeared as *mise-en-abyme* in the account of an Easter parade in *Pérégrinations*:

> The history of the Passion, no circumstance omitted, is enacted; the whole accompanied by songs, by recitals: then comes the death of Christ; the candles go out, darkness reigns .... The descent from the cross is the second performance: a confused crowd of men, of women, white, Indian and negro alike, storm the *calvary* uttering lamentable cries; soon uprooted trees, stones torn from the ground are in their hands; they drive out the soldiers, take possession of the cross, unfasten the body; blood runs from the wounds of this cardboard Christ, the howls of the crowd redouble.[22]

Of course, Flora's own Way of the Cross, as champion and heroine of the working class, was as real as her journey into the desert, but she was also always conscious of the myth she was enacting. Of the trial after the assassination attempt she wrote: '8 days ago today at this time I ascended my Calvary – I was crucified, like my master, between two female thieves ... the populace of Paris [was] as stupid, as nasty as that of Jerusalem. . .'.[23]

Although *Promenades dans Londres* (Walks in London) (1840) appear as another journey into the desert, and are extremely successful in depicting the worlds of those who dwell in darkness, they can also be seen, given her views on England, as a descent into Hell. *Promenades* and *Union ouvrière* are addressed to an exclusive narratee, the working class. But they appealed and sold to all the socially or politically delegitimated. *Union ouvrière* was financed by subscription, and two of those subscribers were George Sand and Marie Dorval (Tristan 1983b: 31,33). The bonds of pariahdom were a constant theme, and Tristan saw herself more and more in the light of a persecuted saviour. Most of her travels from then on, and particularly the last unpublished journal *Le Tour de France*,[24] should be seen as Stations of the Cross. Indeed this was how she saw it. On 3 July 1844 she notes: 'Gods [her Father, Mother and Embryo trinity] definitely want me to go through all the stages of crucifixion.'

But the final torments do lead to moments of true apotheosis, of, as Desanti says, effusion, hope, ecstasy, euphoria. Desanti goes on:

> It's the evening of 7 July [1844], at the Croix-Rousse. [Flora speaks and] . . .
> The Saint-Simonian Pérelle, his face flooded with tears, called out: 'The Woman-Messiah. We've been waiting for her for twenty years!' Another workman, Jacob, cried: 'On your knees!' and the front rows all knelt while there rang out the *Workshop Marseillaise*, learnt from the 'little book' [*Union ouvrière*].
>
> (Desanti, 1972: 287)[25]

As Tristan lived, she wrote, using the master tongue and particularly the biblical tongue to set up her own oppositional and authorising narrative, her autothanatography. Her peripatetic ministry was as much a journey in the imagination as it was one in reality. Of the two books that she planned as her memorial, one, *Le Tour de France,* never appeared and the other, *Le Testament de la paria,* appeared posthumously in 1846, taken over by the Abbé Constant for his own ends. We know, however, that the planning was hers, because she signed a letter to him (3 March 1844): 'Votre mère en l'idée du Testament de la Paria' ('Your mother in the idea of the Testament of the Pariah'). The very fact that she called the work a testament points to its function: a testament is a statement of what one bequeaths, whether it be one's property, one's works, one's beliefs or, of course, in the last resort one's life laid down for others. The *Testament,* in other words, was intended to be both autothanatography and encomium, or formalised praise for a life well spent in the service of the public. As Bakhtin has made clear, this ancient genre confirms a mythical status posthumously conferred, but seen as conferred on a career rather than a person:

> The encomium's emphasis on generalized careers, for example, is a structural inheritance from the past of ancient myth: it translates into stories about humans a pattern already present in older tales about demi-gods .... It continued to shape such later genres as the saint's life, where its influence is obvious.
>
> (Holquist, 1990: 127)

124

Flora Tristan died a martyr's death in the cause of the proletariat and that of the *Union ouvrière* in 1844, when she collapsed on her peripatetic ministry as she endeavoured to rally working-class support. The last ironic touch was that the written memorial that she had planned was finally put together opportunistically by her so-called disciple Constant, as *L'Emancipation de la femme, ou le Testament de la paria* (The Emancipation of Woman, or the Testament of the Pariah) (1846). As we have seen, it was not altogether a fake, but Constant shamelessly exploited her audience and her signature, while ending with a partial attack on her under his own name as editor. He depicts as truly satanic her pride in calling herself the new Messiah, and she is even impugned for denying Man the title of Father – this by the man who preached the assumption of the Mother. Indeed, she is seen as the new Circe: 'ceux qu'aime Mme Tristan, elle les tue (au moral entendons-nous)' ('those whom Mme Tristan loves, she kills (of course, we mean morally)') (Tristan, 1846: 118). As a result of both his hyperbolic rendition of her principles and his damning of her as a person, he ensured that her last martyrdom should be posthumous, as was to be her recognition as a precursor of women's liberation and Marxism. However, she had successfully created her own myth, and such a myth, endowed with the power of the word, continues to shape destinies, just as does a signature.

7

My mother the Revolution: Louise Michel

If we move forward to Louise Michel (1830–1905), another heroine of another revolution, the Commune of 1871, we can perceive both striking parallels and enormous differences when she is compared to the earlier revolutionaries. Since she uses the first-person autobiographical form in her *Mémoires* (1886), her writing must necessarily foreground the self, yet, in a discourse markedly different from that of Olympe de Gouges or Flora Tristan, it also backgrounds the self. She writes, as she always seems to have acted, as an equal among equals. There results a major difference in their assumption of their illegitimacy. Whereas, as we have seen, Olympe actively campaigns for the rights of women and of the natural child, and Flora's fictional-isation of the bastard culminates in an apotheosis, Louise discusses the rights and wrongs of women and children but subsumes them within her belief in a Babeuvian vision of a society where all will be equal, happy and without laws or government. In her *Mémoires*, in the passages relating to her childhood, she elides the facts of her birth – indeed, the place and the name of the father are marked only by an absence, a lack in the text. She is named as a bastard only once, towards the end of the book (M: 309),[1] apart from the text given of the prosecutor's speech at the trial of the *communards*, where it forms part of the general indictment.[2] However, her passionate and guilty devotion to the mother whose surname she bears betrays her inner conflict.

Her mother, Marie-Anne or Marianne Michel, was a peasant child adopted, half servant/half daughter, into a family of impoverished *hobereaux* (manorial proprietors), whose name was Demahis. Eventually pregnant to the son of the house, she

126

was, most unusually, given family support. Indeed, one's impression is that it was the son who was thrown out. Paule Lejeune (1978: 37–41) gives an account of an embittered letter of Louise to Victor Hugo, the poet whom she adopted as a kind of literary father figure, which reveals the depth of her true feelings of exclusion, and also the possibility, given her 'father's' constant rejection, that her 'grandfather' might, in fact, have engendered her. This was the gossip in the village, but does not jibe with her acceptance by her paternal grandmother, unless, of course, we are looking at an unusual female manifestation of the St Joseph myth, in which the spouse accepts the bastard out of love for his or her partner (see p. 50).

Her childhood was, in fact, a very happy one. Louise was acknowledged and brought up by her paternal grandparents and her mother. The greatest influence on her development as a writer and her early mastery of the symbolic, was her Voltairean grandfather, who, in bringing her up in the tradition of the *philosophes*, played a much kinder, but similar, role to that of George Sand's grandmother. Louise, like Aurore, was brought up with a freedom more customary for a boy. She was encouraged from an early age to read and to write, both prose and poetry, and to converse without inhibitions with her elders and betters and challenge their views. A major passion throughout her life was her love of and scientific interest in animals. Born 150 years later, she would probably have become an outstanding zoologist or biologist.[3] She eventually trained as a school teacher, and this was encouraged, even after the death of her paternal grandparents forced her return to her mother's family, who, though peasants, had a surprising interest in books. This background stands in contrast to the largely illiterate upbringing of Olympe de Gouges and Flora Tristan.

The signature

Another major difference appears when one considers the question of the signature. Olympe de Gouges was a self-created name, and as a signature it was, from the first, authorial, that is to say, it was text-based. Olympe wanted to be known as a writer, and her plays and pamphlets ensured a notoriety, consciously enhanced by her reputation as a *femme galante,* which entailed conformity to her signatory myth of emancipation.

Flora Tristan's signature was also primarily text-based, although the notoriety conferred by her husband's attack gave impetus to her recognition as an author. Michel, on the other hand, although she achieved some little-known publications, originally acquired her signature as a revolutionary activist.[4] She had practised as a poet from an early age, but it was not as a writer that she achieved notoriety. Thus, when her *Mémoires* appeared, readers came to them with fully formed preconceptions, and they were read for their controversial content rather than for their extraordinarily evocative discourse. Indeed, Michel seems later to have been forced to conform to her readers', or her publishers', expectations, since the posthumously published sequel, *Souvenirs et aventures de ma vie* (Memories and Adventures of my Life) (1905), is rather bland in comparison, and of less literary than historical interest. The problem I am trying to address here is that her writing – essential, of course, to the history of both socialism and feminism – is, generally speaking, still being read for content rather than form, and yet discourse theory tells us that we can make no valid distinction between the two.

Louise also considered, as Olympe and Flora apparently did not, the relative advantages of a masculine pseudonym. She reflected bitterly that she could get published much more easily if she signed her articles Louis Michel (M: 78), and she spent a time of indecision before establishing her authorial name. Martine de Gaudemar, in her enlightening psychoanalytical approach to the *Mémoires*, sums up the history of the author's signature in this way:

That the two surnames which were hers, Demahis and Michel, should give her a new identity, Michel Demahis, which she used as signature on two occasions, is probably not unrelated to the paradoxical identity which was that of Louise. To sign thus was to assume her double naming. But, ordered to sign Demahis no longer, in a repetition of her non-recognition by her father, Louise obliterates this name even on her indictment as a *communarde*. The name of Michel, which she then takes, *surname / masculine given name, but name of the mother*, redoubles the absence of the name of the father. It is as if Louise, who, at twenty-one, had signed a text Louise Michel Demahis, *were deprived of a patronym, reduced to two given names,* one feminine and one masculine.

The determination of Louise to make a name for herself, in literature or in history, is perhaps attributable to this. The father is perhaps put in the position of the reader and, more especially, of the spectator.

(1982: 132)

Mise en scène

De Gaudemar also makes a strong case for a myth/phantasm which has the same importance in Louise's life as the 'equal to the queen' fantasy does in Olympe's. She traces this to the play-acting in which the child indulged with her cousin. On one occasion, when they had created a scaffold on the wood-heap, and she was orating as she went to her fate, she recalls the performance as being stage-managed by her grandfather, who pointed out that a silent ascent to the tribune would be more effective. Louise's first impulse, then reflected in her leading role in a long series of trials, was to enact herself 'on stage':

> What she loves, it is true, is the romantic *mise en scène* of the martyr. She stage-managed them, she writes, with her cousin Jules, *'for two characters'*. And it was said of the two: They don't respect anything.

(1982: 126–7)

This scene is one form of *mise-en-abyme* in her autobiography, just as it is constantly repeated throughout her life, as again and again she demands death before a tribunal, which becomes, according to de Gaudemar, the 'other' of the phantasm. Laurent Taillade, in his preface to her *Oeuvres posthumes* (Posthumous Works) (1905), quotes her as saying to one tribunal: 'Since it seems that any heart that beats for liberty has no right today to anything but an ounce of lead, *I* demand *my* share!' He comments: 'What heroines, Chimène or Portia, ever spoke firmer words?' (Michel, 1905: 16). However, her deep-seated refusal of any hierarchy extends even to her fantasies, in which, unlike Flora Tristan, she is never a leader of the oppressed but merely their representative. Her self-dramatisation also colours her depiction of the events of the Commune, which are presented principally in a very dramatic form, and appear in the *Mémoires*

129

in the light of prologue, and catastrophe, interspersed by a series of tableaux (M: 128).

It may be noted that this is one characteristic Olympe de Gouges, Flora Tristan and Louise Michel share. For all three, the basic phantasm involves a myth of acting a role before an audience. However, whereas Olympe actually puts her fantasies on stage, and sees herself as playwright first and pamphleteer second, Flora and Louise need to envisage their narratees as a dramatic audience. Louise distinguishes her narratees as belonging to three groups: first, women, 'nous autres femmes'; second, communard sympathisers, who know the pirates' motto: 'Turn your prow to the wind ... every coast belongs to us'; and, lastly, the crowd, 'la grande foule, mes amours' (M: 18–19). We may argue, as de Gaudemar does, that this is intimately linked to the need to construct her own name, and that this sympathetic audience is the force that, she hopes, will actually construct her signature.

Myriam or the name of the mother

The other myth, or rather mythical paradigm, which dominates Louise's writing, is that of the name of the mother, with which, more than any other writer I discuss, she is obsessed. She dedicates *Mémoires* to the single name Myriam, which subsumes within itself three names and figures: Marie Anne, her mother; Marie Ferré, her most loved friend; and the mother figure of the Revolution, since Myriam is associated with rebellion. The dedication has a remarkable depth of connotation, and is worth examining in detail. I give the French here and the English in the notes, since (particularly because of the gendered nature of French) any translation of the discourse is approximate at best.

> DEDICACE
> MYRIAM!!!

> Myriam! leur nom à toutes deux:
> Ma mère!
> Mon amie!
> Va, mon livre sur les tombes où elles dorment!
> Que vite s'use ma vie pour que bientôt je dorme près d'elle!

Et maintenant, si par hasard mon activité produisait quelque bien, ne m'en sachez aucun gré, vous tous qui jugez par les faits: je m'étourdis, voilà tout.

Le grand ennui me tient. N'ayant rien à espérer ni rien à craindre, je me hâte vers le but, comme ceux qui jettent la coupe avec le reste de la lie.[5]

Louise Michel

(M: 13)

In using the name Myriam, Louise is reactivating a whole series of very potent myths, beginning with one of the very oldest myths of female rebellion and its savage repression. Miriam, according to a Hebrew dictionary of names, means 'sea of bitterness' and is linked with the *mar* root of Maryam (Marie). However, the *Encyclopaedia Judaica* suggests a link with the Egyptian *mer*, meaning 'love'. Miriam, according to the same authority, was the sister of Moses and Aaron:

The title 'prophetess' was given to Miriam when she appeared, timbrel in hand, at the head of the singing and dancing women after the crossing of the Red Sea (Ex. 15: 20–21) . . . .

Miriam is also mentioned in the context of hers [*sic*] and Aaron's attempt to challenge Moses' exclusive right to speak in the name of the Lord (Num. 12). Miriam is mentioned first, and according to G. B. Gray, the verb appearing in the feminine, *va-tedabber be-* ('she spoke against'), suggests that Miriam led this revolt, or that Miriam alone rebelled and that Aaron's name was added to mitigate her offense. In any event, she alone was punished . . . . Miriam was therefore smitten with leprosy, and was healed only after Moses interceded on her behalf and after being quarantined for seven days. Her punishment is recalled again (Deut. 24: 9), as a warning against leprosy . . . . She is mentioned in Micah with Moses and Aaron as one of the three who led Israel out of Egypt (6: 4). In the Aggadah: Miriam was so called in reference to the bitterness of the bondage of Egypt . . . .

Miriam is portrayed as fearless in her rebukes. As a child, she reprimanded Pharaoh for his cruelty, and he refrained from putting her to death only as a result of her mother's plea that she was but a child (Ex. R. 1: 13) . . . . Like Moses

and Aaron, she too died by the kiss of God since the angel
of death had no power over her (BB 17a).

(Vol. 12: 82-4)

We can, I think, identify a source for Michel's knowledge of the
name and its connotations. She struck up a friendship with a
very devout old Jewish woman, and was interested enough by
what she heard actually to pay a visit to the synagogue, where
the rites and the rhythm moved her to tears (M: 76-8). It seems
possible that her mother's name was mentioned and its ancient
roots discussed, and she thus became aware of a little-known
myth which supplemented her vision of the figure of the
revolution as a female one. Miriam is both a rebel against the
law of the father, an equal to her brothers, and a victim of her
own demand to exercise that equality. She provided an extra
model for the fearlessness of Michel's own rebukes to her
judges and jailers.

Voltaire's tragedy *Hérode et Mariamne* (1725), to which
Louise must have been led both by her grandfather's cult of
the writer and by the coincidence of the name, had early
provided another mythical figure linking the Hebrew name
Miriam, its Aramaic version Maryam, and the French Marianne. It is a tragic story of a tyrant's revenge on his falsely
accused consort. Above all the proud image of the maligned
queen, Mariamne, defying the kingly indictment and going to
a martyr's death, reunited Louise's two obsessions, the public
trial of the innocent, which she was to enact so often, and the
name of the mother. It found its parallel in the childhood
enactment of martyrdom.

All this extended the connotations of the name Marianne. As
we have seen, the very popularity of the names Marie and Anne
among the devout peasantry had caused the name Marianne to
be used, as early as the 1789 Revolution (Agulhon, 1981: 9), as
a jeering reference to the peasant rebellion and to the republic
that it demanded.[6] So the name was at first used pejoratively,
and remained so later, when it was adopted by underground
revolutionaries in the 1850s and 1860s as the figure of the
suppressed French republic, which they hoped to see born again
(ibid.: 119). Only in the twentieth century is Marianne accepted
as the official symbol of France. The name Marianne Michel
(Michel being the recognised sobriquet of the peasant), combines

132

the symbolism of the republic, and the proletarian demand for liberty, with the age-old sufferings of the countryside.

Last but not least, Myriam/Maryam stands for the two Maries. We have already examined the extraordinary dominance of the cult of Mary, and hence of the name Marie, in nineteenth-century France. We have also seen how the very weight and extent of the official Catholic cult made the existence of parallel and subversive 'anti-myths', such as those created by Flora Tristan, possible. According to Maurice Agulhon, during the Commune 'in the décor of a club that met in the church of St Eustache . . . a Republic was apparently improvised by crowning a statue of the virgin with a red cap' (ibid.: 140). Michel, in the same vein, is recycling the official myth as her private possession in several ways. Her own mother is the *mater dolorosa* who must see her bastard child rebel against the establishment, refuse the rich the right to enter the future kingdom on earth, and, finally, be slowly crucified for her ministry. Like her namesake, Marie Anne must watch and weep.

Second, the sister beloved, incarnate in Marie Ferré, is not only a fellow-revolutionary, but also the most adored of that series of female companions with whom Louise chose to spend her life. *Mémoires*, and to a lesser extent *Souvenirs de ma vie*, recount and conflate these close relationships, from those with the peasant girls and women of the village, then with her fellow-teachers and her revolutionary comrades, to the companions of her London days. We will return to the question of the role their discourses play in her writing. The conventional wisdom is that Louise, who, poor thing, was too ugly to attract a man, was hopelessly in love with Marie's brother, Théophile, who was executed as a leader of the commune.[7] This is a nice example of the conventional tendency to naturalise the 'unnatural'. I agree with de Gaudemar and Souriau (in Armogathe, 1982: 131, 178) that it is a mis-reading of a purely fraternal relationship between two comrades impassioned only for the revolution. Indeed, what *Mémoires* makes clear is that it was actually Théophile's sister she was in love with, but the critics, like Queen Victoria, obviously would not believe a story like that.[8] Yet the expressions of this love constantly recur, witness this cry at Marie's funeral:

Poor Marie!
She sleeps in a big red shawl, that I was given to use as a

banner if I needed one; it made a shroud; for us it's the
same now . . . .

I thought I would die after that dreadful blow; my
mother was left to me, my mother and the Revolution.
Now I have nothing left but the Revolution.[9]

Her mother too was shrouded in the red of revolt (M: 149),
and buried in the same tomb as Marie (M: 302). Both women,
by the primacy of the dedication, are fused from the first with
the maternal image of the revolution in the trinity named
Myriam, or the rebel. The same phantasmic trinity, three in one,
also brings the writing to a close:

A bientôt, ma bien aimée!
Myriam! que votre nom à toutes deux termine ce livre avec
le tien, Révolution!

(M: 310)

(We will meet soon, my beloved!
Myriam! may the name of you both close this book with
yours, Revolution!)

Thus Louise's love, her birth and her evocation of a liberated
France are all three coded into the text as acts of rebellion.

Anarchy and heteroglossia

The discourse of *Mémoires* is governed, as is its thematics, by the
principle of anarchy. In the very smallest details of her life and
writing Louise rejects the notion of hierarchy, of Cartesian order,
and of the chronological tyranny of narrative. I was made acutely
aware of this when I looked at the American edition and translation of *Mémoires* (Michel, 1981), which I regard as one of the
greatest pieces of literary vandalism to have come my way. The
editors decided that the memoirs' fragmentation could only be
attributed to Michel's 'nervous collapse' at the death of her
mother, and that they would be unreadable to present-day
readers. They then proceeded to gut and fillet them, removing
'redundancies', such as the greater part of the poetry and apostrophes to the revolution, 'irrelevancies', such as the dedication,
and rearranging what was left in chronological order. One can, to
be fair to Lowry and Gunter, see traces of the same attitude in
Daniel Armogathe's introduction to the *Colloque Louise Michel*:

We question here all the signs of her 'madness', her public assumption of illegitimacy, the relationship with her mother, a source of infantilisation and transvestism, which leads her to the breakdown of 1885, the fabrication of the symbolic father, the revolutionary sublimation and mysticism, the daily experience of hallucination.

(Armogathe, 1982: 5)

My own reading of both the 'signs' and the discourse is very different, as will be seen. However, I found that these editings and readings had in fact done me a service, as my outrage prompted me to ask why the original text was so important, and so 'postmodern' in its structure that it remained, even in the 1980s, in the domain of the unreadable. Michel says, in her introduction: 'if I assume for my thought and my pen the right to wander, you will agree that I have earned that right the hard way'.[10] Her *vagabondage* has three important consequences. It enables her to disrupt the accepted form of the symbolic order in her writing, just as she attacked the establishment by her actions. It shows that the personal is always and inevitably political, by the equal importance it gives to the 'trivial' events of everyday life and the 'great' events of history. (This political importance of the 'trivial' can be clearly seen in the early schoolday reminiscence which follows.) It provides not just one woman's voice, but a whole polyphony of women's voices, and thus inscribes 'women's becoming'[11] into the text far more radically than did, for example, Tristan.

There is one moment in her childhood reminiscences which prefigures the wilful preference for heteroglossia,[12] and the disruption of symbolic authority, and forms a *mise-en-abyme* for the textual strategies as a whole. This is the account of the subversion of the ritual of dictation, a subversion similar to that which will be used against every form of dictation and the dictatorial in later life:

When *monsieur le maître*, as we used to call him, from the height of his big wooden armchair, the *rostrum*, had carefully *recommended* that we write down the dictations exactly, I took care to add to what should be written what was not supposed to be. It produced something of this nature:
'The Romans were the masters of the world (*Louise, don't hold your pen like a stick; – semi-colon*), – but Gaul

135

resisted for a long time. (*You children from up at Querot, you're very late; – full-stop. Ferdinand, blow your nose. – You children from the mill, get your feet warm*). – Caesar wrote the history of it, etc.'

I even added things that the teacher didn't say, not losing a minute, scribbling furiously.[13]

She was only dissuaded from these diversions by the teacher's remark that she might get him dismissed, which, of course, substituted a higher authority as a target. The heteroglossia of childhood, in which the child's worm's-eye view and simple monosyllabic statement of fact subvert adult discourse, has become a privileged genre in the twentieth century. We can see in Michel a first gesture towards the language which Wittig will exploit so skilfully, and also so politically, in *L'Opoponax* (1964). Further forms that this subversion of authority through heteroglossia take in the text of *Mémoires* are multiple. There is not only the mixture of literary and oral forms of speech, like those already juxtaposed by the child in her school dictation, but also the deliberate mix of genres, such as narrative, oratory and poetry; of registers, the political, the legal, the pedagogic and so on; and of actual languages, codes and sub-codes, such as Kanak, local dialects and prison *argot*. She was well aware of the power of these discourses:

> Red *argot*, black *argot*, white *argot* are mixed like writhing monsters among which are entwined charming shapes, for *argot* is alive, it creates bloody or naive images. *Argot* undergoes eternal fluctuations, it changes its flow as rapidly as do the destinies of those who use it. White *argot* is the unmarked dress of words; most are still unknown to the neophyte, circumstances will teach him their meaning. Red *argot* and black *argot* are grotesque in their mortuary stories. Then there is prostitutes' *argot*. Sometimes it flourishes in the mud of the gutters or on the bloody cobbles of the Place de la Roquette. It has the coquetry and the charms of death.[14]

The voices of the excluded

The net result of this polyphony is that her text figures 'minority-becoming' by the inclusion of the voices normally excluded from the hierarchy of the text. Indeed, it gives a voice to those doubly excluded, illiterate women tellers of folktale and song, female prisoners, Kanak rebels. (Michel was a political prisoner in New Caledonia for many years.) There is a specific contrast made between the male, written code – the books which come from the two grandfathers, often stamped with the words *privilège du roy,* licensed by patriarchal approval – and the female oral code, represented by the *écrégne*:

> The *écrégne* [sic.], in our villages, is the house in which, on winter nights, the women and girls meet to spin, knit, and above all to tell or hear the old stories of the *feullot* (will-o'-the-wisp) which dances, dressed in flame, in the *prèles* (meadows) and the new stories of goings on at home or at the neighbours.[15]

It is also from the horrific stories heard at these gatherings, stories of exploitation, and of peasants who endured their lot and went like sheep to the slaughter, that Louise dates her first feelings of revolt. This, and the dialogic relation of the very language of the educated and the uneducated, is shown in the stories of the great famine. To get the tone, I leave Louise's reaction in French and translate in the notes:

> Il me semblait que s'il [the usurer] était rentré je lui aurais sauté à la gorge pour le mordre, et je disais tout cela; je m'indignais de ce qu'on croyait que tout le monde ne pouvait avoir de pain tous les jours; cette stupidité de troupeau m'effarait.
> – *Faut* pas parler comme ça, *petiote*! disait la femme. *Ça fait pleurer le bon Dieu.*
> (M: 158–90)[16]

As with George Sand, we may learn a great deal about Louise's use of the dialogism of textual discourses if we see her practice of, and attitudes to, cross-dressing as a sort of metaphor. An early lesson that both women learned was that male attire provided a merciful cloak of invisibility. As Louise tells her female narratees: 'Remember this, women who read me: We are not judged like men' (M: 274). But there is one way to rejoin the norm and its useful anonymity (only, of course, to be later judged even more harshly for exposing the fragility of the dominant code), and that is to wear male clothes:

While certain reporters were talking to me in a house where *I was not*, others saw me *on a picnic to the Bois* where I was not either. I was living with the families of my friends Vaughan and Meusy, whence I went, dressed as a man, to visit my poor mother.

Wearing this dress, I should have been able to stay in Paris, or take my mother abroad.

I should even have been able to go on with my propaganda work. How often I went to meetings from which women were excluded! How often, in the days of the Commune, I went, dressed as a national guard or a foot soldier, to places where no one dreamed they were dealing with a woman![17]

This cloak of invisibility is the same as prevents much discourse being seen as gendered male, so that we read the discourse of capitalism or that of socialism as a single ideology without reading the other deeper ideology that subsumes it. Louise exposes this hidden gendering in criticising the views of Proudhon, the ultimate misogynist, and demanding liberty for all, regardless of sex (M: 274), but, to my mind, her realisation of the sheer convenience and freedom conferred by male garb puts her message over even more effectively.

Textual delegitimation

Another piece of heteroglossia is the generic infringement, which mixes verse (her own and that of others), generally in rather hackneyed literary forms, with prose narrative, but also with speeches, newspaper articles and legal documents. It is a way of delegitimating the authorised form of structured narration by infusing it with the random play of memory, represented by shifts in form as well as voice. As she says:

There are perhaps a lot of verses in my *Mémoires*; but it is the form that best conveys certain impressions; and where will one have the right to be oneself and express what one feels, if not in one's reminiscences?[18]

Michel's writing in her poetry is at first legitimated by such things as the intertext of the conventional literary style of the period, seen in the verses she sent to her literary 'father figure',

Victor Hugo, and later by that of the popular revolutionary style of writers like Dupont and Béranger (cf. M: 73–4). In the same way, her political ideas (e.g. 'From each according to his capacity, to each according to his needs', cit. M: 184), the received ideas of the movement to which she belonged, are at first quoted, then paraphrased. However, the writing is delegitimated by the insistent intrusion of female voices, and more particularly by the empowering of the illiterate in her text with what they lacked in life, the gift of written expression. An example is the dialogues of women prisoners, speech perhaps never inscribed until that moment (M: 280–6).

Ross Chambers has pointed out, in a recent study, that, while narrative always contains description, the usual pattern is for the syntagmatic axis to dominate the paradigmatic axis. However, in what he felicitously calls 'loiterature', a different textual economy prevails, a literature which functions according to the relaxed 'etcetera principle', allowing constellations and clusters of incidents and events, and indulging in the free play of textual *jouissance*:

> In short, the openability of seemingly closed structures is what the etcetera principle affirms. And it is this openability of apparently closed structures that is illustrated by the phenomenon . . . whereby the closed, or syntagmatic, structure of narrative proves to be openable to a disordering, paradigmatic, or listing principle that *changes the context* and turns it into a limitlessly openable encyclopedia or inventory, a description of the endless diversity of the world.
>
> (1992: 5)

The listing principle is what governs the greater part of Michel's text, as in the extraordinarily powerful attack on cruelty to animals, and the cruelty to people which breeds it (M: 155–64), or the evocation of the flora of New Caledonia (M: 223–30). Seemingly random, this diversity opens onto freedom and produces a radically different form of text.

Another process as vital to the autobiographer as to the averred writer of fiction, and as dependent on the workings of the paradigm, is the reactivation of memory, both that of the writer and that of the reader. Proust later demonstrated most memorably the metonymic power of the object and found in its capacity to re-invoke a whole cluster of sensual experience the key to anamnesis. Michel, writing her 'memoirs/memories' at 55, after the traumas of her mother's death and her own breakdown, constantly uses what she calls 'the terrible eloquence of things' (M: 135) as an entry into the 'house' of the past. Her entrance into each 'room', to use the ancient metaphor of memory, permits her to re-experience and re-member the scattered elements of sensual, emotional and intellectual paradigms.

To take the example of one such metonymic and paradigmatic cluster, she reunites, by the associations of flowers, the climactic and tragic moments of loss, rather than narrating them in chronological sequence. Red carnations stand for the Commune in her two best-known poems (printed in full M: 113–14). These red flowers are the means of rebirth, not just of hope, but of memory itself:

> De ces rouges oeillets que, pour nous reconnaître,
> Avaient chacun de nous, renaissez, rouges fleurs.
> D'autres vous reprendront aux temps qui vont paraître,
>   Et ceux-là seront les vainqueurs.[19]

This last verse of 'Les Oeillets rouges' leads on to 'A Théophile Ferré', an epitaph for the executed leader of the Commune, which asks for the same flowers on her own tomb and, in the wider context of this constellation of reminiscence, remembers their use on his. The carnations evoke, in their turn, 'the red roses loaded with bees at the end of the farmyard, the white lilac that Marie wanted on her coffin, and the flesh-coloured roses stained with drops of blood which I sent from Clermont to my mother!'[20] In other words, this floral paradigm links with another, functioning both metonymically and metaphorically, and evokes the same trinity as begins the text: her origins and the name of the mother, her love, and the revolution; but this trinity is here expressed in 'the terrible eloquence of things'.

Perhaps the most radical, because most deeply inherent in the textual structure, of Louise's delegitimatory tactics is this substitution of the workings of memory, fragmentation, diversion, free association and random patterning, for the cause and effect, a then b, then as a result c, of accepted narrative. I think Michel's text opens to question Nancy Miller's assumption that, in the use of such textual strategies, we are dealing with a local and post-Barthesian phenomenon, which is, politically, merely oppositional and not revolutionary:

> Dispersion and fragmentation, the theft of language and the subversion of the stereotype attract Barthes as critical styles of desire and deconstruction, rupture and protest. Certain women writers in France like Hélène Cixous, Luce Irigaray, and I would argue, paradoxically, Monique Wittig, have also been attracted to this model of relation: placing oneself at a deliberately oblique (or textual) angle to intervention. Troped as a subversion – a political inter-textuality – this positionality remains in the end, I think, a form of negotiation within the dominant social text, and ultimately, a local operation.
>
> (1986: 111–12)

Narrative based on the 'etcetera principle' is a form which is freed from the ideological demands of structural hierarchies. It may therefore be oppositional in a purely literary way. What I would wish to add, however, is that such a discursive economy, resisting the structural demands of the canonical, in both literature and politics, can also be used to make an ideological, even a political, statement, which subverts the 'dominant social text'. Using the well-springs of memory, Louise demonstrates in her text the very principles of equality, of including the excluded, of taking from each speaker according to his or her capacity and of giving to each hearer according to her or his needs, for which she fought all her life. Her text is a demonstration of anarchy in action and of the governing political principle of her struggle.

8

Symbolic delegitimation

Our case studies until now have been of authors who have spoken from beyond the pale. Each of these women has, in her own way, questioned both the bounds of gender and and the norms of social exclusion. Each has used her illegitimacy to reach that threshold position of which Serres speaks (1987: 90), and which permits the energies of social and discursive freedom to be exploited. Each has refused the name of the Father and appealed for a different law. This *dynamis* of the border, this emancipation from the seemingly immutable laws of convention, has always been the goal of the artist as much as the revolutionary. Indeed, in the case of a poet like Aragon (1897–1982), his actual experience of illegitimacy and its social stigma is the factor, I would contend, which keeps the two strands of art and revolution firmly combined, often to the detriment of the art and in the service of a revolution already turned to tyranny. It is time to look more closely at the artists, and I begin with the autobiographical or semi-autobiographical texts of four male artists who, in different modes, choose the way of the mother.

For male as for female writers delegitimation may be real or symbolic. One male example of the defiant assertion of actual illegitimacy, with all its implications for good and for evil, and of the assumption of the name of the mother, may be seen in the work of Jean Genet. It finds its *locus classicus* in *Journal du voleur* (The Thief's Journal) (1949), which we will examine in the next chapter. But for the moment we will consider the symbolic delegitimation which, for some writers, is the chosen surrogate for real illegitimacy. It is not only a denial of the law of the Father but access to the way of the mother. By putting oneself beyond the pale, by participating in the *mundus mulie-bris* (the world of women) (Baudelaire, OC I: 499)[1] or in the world of the outcast, one also puts oneself beyond the herd, since one has moved into another possible world, where the very marginality of existence involves a multiplication of self. Those who construct that other compelling narrative where the way of the mother prevails often give themselves paradoxical sobriquets which mark their access to alterity. Thus Flora Tristan calls herself Pariah; Nerval, among his multiplicity of names, is Peregrinus; Baudelaire identifies with the Monster; and Sartre fictionalises himself as Bastard.

There are many variations in the strategies of writers who achieve symbolic delegitimation by following the way and the name of the mother, even though a stable identity and a legitimate name is their birthright. Perhaps not surprisingly, all of those I examine are male. Their female equivalent would, I suppose, be a writer like Colette, who uses as signature not only her maiden name (Colette was her father's surname), but a version of it (the name as single sign – both male surname and female given name) which emphasises its sexual ambiguity. The four male writers are chosen as case studies because each has used a different approach in presenting himself as a pseudo-(or symbolic) bastard.

STENDHAL AND THE MOTHER'S LINE

The first, the novelist Stendhal (1783–1842), constructs a private world in which not so much his own legitimacy, but that of his father, Chérubin Beyle, is phantasmatically denied, thereby calling the male line into question.[2] His is not the 'family romance'.[3] Rather than by dreams of bastardy, his delegitim-ation is constructed by giving precedence to a 'female genealogy': 'I considered myself a Gagnon and I never thought of the Beyles without a disgust that still endures in 1835.'[4] Genealogically speaking, the appeal to the name of the mother always involves not only an inescapable diversity, but also a continual branching movement into absence, as each move towards the absent mother, and *her* absent mother, only reveals yet another patro-nym, while the female line remains fragmented and occluded. But this apparent frustration is the source of a drive towards plurality and diffusion, quite different from the pseudo-unity and verticality of the name of the father as embodied in paternal genealogies.[5] In Stendhal's case, although he dreams of assuming the maternal patronym, Gagnon, this is given immediate fluidity by being mythologised as Italian (Guadagni or Guadaniamo). And, in fact, rather than assume a single signature, even the 'sacred' name of the mother, Gagnon, Stendhal chooses multiple pseudonyms and endless protean transformations.

The best study of this passion for pseudonymity is that of Jean Starobinski, 'Stendhal pseudonyme', partly translated as 'Truth in Masquerade'.[6] It is, however, imbued with both the existentialist vogue of its time of writing, and a certain feeling of Oedipal guilt, seeing the rejection of the name of the father as a murder in effigy (Starobinski, 1962: 115):

> In the equation $I=I$, the name (in the eyes of others) acts as the equal sign. Confined to our name, our identity becomes alienated; it comes to us through and from others . . . . A pseudonym eliminates perjury and allows the invocation of a plurality of I's as a splendid alibi . . . . The mask and the pseudonym generate a perfect dynamics of irresponsibility . . . . The mask must be a procession of masks, and pseudonymity a systematic 'polynymity'. Otherwise the egotist is recaptured by others.
>
> (ibid.: 117–18)

The egotist is, in any event, always recaptured by the mechanism of the signature. Stendhal uses the pseudonym to produce multiple lines of flight, some private, some public. However, one of these pseudonyms, Henry Brulard, belongs to the female genealogy, and will be used to demonstrate the mythopoesis involved.

When Stendhal comes to write his autobiography, *The Life of Henry Brulard*, which will remain unpublished until well after his death,[7] he chooses a pseudonym which enables him to remain himself (Henri, H.B.) and yet become other. Henry comes from Henriette, the given name of his beloved mother, but it is anglicised to free it from any lingering taint of having been conferred by the father. It is thus derived from the name 'of my dearest mother', which is written in English in the margin of the manuscript at the spot where her birth certificate is mentioned (HB: 462). The given name, of course, is beholden only to the mother–son relationship, and not to either patronym. The pseudo-patronym, Brulard, also has an interesting history. It was conferred on the baby Henri as a joke by the maternal uncle who was his favourite and his masculine ideal, Romain Gagnon:

> My uncle was teasing his sister Henriette (my mother) about my ugliness. Apparently I had an enormous, hairless head, and I looked like Father Brulard, a wily monk, a gourmet and very influential in his monastery, my uncle or great-uncle dead before I arrived.[8]

Thus the name Brulard encapsulates both a re-baptism by the mother's side of the family *and* a denigration of the paternal side, since *Father* Brulard was not only a paternal great-uncle, but a representative of the hated patriarchy of the Church. Henri can never rid himself of the paternal ugliness, but he can assume it, and by laughing at it, choose to delegitimate himself. The insult itself is transformed into that object of desire, the mask. As Starobinski says:

> A name, a body, a social status, all are prisons. But their doors are not so well locked that a dream of escape is impossible. Of course one takes leave of one's name more easily than one's body, and a pseudonym is a substitute for the desired metamorphosis.
>
> (1962: 119)

Even the 'seven letters: B,R,U,L,A,R,D, which form [his] name and involve [his] self-esteem' (HB: 283) are merely an invitation to another transmutation.

As Rebecca Pauly points out in *Le Berceau et la bibliothèque* (The Cradle and the Library) (1989) Henry's adherence to the female line is emphasised in terms of space. Not only the sacred space of the mother's bedroom which Henry alone is allowed to enter and use as a study, but the rooms of his maternal grandmother and great-aunt become spatial representations of the female genealogy. He recreates in his accounts of them a geography of the emotions. This is made especially clear because the autobiography, while also, as we shall see, poly-semic in other ways, takes its major structure from its dialogism between the verbal and the iconic codes. Each stage in the young life is illustrated but, more particularly, mapped and charted. Thus the movements in time in one textual form are comple-mented by the movements in space in the other, and both reinforce the peculiar ascendancy of the maternal line. What has been less remarked is the importance of the double mothering provided by the servant, Marion, and the parallel ascendancy she exercises.

Stendhal's use of heteroglossia is also linked to the way of the mother (cf. Didier in HB: 11). It is not only a means of giving voice to alterity, as does Louise Michel, but, in the first instance, an excursion into the 'mother' tongue, Italian, or a 'masking' by the use of code (in both senses of the word). Most often, English is used for this second purpose. The particular use of foreign languages, which sees them employed, in the most high-handed way, for emotional rather than communicational reasons, raises some pertinent questions about the linking of the maternal with the 'pre-symbolic'. If, as Béatrice Didier says, when he learns Italian 'The initiate relearns the use of a new language which is, in the last resort, no other than the maternal tongue, obliterated by death, the language of the unconscious which unites him to the mother' (1983: 213), then not only the symbolic, but the meta-symbolic, in the form of a second language, can perform the function attributed to the Kristevan 'semiotic'.

As with Baudelaire, the maternal language and, indeed, a whole maternal semiosis, are constantly sought after and phantasmatically recreated in the *mundus muliebris*. The names of the women who have attracted him with the same intense sensuality as his mother did, or rather the initials of these women, constantly inscribe another female line, one which has, as he puts it, 'to the letter, occupied my whole life' (HB: 37). Talking of this world, Stendhal produces an almost textbook example of heteroglossia:

> *Now you know* [*Par ainsi*], as children say, why I'm so far from being blasé about their [women's] tricks and engaging ways, that at my age, 52, and, [*sic*] writing this, I'm still under the spell of a long *chiacchierata* I had with Amalia yesterday evening at the Valle Theatre.
>
> To consider them as philosophically as possible and so endeavour to strip them of the halo which makes me *goggle-eyed* [*aller les yeux*], which dazzles me and deprives me of the faculty of seeing clearly, I will *class* these ladies (mathematical language) according to their differing qualities.[9]

The discourse combines past and present in the double registers of childhood in Grenoble and maturity in Italy, dialect (*Par ainsi* and *aller les yeux*), a foreign language, cliché ('under the spell' and 'the halo'), and the discourses of philosophy and mathematics ('the faculty of seeing clearly', and *class*). There is also the sub-text that mathematics (usually seen as a masculine code) was actually the passport that enabled him to escape from Grenoble and the law of the Father, enshrined by Chérubin Beyle in property, patois and piety.[10]

The figure of the dead mother governs the discourse and the signature in the autobiographies of both Stendhal and Nerval, all the more readily because it is also inscribed as an addressee. Stendhal speaks either to the future (the well-known 'happy few' of 1935) or to the dead – his mother or that other ideal mother, the revolutionary leader Mme Roland, who died on the scaffold in 1793, three years after his mother died in childbed (HB: 11, 53). The novelist, essayist and poet, Nerval (1808–55) (OC: 461–8) also at times appeals to the same ghostly addressee. Derrida grasps the importance of this obsession, perhaps because it is also his own:

> If, therefore, every name is the name of a dead person, or of a living person it can do without, from then on, if one writes with names in mind, to call up names, one also writes for the dead. Perhaps not the dead in general, as Genet says. Genet says, more or less: 'I write for the dead, or I made a theatre intended for the dead.' But for *such and such* a dead person, and perhaps in every text there is a dead man or a dead woman to be sought, the particular figure of the dead person for whom the text is destined, and who signs.[11]

NERVAL AND THE MATERNAL SPACE

We have seen Stendhal play with the toponym, and construct an entire mythology of place, centred on Italy, the 'maternal paradise'. Even more dramatically, the toponym, Nerval, chosen as signature by Gérard Labrunie, is the key to the construction of a syncretic and mythical country, which is at the same time a real place, the Valois region of the Ile de France, to which only the way of the mother can lead, and where the name of the mother is deeply encoded. When his mother followed his father to the front in Germany, where she died two years later, she left the baby in her brother's charge. His property was called the Clos de Nerval.[12] The child was fostered to a local peasant wet-nurse, in whom he was lucky enough to find a true second mother. I find it quite characteristic of literary scholarship that I know the name of every female association of Nerval's in his beloved Valois countryside (aristocratic, royal, mythological, toponymic), but I have been unable to discover either given or surname of this foster-mother. Just as the second peasant mother and her family stand for life and the gates of horn, the absent true mother stands for dreams and the gates of ivory (N: 753). This is seen not only in the name Nerval but in the place-name Mortefontaine, often changed or repressed in the texts because of its symbolic association with the death of the first mother, since Marie Marguerite Antoinette Laurent, Madame Labrunie, had died in Germany before Gérard could know her and was only a fantasy to him, a fantasy completely centred on her native region, the Valois:

> The Valois region near Paris is produced in Nerval as the space of the (always already) absent mother as against the city of Paris where the law of the father prevails, history (as the economic and material 'progress' of the bourgeoisie) is made, and alienists minoritize 'madness' by producing it in the diagnostic language of the other.
>
> (Chambers, 1991: 107)

It is true that, in the cases of both Stendhal and Nerval, the rejection of the law of the Father has been interpreted primarily in terms of the Oedipus complex. The symbolic murder of the father by rejection of his name is seen as the necessary prelude to the forbidden dream of marriage with the lost mother, which gives phantasmatic access to the lost paradise, the world of sensual freedom and polymorphous perversion. In staging their fictionalised signatures, Stendhal, Nerval and Baudelaire, who adopts yet another tactic by an actual, if temporary, adoption of his mother's maiden name, are usually read in these terms. They are seen as eternal victims of the Oedipal, threatened with castration by the father figure they reject and unable to assume their true masculinity in the possession of the phallus. And indeed it is not difficult to read their texts in this light (cf.

Quesnel, 1987). The problem with this commonly accepted myth is that it views a preoccupation with the female only in terms of sexual desire, and union with the mother as the Garden of Eden subject to the rule of a jealous God. It does not come to terms with male desire for female potential.

The drama of regendering

A basic repressed desire is, as I suggested earlier, one for two female powers: the power of reproduction and the power of transformation. Female multiplicity and lability are seen to challenge the male order. The envied and dreaded power of female reproduction is controlled by the fiction of the imposition of masculine identity and a masculine order, the so-called name of the Father. As Deleuze says (thereby, in a certain sense, once more imposing masculine order):

> A minority never exists ready-made, it is only formed on lines of flight, which are also its way of advancing and attacking. There is a woman-becoming in writing. *Madame Bovary, c'est moi* is the sentence of a hysterical trickster. Even women do not always succeed when they force themselves to write like women, as a function of a future of woman. Woman is not necessarily the writer, but the minority-becoming of her writing, whether it be man or woman. Virginia Woolf forbade herself 'to speak like a woman': she harnessed the woman-becoming of writing all the more for this.
>
> (Deleuze and Parnet, 1987: 43–4)

Many male artists feel therefore impelled to play out a drama of feminisation, hoping thereby to attain full access to the powers of creation (cf. Burton, 1988). But, as we will see in the cases of the poet Charles Baudelaire (1821–67) and the uncategorisable Jean-Paul Sartre (1905–80), the access to the world of textual reproduction, which is lived as a dangerous loss of identity, a seductive polymorphism, may be compensated for by a symbolic, and even actual, refusal of biological reproduction. A demand for non-reproductive sexuality and for female sterility seems to bring the scenario back under male control. One must, however, remember that this can also be used as a means of control by females. We have seen the classic case in Elizabeth I and her exploitation of her virginity. Indeed the re-gendering of language in her quest for relegitimation, and the frequent use by females of male codes when they wish to gain power from the law of the Father, provides the other side of the coin to the male use of the *mundus muliebris* as a means to delegitimation.

As I have indicated elsewhere (Maclean, 1982), the 'paradox of procreation' which emerges is the impossible desire to be female, multiple and gravid and *at the same time* male, unified and seminal. Frequently linked with this desire to be at once single and multiple is a male envy of the female capacity to switch roles, masks and identities. The refusal of the father's law is linked with a refusal of the self as the unitary 'subject', the conventional site of patriarchal authority. There is a remarkable paradox in the determination of many male writers to exploit the very emancipation from the law of the Father which they condemn in their female contemporaries.[13]

Pseudo-illegitimacies

Moving on to the *faux bâtards* or pseudo-illegitimacies, I wish to consider as paradigmatic the parallel and complementary cases of Baudelaire and Sartre. There are three recurring narratives in Baudelaire's work which gain their dynamism and their 'mobile and virtual power' (Derrida, 1982: 41) from belonging to the border between life and work, between inside and outside, between active and passive and, most importantly, between male and female. As Derrida says: 'This divisible border passes through the two "bodies", the corpus [or body of work] and the [physical] body, according to laws which we are only beginning to perceive' (1982: 41). Each of the three narratives is, in its own way, a narrative of delegitimation. Each opens a window, the window of a possible world in which the narrator can live and suffer both as self and as other. The making of such narratives is, of course, evoked in *Les Fenêtres* (The Windows) (OC I: 339).

THREE BAUDELAIREAN NARRATIVES

1 The abortion

The first of these narratives is what Mauron would call a *mythe personnel* (1972), although, oddly enough, he himself in *Le*

Dernier Baudelaire (The Last Baudelaire) (1966) does not identify it as such. It is based on what many have argued (and Sartre the chief among them) to be the most traumatic event to affect the whole of Baudelaire's life. This was the remarriage of his mother after a year and a half had passed since the death of his father in February 1827, a period in which Charles had enjoyed solitary possession of her. She thus assumed a third identity; born Defayis (or Dufaÿs or Dufays), she had become Baudelaire and now became Aupick. We will return to the significance of this name-changing. But it was not just the remarriage that was traumatic, but its circumstances. The marriage was both sudden and forced. Married on 8 November, Mme Aupick gave birth on 2 December to a still-born daughter. (Sartre was unaware of these circumstances when he wrote his *Baudelaire* in 1947.)

As I have shown in my study 'Baudelaire and the Paradox of Procreation', the basic story of these events undergoes various transformations and fictionalisations in the correspondence, poems and prose poems, and its echoes may be heard in texts which span almost the whole of Baudelaire's literary career. The most startling mutation of the trauma is that of the dream work and its secondary revision. The letter of 18 March 1856, which relates a nightmare, shows the depth of the obsession (C I: 338–41).[14] The dream takes place in an imaginary museum where the displays are malformed foetuses and other monsters of the imagination. Each abortion is presented as a work of art, as a framed picture, though frequently unfinished or distorted:

> In a mass of little frames, I see drawings, miniatures, photographic proofs. They represent coloured birds, with very brilliant plumage, whose eye is *living*. Sometimes *there are only halves of birds*. – They sometimes represent images of strange, monstrous, almost *amorphous* beings, like *aeroliths*. – In a corner of each drawing, there is a note: *The girl [la fille] so and so, aged . . ., gave birth to this foetus, in such and such a year.*[15]

There are two identifications, two transformations in narrative identity, possible with such an obsession. The first is that the textual identification should be with the mother/prostitute who can give birth to nothing but abortions. In all Baudelaire's work there recurs in various forms the story of the male

151

pregnancy, the textual travail that can only produce still-births or monsters. For instance, the poet in 'Bénédiction' is 'un arbre misérable/ Qui ne pourra pousser ses boutons empestés!' ('a wretched tree/ unable to produce its diseased buds') (OC I: 375) or elsewhere the soil from which spring 'fleurs maladives' ('sickly flowers') (OC I: 4). The scenario of the writer in labour and giving birth to the book[16] is, of course, widespread and relates over and over again the basic male womb envy which is studied by Christiane Olivier (1980). This may be a simplification, but no more so than is the famous 'penis envy'. The peculiarly Baudelairean twist is the link with abortion and still-birth in which the writer, as prostitute, must also suffer the maternal penalties of prostitution.

The other fiction and the other mask which can be linked with this narrative is the one where the poet figure, rather than identifying with the 'vieilles mères portant des avortons accrochés à leurs mamelles exténuées' ('old mothers carrying abortions attached to their exhausted breasts') ('Les Tentations', OC I: 309), identifies with the *avorton* instead. The poet is a figure of exclusion, of alterity:

> Comme une enfant chétive, horrible, sombre, immonde,
> Dont sa famille rougirait,
> Et qu'elle aurait longtemps, pour la cacher au monde,
> Dans un caveau mise au secret.
>
> ('Confession', OC I: 45)

(Like a sickly, horrible, dark, unclean infant / Who would make her family blush with shame / One that, to hide it from the world, she would long / Have hidden away in a cellar.)

It is revealing that this verse, the nearest thing in his work to a straightforward reference to the events of his childhood, (note the female forms *une enfant, la, mise*) is given a certain protection by being presented as a simile. This simile is linked with the narrative of the monster birth. The monster is itself a figure of the border, a figure of doubleness incorporating both animal and human, human and divine, and, of course, male and female (see Maclean, 1988: 156–7). The monster, like the angel, may be hermaphrodite and sterile ('La Fanfarlo', OC I: 577). It is also a *monstrum*, a showpiece. The identification it provides is with alterity, with the marginalised, the female, the excluded, with the *monstres innocents* ('Mademoiselle Bistouri', OC I: 355). This identification is in itself a form of delegitimation.

2 The transformations of the snake/woman

The second narrative identification with illegitimacy and at the same time with the *mundus muliebris* becomes what I shall call the story of the *femme serpent*. Woman as snake not only has flexibility and lability but, most importantly, infinite powers of transformation. She is a protean figure, as were the women who inspired the three main love cycles of *Les Fleurs du mal*. Each has been exhaustively studied biographically as a sensual figure (one can practically quote their measurements), and yet what they represent as figures of alterity is little considered. Each, like the snake changing its skin, assumed the right to change her identity and her name as she wished. All three women were illegitimate. We do not know Jeanne's real name; she was also known as Berthe, and she called herself Duval, Lemer and Prosper. One can even make a case that phonetic traces of these names, scales of the snake's skin as it were, may be found in Baudelaire's early writings. For example, the phonemes of Lemer are present in the name Samuel Cramer, and the trace of Prosper may be read in the phonetic and semantic play of 'Dans l'enfer de ton lit devenir Proserpine!' ('Become Proserpina in the hell of your bed!') (OC I: 28). Marie Daubrun was born under her mother's name, legitimised Marie Bruneau, and assumed the stage name Daubrun. Aglaé Joséphine Savatier, also born under her mother's name, renamed herself Aglaé Apollonie Sabatier and was generally known as La Présidente.

One can see here the same process to which I referred earlier; uncontrolled by the law of the father, these women use their marginality as a right and choose names which can serve as masks in the changing circumstances of their lives. One can ask, like Baudelaire, 'Laquelle est la vraie?' ('Which is the true one?') (OC I: 342). As in the poem in prose of this name, the possibility that the *fille miraculeuse* (miraculous girl – or prostitute: one should note the allusion to the *enfant du miracle* – the divine child) will also prove to be the *fameuse canaille* (downright bitch) is in the last resort part of her attraction. The love of the snake woman is also 'L'Amour du mensonge' (The love of the lie) (OC I: 98–9). So the second form of delegitimation is the deliberate association with the unstable, the protean and the marginalised. It is the choice that made Baudelaire issue his first poems under the names of his friends; it is the delegitimation he is still celebrating right at the end of his writing life in 'Perte d'auréole' ('Loss of a halo') (OC I: 352), which was not published until after his death. In this poem, the halo of social recognition, the *insigne* of the law of the Father, is dropped in the mud, and the relieved poet, one of the many Baudelairean *alter egos*, can at last enjoy the pleasures of being *incognito*, having lost his 'good name'.

3 Destabilising the signature

This brings us to the third narrative form, the most obviously linked to delegitimation, the destabilising of the signature and the refuge in pseudonyms. This, like the first, has a very particular link with his mother. In 1842, Charles entered into adulthood and his father's inheritance, and so into the name of the Father. He proceeded to dissipate that inheritance so fast that, at his mother's and stepfather's request, a family council reduced him to tutelary status and to the care of a *conseil judiciaire*. This was experienced by Baudelaire as a form of 'illegitimation'. Like a bastard, or a woman, he had humbly to request an allowance from a well-meaning but philistine trustee, and he had to beg, threaten or cajole his mother for the supplements he constantly needed. This had the paradoxical result of leaving her in his power for life as much as he was left in hers. Their relationship, just as much as his with Jeanne, was the mutual mastery of victim and executioner, or of the man who keeps a woman and the woman who is kept, here interestingly reversed, as mother keeps son. The 'Duellum' (OC I: 36) and the savage promise of reciprocal suffering (OC I: 78) are as much characteristic of the passionate love-hate relationship with his mother as that with his mistress.

It is against this background that we must see the choice, between 1843 and 1847, of his mother's maiden name as a pseudonym. Sometimes in this period he signs himself Baudelaire-Dufaÿs, sometimes he uses his mother's name alone. The Deroy portrait of 1843, of which he was extremely proud, is simply titled 'M. Dufaÿs', and *La Fanfarlo* (1847), his first major literary

154

publication, is signed Charles Defayis. Nobody, least of all Baudelaire, seems to have been aware of the correct spelling of his mother's name, but no doubt the uncertainty lent to its charm (see C I: 133). Even more here than in the use of his friends' names as pseudonyms, the will to delegitimise is apparent, but also the hesitation. Was he, as 'monster', to assume his double nature as Baudelaire/Dufaÿs, both male and female, and subject to the law of the father as well as that of the mother, or was he to opt as Charles Defayis for childhood status and the law of the mother alone?

La Fanfarlo presents us with a parody of the whole dilemma, just as it presents the rejection of the law of the Father in parodic form, when its hero Samuel Cramer cries: 'Malediction, a triple malediction on the infirm fathers who made us scrawny and stunted, predestined as we are to engender only still-born children!'[17] The story of Cramer, a writer whose nature is 'féconde en desseins difficiles et risibles avortements' ('fertile in difficult designs and ridiculous abortions'), combines the narrative of the monster birth with that of the snake woman (he can only love a woman who can metamorphose herself). He, like his creator, is torn between two natures and two genders, 'dieu de l'impuissance, – dieu moderne et hermaphrodite' ('god of impotence, – modern and hermaphrodite god') (OC I: 553), and uses the signature to express the ambivalence of his nature. The story begins: 'Samuel Cramer, qui signa autrefois du nom de Manuela de Monteverde quelques folies romantiques' ('Samuel Cramer, who once signed the name of Manuela de Monteverde to a few romantic follies') (OC I: 553). Samuel's monstrous and protean nature is expressed in this double signature:

> He was at once all the artists he had studied and all the books he had read, and yet, in spite of this talent for performance, remained deeply original. He was always the gentle, the fantastic, the lazy, the terrible, the learned, the ignorant, the sloppy, the stylish Samuel Cramer, the romantic Manuela de Monteverde.[18]

One can see here, in the very semantics and syntax, the fragmentation, the multiple skins of the snake, which represent the denial of the unitary law of the Father. This principle will remain with Baudelaire all his life and will prove a guiding factor in elaborating the 'snake' of the *Petits poèmes en prose*

(Little Prose Poems), a text designed to be hacked into many fragments as desired (OC I: 275), as I have shown in *Narrative as Performance* (Maclean, 1988).

The addressee

But the narrative of delegitimation in *La Fanfarlo*, ironically underscored by the fact that poor Samuel has to relegitimise himself in the end, has another target. We may see it as a letter sent to an address, an address which explains the skill, the 'address', of the sender.[19] One could compare it with the savage fantasy of the 'Galant Tireur', where the marksman shoots and decapitates the doll by imagining it to be his wife. He remarks: 'Ah! mon cher ange, combien je vous remercie de mon adresse!' ('Oh! my dear angel, how much I thank you for my address!') (OC I: 349–50). The address of *La Fanfarlo*, in both senses of the word, is of course in the signature itself, the Defayis which flaunts the name of the mother, but does it in the way most wounding to Caroline Defayis-Baudelaire-Aupick herself. Baudelaire seems to have sent her the manuscript as early as 1843: 'Do me the pleasure of reading this manuscript, which is complete . . . . You don't know the ending; read it and tell me honestly *the effect it has on you.*'[20] Each barbed reference to the tragedy which never officially happened, and which Charles as a child was never supposed to have known about, is a code within a code, addressed to a *destinataire* who, in a way that forestalls Derrida by some 150 years, 'signs' the text destined for her.[21] The early description of Samuel Cramer is an 'autobiography' in the Derridean sense described in *L'Oreille de l'autre*:

> If I want to tell my life, well, it is an addressee, it is an 'I' marked as female who will sign and who will thus be – I will not say the author because the word destroys everything straightaway – but who will be the place from which something like my biography, my autobiography will be signed. In other words, it will naturally not be an autobiography but a heterobiography . . . . Thus, the autobiography of the woman, hers, or of her, descending from her, as it were inherited from her, from a woman, from woman.[22]

Thus every signature entails the choice of a history and the choice of a law. The name of the mother may be seen as a signature which both delegitimises and relegitimises by the left hand. It is a fiction which still relies on authorisation. Baudelaire might decentre himself, but, like Sartre, he always needed a judge. In fact, as we know, he not only returned to the patronym as his authorial signature, but kept the law of the Father present in the other symbolic form of a portrait which he carried with him. It is a portrait which gave rise to yet another story (never written), number 52 of *Le Spleen de Paris* (an alternative title for *Petits poèmes en prose*), which was to be called 'Reproches du portrait (portrait de mon père)' ('Reproaches of the Portrait (Portrait of my Father)') (OC I: 368). He prayed to his father too. Alas, there is no freeing oneself from the super-ego, whether it be maternal or paternal.

SARTRE THE *FAUX-BATARD*

Now Sartre, as he tells us himself, in one of the most manifestly inaccurate statements in the history of literature, never had a super-ego (1964: 11). This is an assertion to which we will return. On the other hand, he almost invariably used the patronym and seems only once to have signed with a pseudonym, which was, revealingly, 'the borrowed maiden name of his maternal grandmother' (Cohen-Salal, 1987: 55). So how does he belong in this discussion? His process of delegitimation is rather an involved one, but one manifestation of it is an extraordinary identification with Baudelaire, an identification which takes the form of castigating Baudelaire for the very *mauvaise foi* of which he feels himself guilty, especially the *faculté comédienne*, the multiplicity and self-division which Baudelaire so freely acknowledged in himself. The familial drama of the two bears strong resemblances, including the death of Charles' father when he was 5, and that of Jean-Paul when he was 2. In both cases, a perception of an idyllic relationship with the mother was rudely shattered by the mother's remarriage when Charles was 7 and Jean-Paul was 11: 'There was only one home, one family, one incestuous couple. "I was always alive in you" he would write to her later, "you were mine, only mine. You were at the same time an idol and a comrade".'[23] The mothers thus both bear three names: Defayis–Baudelaire–Aupick and Schweitzer–Sartre–Mancy. Sartre uses Baudelaire as his *porte-parole* to say what he merely suggests about himself:

> There was, in his existence, an event which he had been unable to bear: the second marriage of his mother. On this subject, he was inexhaustible and his terrible logic always boiled down to this: 'When one has a son like me – like me was understood – one does not remarry.'[24]

Josette Pacaly in her psychoanalytic study *Sartre au miroir* (1980), points out that this disbeliever in the unconscious manages to repress all mention of his mother's remarriage in the autobiographical *Les Mots* (*Words*). Actually this is not quite true, and one mention is interesting in itself. The *absence* of Sartre's father was marked, like that of Baudelaire's, by the *presence* of a portrait: 'For some years, I saw, over my bed, the portrait of a junior officer with frank eyes, a round, balding head and a heavy moustache: when my mother remarried, the portrait disappeared'(W: 15).[25]

In fact we may say, in Derridean terms, that *Baudelaire* by Sartre is in many ways *Sartre* by Baudelaire; it is the subject/ addressee who signs the text, and the name of the dead that governs the living. In this savage attack the mother is again the hidden addressee, the target of the message ostensibly directed to another. Baudelaire is roundly condemned for the very feminisation so essential to Sartre's own development, and which stands for the way of the mother to him. The clash between the feminising way of the mother and the castrating law of the Father is beautifully summed up in *Les Mots* by the episode of the grandfather's cutting of the long blonde curls which are the mother's pride and joy: 'she would, I think, have liked me to be a real girl . . . . Heaven had not granted her prayers, so she made the best of it. I was to have the sex of the angels, indeterminate but feminine around the edges' (W: 65).[26]

Sartre as 'no man's son'

His grandfather, Charles Schweitzer, is of course the dominating super-ego figure of Jean-Paul's life, and it is this patriarchal presence – 'he was so like God the Father that he was often taken for him' (W: 16) – that enables Sartre to perform the neat sleight of hand of his delegitimation. It was Francis Jeanson in his *Sartre par lui-même* who first identified the recurrent theme of the bastard in Sartre's work and confirmed its personal application:

> But it was Sartre himself who said that I was right, from the moment he undertook to go back over those years to recapture the general climate and the most telling aspects: 'I was the *pseudo-bastard* [*le faux bâtard*].' Totally accepted, and so legitimate (rather too legitimate, to be honest, he was so fêted), the net result was that he felt in no way justified.
>
> (1969: 111)

In *Les Mots*, Sartre calls himself 'Nobody's son' (W: 71) ['le fils de personne' (91)), and Jeanson promptly reads into this a patriarchal message: 'No man's son, that is to say one's own son: father and son in a single person' (ibid.: 126), and develops the theme of the Messiah, which certainly is one of the hidden narratives of *Les Mots* and, as we have seen, one of the recurring narratives of illegitimacy. The book provides a startling example of the conscious creation of an anti-myth of the divine child.

Sartre's delegitimation is possible precisely because, in his myth, his grandfather has assumed the patriarchal position and represents the law of the Father. A greater reason than mere lack of interest prompts Sartre to throw the Schweitzer family tree into the waste basket (Cohen-Salal, 1987: 41). In a household where the name of the father is very emphatically Schweitzer and where Charles enacts the part of the super-ego, an obvious reversal takes place. Sartre, Jean-Paul's patronym, becomes merely the devalued name of the mother, who becomes 'maiden' again, 'a virgin tarnished' ('une vierge avec tache' (10)) (W: 14). Derrida says that every male bastard can rejoice in 'an immaculate conception' (1981, I: 66). Sartre sees his mother rather as maculate, *avec tache*, but becoming a 'bastard' in his case means taking the mother's 'maiden' name, and this name is Sartre, which is the despised patronym of a progenitor irresponsible enough to die young:

> I was shown a young giantess [note the Baudelairean allusion], and I was told that she was my mother. On my own, I should more likely have taken her for an elder sister. This virgin, who lived with us, watched and

domineered over by everyone, was there to wait on me. I loved her: but how could I respect her if no one else did? There were three bedrooms in our house: my grandfather's, my grandmother's, and the 'children's'. We were the 'children': both minors and both maintained [another Baudelairean note].

(W: 16)[27]

The very excess of the Sartrean rejection of the law of the Father, at its most virulent in 'L'enfance d'un chef' (Childhood of a boss) (Sartre, 1939), in fact marks the ambiguity of his reaction against the patriarchal fiat. He carries on this rejection in *Les Mots*, which was originally to have been called *Jean sans terre* (John the Landless):

> To an owner, this world's goods reflect what he is; they taught me what I was not. *I was not* stable or permanent; *I was not* the perpetuator-to-be of my father's work; *I was not* necessary to the production of steel; in short, I had no soul.

(W: 56)[28]

The narrative of lack

The most interesting aspect of the Sartrean delegitimation is what I shall call the narrative of the empty square (*case vide*) which suggests *en abyme* the basic paradox of the whole autobiography. It first occurs on the occasion of the Institute party:

> my grandfather, from the height of his glory, made a pronouncement which pierced me to the heart: 'Someone's lacking here: it's Simonnot.' I . . . took refuge in a corner, and the guests disappeared; in the centre of a tumultuous circle I saw a pillar: Monsieur Simonnot himself, absent in flesh and blood. This astonishing absence transfigured him . . . . Only Monsieur Simonnot was *lacking*.

(W: 58)[29]

The original play on the word *manquer*, which is at once to be lacking and to be necessary, leads into the next narrative built on the *case vide*, one of the child Jean-Paul's fictions. In this adventure, at one point 'a groan would run through the desert and the rocks would say to the sand: "Someone's lacking here:

it's Sartre"' (W: 72).[30] It is in the multiple resonance of this exclamation that we see the basic thematics of the empty core, the decentredness to which one is sentenced by the way of the mother. 'Sartre' is what is lacking throughout the book, not only the father, 'absent in flesh and blood', but the son, absent as subject, as fixed identity, a child who has become instead a feminised and shifting play of roles. At the same time, also implicit in the way of the mother is that 'Sartre' is needed. The bastard needs to be needed, it is one of the rules of exclusion. In the third story of the *case vide* 'There's someone lacking: it's Dickens', and here the figure of the celebrated author is created by the enthusiasm of the crowd waiting for him on a wharf which is 'depopulated simply by the absence of the man it was expecting' ('dépeuplée par la seule absence de l'homme qu'elle attend' (140)) (W: 106). In other words, it is once again the addressees who in the last resort create the signature. 'Dickens' can only be lacking if his audience needs him.

The signature by others

It will be noticed that these ambiguous narratives of lack nevertheless also suggest an unfulfilled desire to be the absent phallus, the 'column', the hero, the male genius. The dominant super-ego constantly reproaches him for that feminisation, 'that holy prostitution of the soul' ('cette sainte prostitution de l'âme') (OC I: 291), as Baudelaire puts it, which Sartre condemns in his *alter ego*. He struggles against 'viscosity', that female fluidity which is the very condition of creation. His recurring nightmare of the crab, the octopus, the creature emerging from the sea is extremely revealing in this regard (need I say that neither Baudelaire nor Sartre escapes from the *trace* of the mother in the sea, the inescapable unity and duality of *la mer–mère?*). Like Baudelaire's Samuel Cramer, Sartre approves only of textual procreation. He too, considers 'reproduction as a vice of love, pregnancy as the sickness of a spider'.[31] Perhaps he also remains the 'hermaphrodite' of the narrative his mother originally constructed for him, the girl hidden in the boy. For our narrative fictions, no matter how artfully constructed, are finally beyond our control. Every name has its hidden story, and every story in its turn depends on its reception. It is a point on which Derrida and Sartre are oddly at one. According to the former:

the signature will be effective, performed, performing, not at the moment when it apparently occurs, but only later, when ears will have been able to receive the message.[32]

In the same way, for Sartre the book, like the essence, exists only when it is seen, when it is read:

> Other consciousnesses have taken charge of me. They read *me* and I leap to their eyes; they talk about *me* and I am on everyone's lips a universal and singular language . . . . I exist nowhere but I *am*, at last! I am everywhere.
>
> (W: 122)[33]

There is a wonderful Sartrean allegory of how essence depends on others in *Les Mots*:

> In the drawing-rooms of Arras, a cold and affected young lawyer is carrying his head under his arm because he is the late Robespierre; the head is dripping blood, though it does not stain the carpet; not one of the guests notices it, yet we see nothing else; some five years go by before it rolled into the basket, and yet there it is, chopped off, making gallant speeches, in spite of its sagging jaw.
>
> (W: 126)[34]

So the very name Robespierre carries its history inscribed in it. We might venture the thought that, for Derrida, it is the text that conveniently carries its head, its signature, underneath its arm as it waits for execution by the reader. Just as the name Robespierre stands at the border between life and death, waiting for the one to define the other, so Jean-Paul Sartre, as he would be the first to agree, waits between life and work, between *corps* and *corpus*, waiting to be signed by the reader.

These examples show that delegitimation is not necessarily linked to illegitimacy as such, or to the mere assumption of a matronym. It is an entry into the way of the mother, which gives rise to narratives, sometimes conscious, sometimes unconscious, which are inscribed not just in one text but in a whole *oeuvre*, and particularly marked in the crucial paratextual inscription of the signature. The signature acts as the coded point of entry into the narrative, but neither name nor story is complete until it has been cosigned by the addressee. The choice of the name of the mother is the choice of alterity, of a decentred experience of multiplicity and exclusion, which complements the regime of the law of the Father and thereby facilitates creation. In a world where the 'natural' child is deemed unnatural, and the bearing of a matronym is perceived as gendered and abnormal, an exception to the father's rule, delegitimation, even that of the *faux bâtard*, marks both a political and an artistic choice. It implies a refusal of preconception and preconceptions, and an endeavour to reconceive oneself. Yet there is no escape from the power of the name or that of the word. Changing the signature changes the rules, but provides no guarantee of escape, only a move sideways so that the game can begin again. Whatever name we choose, our stories tell *us* in the end.

9

'Better to reign in Hell . . .'

When we move into the twentieth century (not merely that pseudo-nineteenth century in which Sartre proclaims his delegitimation), and examine two of the most outspoken and aggressive narrations of illegitimacy, the move is actually as far back in mythologising as it is forward into narrative modernity. The work of Jean Genet, poet, playwright and novelist (1910–86) and Violette Leduc, innovator in prose narrative (1907–72) reverts to the ancient traditions of bastardy as excess, a badge of shame and evil, a latter-day mark of Cain, which at the same time distinguishes the bastard from the herd and confers a sort of perverse and even grandiose power. Emphasising excess by the traditional metonymy of the body, Genet and Leduc also see their exclusion reinforced by physical ugliness, the outer mark of a social branding. They create themselves, and it is impossible to distinguish fact and fiction in their writing. Their self-mythologisations are similar, and yet different, as are their family histories. They were fraternal enemies. Each admired the other's work as much as they eventually came to loathe each other personally. Both owed their breakthrough partly to Cocteau, but most particularly to Sartre in Genet's case and Simone de Beauvoir in Leduc's.[1]

Whereas Leduc conforms to the now familiar pattern of the offspring of a seduced female servant, brought up by her mother and grandmother, and able to construct a female genealogy for herself, Genet is the only example among my case histories of a real foundling, left by his mother with an institution from the day of his birth.[2] It is, in fact, extremely rare for such children, institutionalised and then fostered out to peasants almost as slave labour, to make the breakthrough into the power of the symbolic order. It makes Genet's case as interesting to the sociologist as to the literary critic.

The study in this chapter of the writing of illegitimacy as a discourse of revenge and as a vindication of exclusion is a necessary complement to the more positive view from those secure in class and status, such as the symbolic delegitimators we looked at in Chapter 8. I am limiting myself to autobiographical and para-autobiographical works, with special attention to Leduc's *La Bâtarde* and Genet's *Journal du voleur*. It is instructive to compare these titles and their intentional provocation with the ones we saw in earlier centuries, like *The Natural Son* or *Peregrinations of a Pariah*, which call for a positive reading or, at the very least, for compassion. Why, for instance, is the title *La Bâtarde* left in French in the English translation? Is it somehow to reduce the offence, or simply because the feminine form is untranslatable? I am not sure that it is just because of the increased pejorative associations in English.

The negative mythology

What we see in both autobiographies is the social imposition from an early age of the negative mythology of bastardy. The roots of this negative branding of hybridity, but also those of the positive complementarity of its divinisation, lie deep in the human psyche. The most ancient Judaeo-Christian myth of illegitimacy confirms the doubleness of the bastard, both outcast and progenitor of a new race. Remember the story of Ishmael and God's words to his mother, Hagar:

> Behold thou art with child, and shalt bear a son, and shalt call his name Ishmael; because the Lord hath heard thy affliction. And he will be a wild man; his hand will be against every man, and every man's hand against him; and he shall dwell in the presence of [opposed to] all his brethren.
>
> (Genesis XVI: 11–13)

And yet the Lord also promised his father Abraham:

> And as for Ishmael, I have heard thee: Behold, I have blessed him, and will make him fruitful, and will multiply

165

him exceedingly; twelve princes shall he beget, and I will make him a great nation.

(Genesis XVII: 20)

The fruitfulness which distinguishes and blesses our latter-day Ishmaels is rather the flowering of the symbolic. It is the power of the word, the fascination of metaphor and the seduction of narrative that confer royalty upon them, a royalty which Genet, at least, actively asserts.

The initial stigma of otherness is socially imprinted by neighbours, by playground bullying, in Genet's case by institutionalisation, and in Leduc's case by her mother's constant assertions of shame and guilt over the 'burden' of the unwanted child.[3] Both she and Genet tendentiously assert the popular linking of illegitimacy and inclinations to crime and 'perversion': 'A bastard must lie, a bastard is the fruit of evasion and lies, a bastard is an infringement of all the rules' (BA: 56).[4] Both fulfil social expectations that the 'natural' child is sinister, a liar, a thief and sexually deviant. As Genet says:

> Abandoned by my family, I already felt it was natural to aggravate this condition by a preference for boys, and this preference by theft, and theft by crime or a complacent attitude in regard to crime. I thus resolutely rejected a world which had rejected me.
>
> (TJ: 77)[5]

Yet to be refused by the world confers a strange power, that aura of evil which is envied and feared. Leduc's cry of anguish is at the same time an affirmation of difference:

> Bastards have a curse on them: a friend told me so. Bastards have a curse on them . . . . Why don't bastards help each other? Why do they avoid each other? Why do they detest each other? Why don't they form a brotherhood? They should be able to forgive each other everything since they all hold the most precious, the most fragile, the strongest, the darkest part of themselves in common: a childhood twisted like an old apple tree.
>
> (BA: 52)[6]

The internalisation of negative social attitudes is seen as producing a positive poetry, a different angle of vision, and yet that very poetry of difference reinforces the social attitudes. Each time the myths of bastardy are reworked and recomposed, they are given new power. This could be seen either as a vicious circle or as an inbuilt and necessary corrective to social and narrative conformity.

GIVING BIRTH TO MY GRANDMOTHER: LEDUC

Violette Leduc says that her work is autobiographical even when it masquerades as fiction, but this may be a statement to rank with the famous liar paradox. Though *La Bâtarde* (1964) purports to be the 'factual' account of her childhood and youth, it is even more mythologised than many such accounts. According to Violette's own account, her peasant grandmother, Fidéline Leduc, herself illegitimate, (A: 115, or is this more wishful thinking?) and left a widow at 20, had been forced to abandon her own children to fostering and then an orphanage. Her daughter, Berthe Leduc, sent out to service, soon found herself pregnant to the son of the house. She chose to protect him by silence and bore her child in circumstances of extreme destitution. Intelligent, resourceful and bitter, she raised her daughter with steely resolution. Determined to escape the trap of social exclusion, she insisted that her daughter should be the best-dressed and best-educated in her peer group at any price. In her single-minded attempt to counter stigma, she unconsciously reproduced in her child's life the emotional deprivation she herself had suffered. She instilled in her a distrust of men and a terror of intercourse and its results. Violette[7] found human warmth and love only in the arms of the simple, peasant grandmother who lived with them. The child only perceived the overwhelming, and stifling, devotion of her childlike confidante, not the guilt for the unavoidable betrayal of her own children. Not altogether strangely, the pattern repeated itself, and Berthe, the cool, distant mother, turned into a grandmother dangerously devoted to her son's daughter, Christine (CA: 304–26).

Using this story, Violette constructs a female genealogy for herself which functions by inversion: she sees herself not as the *product* of a long line of women, but as their *producer*. 'Qui est-ce Violette Leduc? L'arrière-grand-mère de son arrière-grand-mère après tout' ('Who is this Violette Leduc? The great-grandmother of her great-grandmother when all is said and done') (B: 26, BA: 20). She inverts her own birth to fit the pattern:

> I believe, I shall always believe that all servants despise
> me totally. They are blaming me for having brought my
> mother into the world, for having made her a housemaid.
>
> (MP: 96)[8]

When Leduc, at 35, finally writes the first line of her first book, *L'Asphyxie* (Asphyxia), 'Ma mère ne m'a jamais donné la main' ('My mother never held my hand') (A: 7),[9] she is not only exacting revenge, but taking control of her past life. She feels she is at last about to give birth . . . to her grandmother:

> The birds suddenly stopped singing and then I sucked my
> pen: the pleasure of foreseeing that my grandmother was
> about to be reborn, that I was going to bring her into the
> world, the pleasure of foreseeing that I was going to be the
> creator of my grandmother whom I adored, of my grand-
> mother who adored me. To write . . .
>
> (BA: 404)[10]

The angel maker

And yet this birth into the word only occurs at the very end of *La Bâtarde* and is introduced and made possible by a series of deaths, real death-beds like that of Fidéline, and ritual 'murders' as Violette destroys those she loves by her self-centred passions. Her mother, as I said, had imbued her from an early age with a hysterical fear of pregnancy, encouraging her long lesbian liaison because it provided security from pregnancy (R: 57). So it is no surprise that the most significant killing, and one that nearly ends her own life, is her decision to abort a foetus at five months, in a refusal of any 'female', and more especially maternal, role. To enforce this decision she must have recourse to the back-yard abortionists known as 'angel makers', *faiseuses d'anges*. It is, I think, significant that her way of writing illegitimacy is to become in her turn an 'angel maker'.

When she reinvokes those she sees herself as having loved and killed, 'by thought or deed or word', they appear as angels, sexless or hermaphroditic. The first is the 'angel Fidéline' (B: 28, BA: 22), the grandmother so often referred to as angel that she acquires a curious ambivalence of gender, since *ange* is masculine in French and *grand-mère,* of course, feminine. Fidéline is seen as the embodiment of love, saintly in her simplicity and sexless in her old age. Hermine, the first lover/ partner, and her predecessor Isabelle, the initiator of the schoolgirl to sexual pleasure, are masculinised, not so much by their lesbianism, as by the fact that they assume the 'masculine' role in the relationship.

Gabriel, the 'archangel' (B: 168, BA: 124), Violette's lover and later husband, initiates a relationship just as sexually ambiguous, at first expressed in buggery with the woman he calls 'petit bonhomme'. He always remains the 'feminine' partner in the relationship. Both the name Gabriel and the appellation of archangel were taken by Leduc from Genet's *Notre-Dame-des-Fleurs* (Our Lady of the Flowers) (146), where the relationship of the drag-queen Divine and her/his soldier lover partake of the same ambiguity. Indeed, all these names are fictitious ones, chosen by Leduc for the early actors in her life. Even the name Violette, it has recently been suggested, she may have chosen to use in preference to her given name Thérèse.

Maurice Sachs, artist, writer and con-man, the mentor who dominates the last part of *La Bâtarde,* is the first in a series of homosexuals for whom she conceives ill-fated and abortive passions.[11] He acts as 'father' to Violette's texts and achieves his ascendancy by the very sexlessness of their relationship.[12] Both 'father' and 'daughter' are sterile and hermaphroditic like the angels, a fact sadly stressed by his final desperate plea that she should pretend to be pregnant by him so that he could get compassionate leave from a labour camp. She gets the certificate of pregnancy but, in rage and despair, finally burns it (B: 594, BA: 438). By this act she murders his love for her and, however improbably, also sees herself as his murderess. In burning the certificate, which mirrors her own birth certificate, the 'writing' which begins her life and her autography, she ends the story as an 'angel maker', even if the child she destroys this time is only a fiction. Finally, by writing her autobiography, she achieves her ambiguous aim of reproducing without reproduction, of creating a past while aborting a future, and of controlling at the level of the signifier the life which defeated her demands.

The law of the Father or that of the mother?

The female genealogy which inscribes the past is also written into the very structure and discourse of the book. Working on a variety of temporal levels, and also a variety of emotional levels, the narrative oscillates between a series of journal entries, set in the warm present of a Provençal landscape and making immediate and intimate appeals to the narratee (Violette's *lecteur* and addressee), and a devastating account of the past which sets out to outrage that same narratee. The account of the past also varies between sparse, controlled, hard-edged statements of fact and sudden outpourings of metaphor piled on metaphor and of stream-of-consciousness techniques.

Martha Evans (1985), in one of the few serious attempts to theorise Leduc's work, makes a suggestive division between her writing of the past and that of the present. She sees the writing of the past as marked by and belonging to the harsh law of the Father and Leduc's difficult birth into the symbolic, which is metonymically present in the first page of the book and of her life:

> And yet my birth certificate fascinates me. Or else revolts me. Or bores me. I read it through from beginning to end whenever I feel the need; I find myself once more in the long gallery as it echoes with the clicking scissors of the doctor attending my birth. I listen, I shiver. We are no longer the communicating vessels we were when she was carrying me. Here I am, born, on a register in the town hall, at the point of a town-hall clerk's pen. No nastiness, no placenta: writing, a registration.
>
> (BA: 19–20)[13]

The writing of the present, on the other hand, Evans sees as belonging to what I have called the way of the mother. To me this is the way of female multiplicity and transformation, but also of maternal sexuality and independence. Evans has a more traditional view and regards it as limited to the world of love and natural emotion, of the 'communicating vessels'. While this reading has a lot to recommend it, I see it, as I also see Schoenfeld (1982) in his psychoanalytic reading, as making too many Oedipal (and Lacanian) assumptions. Nor does it take into account the structural importance of the female genealogy.

Leduc's childhood experience is based not on a paternal

170

presence, but on a paternal absence. It is precisely this absence she re-enacts by the choice of the men on whom she lavishes her adoration. She creates situations in which she is kept at arm's length by one man after another. These 'father figures' are all as gentle and indulgent as they are gay (except Genet, fellow-bastard and peasant, who responds to her embarrassing adulation by tipping a tableful of food and wine into her lap (MP: 149–59)).

The main problem with Evans's traditional identification of the move into the symbolic with the law of the Father is that in the pattern of double mothering (on the St Anne model), which lasts until her grandmother's death when Violette is 9 years old, the harsh law is that of the *mother*. The mother embodies the super-ego, and the grandmother the domain of physical pleasure and reassurance. The father, seldom seen, is a weak and indecisive shadow, bound by class prejudice, a victim of consumption in both senses of the word (his clothes had to be bought in London, yet he could not support his own child; nor could he embrace that child because he was dying of tuberculosis).

The mother's assertion of strength is not based on her playing the male part in the usual Oedipal model. Indeed, until her mother's remarriage when Violette is 14, Violette sees herself as the 'husband' of this intensely feminine woman (BA: 40). Berthe Leduc's quite extraordinary attributes emerge in spite, or because, of Violette's negative, or, rather, ambivalent, presentation. Berthe's sense of style, as with many women of her generation, was a way of appreciating art. It also gave her an edge as saleswoman and business woman which compensated for her poor education. Her daughter learned and loved the lessons of style (a not unimportant factor in her acceptance by the Paris intelligentsia) and, at the same time, saw herself as a martyr to her mother's insistence that they both be well dressed, even when they were living on stolen potatoes.

Feast and famine

Leduc's first 'prose poem' to her mother (B: 26–7, BA: 20–1), with its ambiguities, its anguished tribute and its outpouring of love and hate, also exemplifies what I call the maternal discourse. Berthe complained of the 'heaviness' of Violette's first efforts, and the result is a pared-down, clipped, harsh discourse of great discipline and power. It is the dominant language of *L'Asphyxie*, the book which made her reputation, and that of this early poetic paragraph from *La Bâtarde*. In my view, it is the deeply imprinted dictate of the maternal super-ego that saves Leduc from the excesses to which she is naturally prone and which fuel the other discourses which I call paternal and grandmaternal.

> You become my child, mother, when, as an old woman, you remember things with your clock-like precision. You talk, I take you in. You speak, I carry you in my head. Yes, for you my belly is hot as a volcano. You speak, and I am silent. I was born the bearer of your misfortune as one is born a libation-bearer. To live, you know you must live in the past. Sometimes I'm so tired of it I could fall ill.
>
> (BA: 20)[14]

Yet the dictate also produces a kind of artistic anorexia, a minimalism, a fear of consumption and enjoyment, which parallels the bodily anorexia of Violette, the unhappy child. 'J'aurais vécu dans l'obsession des nourritures' ('I shall have lived my life obsessed by the thought of food') (B: 301, BA: 223). This anorexia is linked with the fear of pregnancy. Force-feeding, like intercourse, is seen as a form of penetration:

> Anaemic and on the verge of rickets when she left the nun's sewing room, a young girl – my mother – found her insides swollen with a phenomenal amount of food: a child. For every million sperms in one jet of semen she countered with a million calories for the daughter they produced.
>
> (BA: 223)[15]

Leduc's 'short sentences', which she frequently laments, are a means of limiting superfluity. Like anorexia itself, they are at once an indulgence and a penance.

They alternate with a wild excess of language, a bulimia of epithets, of metaphors, of free association which invariably ends in nausea and rejection. Even in the invocation to Berthe, we find traces of this other discourse, but see it immediately chastised by the maternal free indirect discourse (I will quote in French here, because the translation loses the very excess I wish to stress):

172

Mon élégante, mon infroissable, ma courageuse, ma vain-
cue, ma radoteuse, ma gomme à m'effacer; ma jalouse, ma
juste, mon injuste, ma commandante, ma timorée. Qu'est-
ce que vont dire les gens? Qu'est-ce que vont penser les
gens? Qu'est-ce diraient les gens?

(B: 27)

[My elegant, uncrushable, courageous, vanquished, ram-
bling mother, you are my eraser to rub myself out with;
my jealous mother, you are my justice, my injustice, my
commander, my shy mother. What are people going to
say? What are people going to think? What would they
say?]

(BA: 20)

The bulimic discourse, in which excess always leads to, and
indeed courts, nausea and retribution, is, to my mind, Leduc's
paternal discourse, an echo of that first seduction, the consumption that made the heart sick. The *mise-en-abyme* of this
bulimia, in the life and in the discourse, is the shoplifting
episode (B: 243–6, BA: 179–81) in which Violette keeps stuffing
into her bag feminine luxuries, described in a feverish cumul-
ation of nouns and adjectives, until she is, must be, arrested.
There follows public degradation and the self-humiliation from
which she emerges drained. The whole is echoed in the debasing
and obsessive involvement in the black market (B: 557–634, BA:
441–63), carried on beyond decency and reason until the inevitable arrest, and the retribution avoided only by sinking even
lower and betraying her sources. Again, the bulimic obsession,
shown in the money bag she wears as paunch (or pregnancy, and
she equates the two (B: 302, BA: 223)), is depicted in language
guaranteed to nauseate the narratee and to ensure that Violette
herself is rejected/vomited. There must be a triple retribution,
one in life, one in the text, and the last in the reception.

However the reader, that 'dear reader', is not allowed the
luxury of pure opprobrium. The text begins and ends with, and
constantly recurs to, that lyrical discourse in the present, which
I see as grandmaternal, since it is generally a discourse of simple
acceptance, of nature and of a yearning for love. The child
Violette's need for Fidéline to drive out fear, hunger and
indifference is echoed in her appeal for sympathy to the narratee,
in the first sentences:

My case is not unique: I am afraid of dying and distressed at being in this world. I haven't worked, I haven't studied. I have wept, I have cried out in protest.

(BA: 19)[16]

And the last:

22 August, 1963. This August day, reader, is a rose window glowing with heat. I make you a gift of it, it is yours. One o'clock. I am going back to the village for lunch. Strong with the silence of the pines and the chestnut trees. I walk without flinching through the burning cathedral of the summer. My bank of wild grass is majestic and full of music. It is a fire that solitude presses against my lips.

(BA: 469)[17]

At the end of the last volume of her autobiographical trilogy, *La Chasse à l'amour* (The Hunt for Love), she returns to the same need for bodily contact with which she began. She begs her reader for the hand that her mother denied her: 'Lecteur. Partageons. Comment? Avec ta main. Ta main sur mes genoux' ('Reader. Let's share. How? With your hand. Your hand on my knees') (CH: 355). The grandmaternal presence and discourse are, mercifully, the ones that save narrator and narrative and unite narrator and narratee in the end.

The three discourses infiltrate one another. The strict, fragmented, maternal discourse dominates, but it can always be subverted by a sudden proliferation. The result is a bastard language which at first seems ruled by the strict law of the mother rather than the lax law of the father, a poor, cursed, abbreviated language, rejoicing in the very sterility of its own reproduction. Yet this same language is constantly breaking boundaries, stuffing itself to bursting, heaving with the pains of its enunciative labour, ignoring the demands of reason, moderation and good taste. It seduces the reader into similar patterns, often forcing the reading to abort or to be regurgitated, but at others encouraging a difficult labour, as the reader attempts to resolve the ambiguities imposed by the clash of the maternal, paternal and grandmaternal discourses, abbreviated yet racing out of control, loveless and obsessive one minute, warm and lyrical the next.

174

GENET: THE FLOWERING OF THE NAME

An obsession which Leduc shares with Genet is that of the symbolic value of the name. Both choose to bear their mother's name; both are acutely aware of the symbolic value not only of given name and surname, but of the individual phonemes they contain and of the semantic trace of multiple associations within them. Names are a sort of predestination: 'We bear the names we deserve. Mine is a blow from a stick. Simone de Beauvoir's is a carriage and pair' (MP: 26). If Leduc is a harsh, peasant, masculine name, it is at one with the 'masculine' appearance and the great beak of a nose, source of both strength and despair, which identify the child with her father and hence with the bourgeois world that rejects her and that she rejects. Violette, the name she prefers, seems an ironic choice for the fruit of seduction. Violette is a name with strong sexual associations for every French child, thanks to a well-known folk song in which picking the violet stands for intercourse.[18] Leduc constantly presents herself as either violator or violated, in either literal or metaphorical terms. At the time of writing *La Bâtarde*, her given name, Violette, actually acquired the force of a surname for her, as she was given the sobriquet of La Violette in the Provençal village where she eventually made her home, having, as so often, forced her presence on her unwilling hosts in a kind of rape, fraught on both sides with pain and fear (CA: 372).

Genet, the foundling, had no contact whatsoever with the mother whose name he bore; indeed we do not even know if his given name, Jean, was bestowed by her:[19]

I was born in Paris on 19 December 1910. As a ward of the *Assistance Publique*, it was impossible for me to know anything about my background. When I was 21 years old, I obtained my birth certificate. My mother's name was Gabrielle Genet.[20] My father remains unknown. I came into the world at 22 rue d'Assas.

'I'll find out something about my origin', I said to myself, and went to the rue d'Assas. Number 22 was occupied by the Maternity Hospital. They refused to give me any information. I was brought up in Le Morvan by peasants. Whenever I come across *genêt* [broom] blossoms on the heaths – especially at twilight on my way back from a visit to the ruins of Tiffauges where Gilles de Rais lived – I feel a deep sense of kinship with them. I regard them solemnly, with tenderness. My emotion seems ordained by all nature. I am alone in the world, and I am not sure that I am not the king – perhaps the sprite – of these flowers. They render homage as I pass, bow without bowing, but recognize me. They know that I am their living, moving, agile representative, conqueror of the wind. They are my natural emblem, but through them I have roots in that French soil which is fed by the powdered bones of the children and youths buggered, massacred and burned by Gilles de Rais.

(TJ: 38–9)[21]

As with Violette, the roots of the name Genet itself substitute for other roots, and an even more involved symbolism than hers links rape and murder with the apparently innocuous yellow blossoms springing from the soil of France.[22] Genet, like those nameless children of the French Revolution, sees himself as a 'natural son of the motherland', a vision which, coming from a bastard, bugger and thief, effectively disturbs, as it is meant to, the complacent mytholog, of blood and soil which flourished in France before the Second World War.

My mother, the reformatory

Genet was brought up first in an orphanage, then by a country foster-family, and finally in a reformatory. His relationship with the matronym is complicated by the fact that it represents pure absence, an empty square to be filled by the imagination. In his case, more than any other, the name is at once imposed by the birth certificate and yet is the arena of choice. It and she, Gabrielle Genet, can be anything that the writer desires, fears or fabricates. Yet this seeming freedom is in fact limited by two negative mythologies, that of the bastard, which I discussed earlier, and the terrifying misogyny of the criminal underworld. This is even more pronounced in reformatory and prison, where Genet says he spent a great part of his early life. In such confinement, a completely womanless culture breeds those curious myths of femininity exemplified by the language and rituals of the *tantes* or queens, on which Genet embroiders with such verve.

Genet sees himself as the product of three mothers: his natural mother who abandoned him, his peasant foster-mother who christened him a thief, and the Mettray reformatory, which enforced a harsh despotism from both warders and inmates, but also provided 'la première consolation, la première paix, la première confusion amicale: c'était dans l'immonde' (JV: 91). TJ translates this: 'Prison offered me the first consolation, the first peace, the first friendly fellowship: I experienced them in the realm of foulness' (76). This fails to convey the untranslatable play on *immonde* as the mirror-image of society or *le monde*. *L'immonde* is not just the foul or the low but the underworld, the world of otherness, a world which requires just as rigorous a discipline in evil, in being 'the coward, traitor, thief and fairy they saw in me' (TJ: 156) as the apparently moral *monde*, the society which shapes us by its conventions and requires a discipline of rectitude. The *immonde*, then, is the inverted, perverted anti-world, a *maternal* world (TJ: 63). All prisons belong to the same paradigm:

> I aspire to Guiana [the penal colony] . . . . The place seems to be most cruelly dry and arid, and yet here am I expressing it by a theme of kindness: it suggests and imposes the image of a maternal breast, charged, in like manner, with a reassuring power, from which rises a slightly nauseating odour, offering me a shameful peace. I call the Virgin Mother and Guiana the Comforters of the Afflicted.
>
> (TJ: 227)[23]

Yet, the core of absence at the heart of this enclosed world is the female itself, the absent mother.

Maternity in drag

This absence requires a supplement. Just as he puts on the empty name, Genet, as one puts on a mask, so Genet puts on 'femininity'. As he sees it, his mother was fucked, probably raped. Exploited, abandoned and betrayed, she abandoned and betrayed her unwanted child. That child obsessively re-enacts what to him is the maternal model. He courts rape and fucking, and the more it fucks him up the better. Yet, in the end, the only femaleness he can achieve is the parodied femininity of the drag queens, and more particularly the male whores.

As he shows in the extended dream of *Notre-Dame-des-Fleurs* (1948), such a femininity is the obverse and the product of the deeply misogynist and macho culture of the *macs* or pimps. This 'femininity' has nothing to do with the female, except as parody, but it does facilitate multiplicity. In *Notre-Dame-des-Fleurs* there is played out a phantasm in which he, as Jean Genet, is at once the male whore/queen Divine, his/her pimp Mignon, and the teenage murderer Notre-Dame, who is fucked by both. He is also Divine's mother, Ernestine, the first of the *pietà* images of a mother worshipping her dead son, which were to haunt him till his death (see CA). The only female mother image in the whole text of *Journal du voleur* is an old beggar-woman just out of prison:

> I know nothing of her who abandoned me in the cradle, but I hoped it was that old thief who begged in the night .... I would weep with tenderness over those moon-fish eyes, over that round and foolish face! 'And why', I went on, 'why weep over it?' It did not take my mind long to replace the customary marks of tenderness by some other gesture, even the vilest and most contemptible, which I empowered to mean as much as the kisses, or the tears or the flowers.
>
> 'I'd be glad to slobber . . . over her hair or vomit into her hands. But I would adore that thief who is my mother.
>
> (TJ: 17)[24]

The female in this case is safely desexualised and at the same time, by the multiple inversions, made part of the maternal *immonde*. On the other hand the maximal sexualisation is accorded to the 'maternal element', explicitly termed 'not feminine', to be found in some old male criminals:

> The tenderness that makes them unbend is not femininity, but the discovery of ambiguity. I think they are prepared to impregnate themselves, to lay and hatch their eggs, but without any blunting of their cruel male sting.
>
> (TJ: 226)[25]

Just as male fantasy creates the drag queen, so a fantasy even deeper and more repressed betrays the male envy of the female capacity to give birth. Here we see how the deletion of the female is extended into a fairly simple manifestation of the

ancient male myth of the pregnant man, associated from the first
with divinity in the myth of the birth of Athena from the head of
Zeus, whose sting was certainly not blunted by this unusual
parthenogenesis.[26] The myth is as ancient and as universal[27] as
man himself and finds an early literary expression in the
Oresteia:

> The mother is not the true parent of the child
> Which is called hers. She is the nurse who tends the growth
> Of young seed planted by its true parent, the male.
> So, if Fate spares the child, she keeps it, as one might
> Keep for some friend a growing plant. And of this truth,
> That father without mother may beget, we have
> Present, as proof, the daughter of Olympian Zeus:
> One never nursed in the dark cradle of the womb.
>   (*Eumenides* 656–64; Aeschylus, 1965: 169–70)

In fact, Derrida in *Glas*, which will be extensively discussed in
Chapter 10, sees the whole replay of the absent mother in these
terms, as the writer endeavouring to replace his mother and give
solipsistic birth to himself in an unending vicious circle.

Dismembering the mother

But the image of the mother is not only parodied but actively
dismembered. Dismemberment is a necessary prelude to fetish-
ising. The fetishisation of flowers, present throughout Genet's
work, can be traced back to that initial dismemberment of the
name of the mother that yielded the broom flower and a string
of other metonymies in its wake:

> Thus, through her whose name I bear, the vegetable
> kingdom is my familiar. I can regard all flowers without
> pity, they are members of my family. If, through them, I
> rejoin the nether realms – though it is to the tree ferns and
> their marshes, to the algae, that I should like to descend –
> I withdraw further from men.
>   (TJ: 39)[28]

A name is a Hydra's head: cut it off, fetishise it and nine more
grow to replace it. Precisely because Genet's use of the name of
the mother has no roots and no stability, it lends itself to the
creation of multiple selves.

179

The proliferation of self, exploited to the full in the para-autobiographical *Notre-Dame-des-Fleurs*, is echoed in a proliferation of discourses, a heteroglossia which stresses not only the polysemy of the text but the narrator's capacity for self-creation. The difference, I suppose, from Louise Michel's first tentative use of heteroglossia to give a voice to the dispossessed is that in the work of Genet, and to a lesser extent Leduc, the voices, codes and *argot* of the dispossessed, the peasants, the poor, the homosexuals, the insane, the criminals, are also the voices of the narrator. The proliferation of self permits all these avatars and their distinctive registers of discourse.

It also permits, indeed necessitates, the inclusion of the voice of their other: the literate language of the bourgeoisie. Whereas, in most literature – in Dostoevsky, for example, whose polyvocalism Bakhtin (1973) made the model for the many present studies of the phenomenon – the master tongue is infiltrated by the voices of otherness, in Genet and Leduc the master tongue is not a habit, but a supplement. It infiltrates, estranges but does not dominate the registers of upbringing and experience. Leduc uses quotation from Rimbaud, from Verlaine, from Gide, from Sartre, and from the once idolised Genet himself, to mark difference more than familiarity, just as the luxurious sale items or impulse buys from Fath or Schiaparelli merely enhance Violette's difference from the *tout Paris*. In the same way, the cadences Genet learned in his cell, from the Bible, from the Mass, from Proust, from myth and legend, are, as he puts it, the marks of Jupiter screwing Ganymede (TJ: 156), though whether he is screwing the cultural tradition or it is screwing him remains unclear. As he reigns in the inverted world, so he achieves in the realm of the word an inverted aristocracy:

> If I use [a] rhetorical device in order to give you a clearer notion of the degree to which I had achieved a solitude that conferred sovereignty upon me, I do so because it is forced upon me by a situation, by a success which is expressed in words intended to express the triumph of the century. A verbal kinship denotes the kinship of my glory with nobiliary glory.
>
> (TJ: 155)[29]

Phantasms of birth

The power of words is, in fact, to be used to facilitate a relegitimation, but one on Genet's own terms. It all starts with the bastard's version of the family romance:

> Without thinking myself magnificently born, the uncertainty of my origin allowed me to interpret it. I added to it the peculiarity of my misfortunes . . . my childhood imagination invented for me . . . castles, parks peopled with guards rather than with statues.
>
> (TJ: 77–8)[30]

There follows an extraordinary passage, an extended metaphor of the prison as castle, which is at the same time a transfer of the family romance into the inverted world, the *immonde*. It is this transfer that is to permit an eventual relegitimation and the constitution of the signature:

> But it is the abandoned urchin's amorous imagining of royal magnificence that enables me to gild my shame, to carve it, to work it like a goldsmith, until, through usage and the wearing-away of the words veiling it, humility emerges from it.
>
> (TJ: 79–80)[31]

Leduc has the same conviction of the power of literature to relegitimate. Her very first publication, inadequate though it is, suddenly transforms her relation to the world and, with it, the value of her name as signifier:

> My name, my first name and my last name, were all I needed, they filled every page. My eyes were sipping absinthe. I counted and recounted the number of letters making up my two names: there I was, round-shouldered Violette Leduc, standing up straight eight times, standing up straight five times, standing up straight thirteen times. I had stars for toes. I pressed my cheek against the paper of the magazine to see if my names were electric. They were.
>
> (BA: 322)[32]

The transformation of the name to a signature is a rebirth, but a legitimate birth, whose certificate is the text and its authorial imprint. But Violette endangers this very legitimation by also succumbing to a more conventional form of social recuperation, that by marriage to Gabriel. 'I had been in exile, but now I had come home again. My fourth finger feels uneasy, the poor thing needs a ring around it. You shall have your wedding ring, I promise you' (BA: 293).[33] Fortunately for her 'reputation' neither the euphoria nor the marriage lasts. Gabriel's magic fades in the bonds of domesticity, and she never uses her prosaic married name, Mercier.

Hermetic myths

Leduc sees the role of the writer as enabling an entry into the world of the dead: dead loves, dead desires, but living torments. Both Leduc and Genet feel a need for Mercury/Hermes, the bastard god of thieves but also of poetry and communication, the one who has entry to the underworld.[34] In *La Bâtarde*, Leduc highlights the role of the psychopomp or conductor of ghosts, and, inventing the names of her loves, plays with allusions to gods and angels. She gives her husband the name Gabriel when she first sees him as the 'archangel', one of the mythical guides of her youth. The other main angelic guides are her grandmother, Fidéline, and her lover, Hermine.

Hermine, named after the god Hermes himself, is a female psychopomp who can lead Violette back to the world of the dead, the world of the village and of her grandmother. But she also gives her the key to a more important Olympus, the world of *haute couture*, where the gods are Schiaparelli, Fath and Hermès. The extravagance of the metaphoric and rhythmic discourse records Hermine's sacrificial gift to Violette of artistic and vestimentary perfection in the form of a complete outfit from the best couturiers. This language marks the ritual nature of the robing ceremony which is the highlight of their relationship (B: 272–7, BA: 200–4). Similarly, at the end of the relationship, Hermine's gift of Hermès sandals is a metaphor for a first consecration of Violette as a writer (B: 321, BA: 237).[35]

Leduc's private myth of herself as a wanderer in an underworld where she suffers the torments of the damned has another, 'noble' dimension: she is also the Dante who will hymn the inferno through which her 'angels' conduct her. Simone de Beauvoir, enacting, as a complement to Leduc's relegitimation, her own delegitimation from the bourgeoisie she scorns, would play, of course, the part of Virgil in this exercise in myth-making. The whole of *L'Affamée* (The Starved Woman) (1948) is a prose poem recording this divinisation of de Beauvoir, and her role as guide into the Hell of unrequited love and the Heaven of writing.

The divine child

Genet has no such humility. Although he needed Sartre and Cocteau as mentors to enable him to escape from the Hell of prison, they are not mythologised as Leduc mythologises 'Madame'.[36] In his personal legend, he plays the divine role. Having been told by a fortune-teller that he would one day be famous, he immediately transforms this into the model of the miraculous child:

> This purely virtual celebrity ennobled me, like a parch-ment that no one could decipher, an illustrious birth kept secret, a bar of royal bastardy, a divine mask or perhaps parentage.[37]

In *Journal du voleur*, this divinity is not only that of the child thief Hermes, or the sodomised Ganymede, but an inverted replica of that of Christ himself. When he arrives in Alicante, the palms remind him of those strewn about the feet of Jesus:

> I was in the heart of my childhood, at its most preciously preserved moment. At a turn in the road I was about to discover beneath three palm trees the Christmas manger where, as a child, I used to be present at *my nativity* between the ox and the ass. I was the humblest of the world's poor.
>
> (TJ: 69)[38]

Genet's stated aim is to be a saint, and he sees that sainthood in terms of living a personal legend, akin to that of an inverted hero of tradition.[39] 'Saintliness means turning pain to good account. It means forcing the devil to be God. It means obtaining the recognition of evil' (TJ: 183). Writing is the means of achieving the legend, and of a rebirth through language. This rebirth into the symbolic produces 'Not my life, but the inter-pretation of it' (TJ: 183). Becoming a writer is in itself a miraculous birth. The act of creation which writing involves confers the imprint of divinity, but also its penalties:

> Creating is not a somewhat frivolous game. The creator has committed himself to the fearful adventure of taking upon himself, to the very end, the perils risked by his creatures. We cannot suppose a creation that does not spring from love. How can a man place before himself something as strong as himself which he will have to scorn or hate? But the creator will then charge himself with the weight of his characters' sins. Jesus became man. He expiated. Later, like God, after creating men, He delivered them from their sins: He was whipped, spat on, mocked, nailed. That is the meaning of the expression: 'He suffers in his flesh.' Let us ignore the theologians. 'Taking upon Himself the sins of the world' means exactly this: experiencing potentially and in their effects all sins; it means having subscribed to evil.
>
> (TJ: 185)[40]

The dangers of subscribing too closely to this curious negative mythology of the divine bastard is that it will lead, in the end, to a divine entropy. Creation will be accomplished once the creator has charged himself with the weight of his characters' sins. Genet moves, like Rimbaud, into a period in which he refuses to write. After that he aspires, like the hero of tradition, to a final delegitimation, and leaves the city for the rigours of the desert. After a life of total disregard for any moral or political values, he chooses in the end to support the revolutionary agendas of the PLO and the Black Panthers. By this move he returns to the humility of his origins. His reward comes when, sharing the long agony of an Arab woman awaiting the inevitable death of her son, he finds in her the mother who has so long escaped him. Like Leduc, he gives birth to this mother by the power of the word:

> Since he [her son] was in the fight that night, in his room and on his bed I was taking the place and perhaps the part of the son. For one night and the space of a simple but multiple act [bringing coffee], an old man, older than she was, became the son of the mother, for 'I was before she existed'. Younger than me, during this familiar – familial? – act, she was, while remaining Hamza's, my mother.[41]

Rites of excess

Genet and Leduc use their personal myths as the basis for rituals: rituals of pride, of revenge, of lust, but above all of that excess which is the mark of the sacred. Performing a ritual is putting on a brief divinity. The forms of these rituals are as polysemous as the language which describes them. Each author enacts and celebrates sexual excess with an almost royal exclusion of any practical considerations. In *Journal du voleur* and its two predecessors *Le Miracle de la Rose* (The Miracle of the Rose) and *Notre-Dame-des-Fleurs* Genet (who becomes Divine in the latter text) draws, as we have seen, on those anti-myths of divinity which celebrate the hero of tradition as bastard, as thief and as sexual pariah.

At her best, Leduc succeeds in an even more difficult task: she creates rituals which can clothe in the mantle of royalty the humble actions of everyday life, and everyday female life at that. Whether it be a manifestation of that bastards' pride, which must turn dross to gold or gold to dross, or of the obsession with perfection drilled into her by an unforgiving mother, she can invest the act of getting dressed with the solemn beauty of a coronation and the preparation of a meal with the dedication of a priest at the altar.

Working on the boundary between genders, between classes, between the sacred and the trivial, between crime and punishment and, it must be said, between sanity and madness, both reverse the angelic choice of Lucifer, and 'force the devil to be God'.

10

Delegitimation by proxy

Le monde mental Messsssieurs
. . .
Travaille arbitrairement
S'érigeant pour soi-même
Et soi-disant généreusement en l'honneur des travailleurs
du bâtiment
Un auto-monument
Répétons-le Messssssieurs
Quand on le laisse seul
Le monde mental
Ment
Monumentalement.

(From Jacques Prévert, *Paroles*)[1]

The critical response to a genealogy which includes illegitimacy
has generally been to enshroud it in a kind of tactful silence.
Writers deemed worthy of critical discussion have, as it were,
already been relegitimated artistically and, hence, it is implied,
recuperated into the law of the Father. An understandable
revulsion against the excesses of biographical criticism led to a
counter-emphasis that criticism should be derived from the text
and the text alone, but this stricture is obviously not applicable
to the criticism of autobiographical literature. While critical
'outing' of the facts of birth may contribute nothing to the study
of a writer who has been happily relegitimated, by adoption for
instance, it is strange to find the origins of authors who have
made major contributions to the writing of illegitimacy en-
veloped in the same discretion. This is not just a phenomenon of
the age of cant. Take the case of Thomas Bernhard, the Austrian

186

writer, whose autobiography, which includes *Die Ursache* (The Origin) (1975), *Der Keller* (The Cellar) (1976) and *Das Kind* (The Child) (1982), is a major modern study of bastardy. I was startled to find that on the back cover of the Gallimard editions of his work the biographical note begins: 'Born on the 10th February 1931 at Heerlen in Holland, Thomas Bernhard is the son of an Austrian farmer . . . .' This bland note gives a totally erroneous impression. In fact, it establishes a paternal genealogy in spite of the author himself, who insists he never saw or knew his father, and who took his mother's name. The traditional critical response to 'canonical' bastards and their writing (did you know Erasmus was illegitimate?) is likely to follow this pattern.

The second critical response mirrors the tendency present in many of these writers themselves to mythologise their origins and experience. There is a marked romanticisation in either positive or negative terms. This romanticising has tended more and more towards the positive mythology in the twentieth century, as the literate and academic establishment has become more politically conscious of the effects of exclusion in its own ranks and in the community at large. Thus there is a tendency to read texts in terms of their author's minority status, rather than for their efficacy either as rhetorical messages or as memorable artefacts. It is extraordinarily hard to point out, for example, that being a heroine of the Women's Movement does not, unfortunately, make one a good dramatist. Ideology can make it difficult to distinguish real textual innovation from didacticism and propaganda. Those who achieve the optimum minority status, excluded on several counts like Leduc and Genet, are particularly prone to benefit from the critical inversion of negative mythology, the 'groves of academe' syndrome.[2] This helps to put into effect the desired relegitimation by literary canonisation.

However, it is the third critical response that particularly interests me and that I propose to study in this chapter. This is a kind of emotive symbiosis, whereby the critics invest not only their time and intellectual powers in the object of analysis, but also involve it in the formation of their own identity, of themselves as subjects. The process is reminiscent of sympathetic magic. Certain aspects of one's own experience are read into the writing of the other, and, by a sort of reciprocal contiguity, parts of the other adhere to one. In its most extreme form, as described and practised by Derrida, for example, it becomes a form of cannibalism, whereby the critic acquires by 'graphophagy' some of the magic of the other and the Other. This fusion of self and the excluded other in the critical enterprise I have christened 'delegitimation by proxy'.

Coming from behind

Derrida, in *La Carte postale* (The Postcard), develops an extensive allegory of just this sort of activity. The postcard from which he derives his argument is one in which the figure of Socrates, seated and apparently in control of paper, pen, stylus and ink, but wearing nightgown and cap, is actually manipulated by his disciple Plato, standing pressed against his chair, with one admonishing finger digging into his back and the other waving in front of his face. Indeed, so strange is the perspective that one might almost see Plato's hand, not Socrates', as holding the stylus. No more than the truth in fact. In a further flight of imagination, Derrida sees the two men's positions as suggesting the act of sodomy and implies that such buggering is what any pupil will do to his master, given half a chance.

Now, for Derrida this is above all a metaphor of the transfer of authority and of self-legitimation by territorialisation. But his playing with textual and sexual inversion also allows the possibility of delegitimation. If Plato is writing Socrates, he is also taking over the part of the Athenian Other: gadfly, 'seducer', scapegoat and martyr. In relegitimating Socrates he is both delegitimating himself and constructing his own identity, in a form of self-generation which erects an 'auto-monument'. It is, I think, symptomatic that each of the three examples of delegitimation by proxy I choose produces a *mise-en-abyme* of sexual appropriation as central to its argument, which is in itself appropriative. In the words of my epigraph, this appropriation is presented in the cases of Freud and Sartre as 'generosity in honour of the workers on the edifice'. Derrida, already enjoying in *Glas* the activity he analyses later in *La Carte postale*, is a little more subtle in his approach.

The examples I want to study involve objects of analysis who were, not altogether coincidentally, doubly or triply minoritised. It is perhaps biasing my study to take three examples of the textual appropriation of the work of bastard homosexuals, and yet, in a way, the choice highlights the delegitimatory drive of the analysis and the analysts. The first is Freud's study of Leonardo, which we have already considered as an example of the remythologisation of illegitimacy in terms of the Oedipus complex. Now I want to look at the way it featured in the construction of Freud's own identity at a crucial period of his career. Then a parallel study imposes itself. It is hard to resist contrasting and comparing the auto-monumental aspects of the two mammoth works in which Sartre and Derrida appropriate Genet for their own purposes. One scarcely knows which piece of disingenuousness to admire more: Sartre's old-fashioned pretence of objectivity in *Saint Genet* as he asserts his mastery of another's texts, or Derrida's delighted admission of postmodern mayhem in *Glas* as the texts reshape him and he them in an infinite circularity.

FREUD

The left-handed and the sinister

Freud's interest in Leonardo covered at least twelve of the most important years of his life, from 1898 to 1910, when his study was published. As we have seen, *Leonardo da Vinci and a Memory of his Childhood* (SE XI: 59–138) was not originally intended as a study of either illegitimacy or homosexuality but was a product of Freud's interest in the wellsprings of the creative processes at work in the arts and, in particular, the need to believe that the true artist sublimates his sexual drives. It is in itself an *écrit*, a very fine piece of creative writing, which claims the extra sanction of the newly formed 'science' of psycho-analysis. Its conclusions are based, as we saw in Chapter 2, on rather shaky evidence, and owe more to self-analysis than to science. The reading of *The Novel of Leonardo da Vinci* by the Russian writer Dmitry Merezhkovsky triggered Freud's interest in Leonardo and the artist's childhood as imagined in the novel. They shared a particular interest in the famous notebooks in mirror-writing. It is in Merezhkovsky that Freud found the 'childhood memory' to which he attached so much importance (Pontalis, 1987: 10). The elaborate edifice of interpetation built on Merezhkovsky and on Freud's other major sources, Vasari's

Vita di Leonardo da Vinci (Life of Leonardo da Vinci) (1550) and Scognamiglio's *Ricerche e documenti sulla giovinezza di Leonardo da Vinci* (Research and Documents on the Youth of Leonardo da Vinci) (1900), proved in some vital respects to be the romanticisation of an already romantic narrative. Freud is led by error, mistranslation and the penchant for romanticising that he shares with Merezhkovsky so far from the facts as we now know them that *Leonardo da Vinci and a Memory of his Childhood* is of interest mainly as an example of almost pure mythopoesis.

We need to turn to his letters to his passionately admired friend Wilhelm Fliess in order to trace, in the best Freudian manner, some of the potential fears and desires which surface in the text. In 1898 Fliess was elaborating a fairly pre-posterous theory equating bilateralism with bisexuality, with some interesting consequences for the left-handed if the right were the heterosexually inclined norm. Freud could see the flaws in the theory; indeed, he broke with Fliess on the subject and developed his own theory of bisexuality. But he was impressed enough to react most emphatically to the suggestion that he might be potentially left-handed himself. Indeed one might feel he protests his disinterest too much in this letter of 4 January 1898:

> It also occurred to me that you may have considered me to be partially left-handed; if so, you should tell me, for there would be nothing hurtful to me in such a piece of self-knowledge. You have known me long enough, and you know me well enough, to know that it is your own fault if there is anything personal about me that you do not know. I am not aware of any preference for the left hand, or that I had any such preference in childhood: I should rather say that in my early years I had two left hands. There is only one point on which I cannot object. I do not know whether it is obvious to other people which is their own or others' right and left. In my case in my early years I had to think which was my right; no organic feeling told me . . . .
>
> That is how it seems to me. But I know very well that it may be otherwise, and that the disinclination I have so far felt to accepting your ideas about left-handedness may be the result of unconscious motives. If they are hysterical,

they have certainly nothing to do with the subject itself, but with the word. Perhaps it suggests to me something 'left-handed' or guilty.

(1954: 242–3)

Indeed the connotations of the German word *links* and its derivative *linkshändig* are considerable and almost always negative. *Linken* is to deceive, *linkisch* is clumsy, but perhaps the two most germane to the argument are *links gewebt* for homosexual, while the result of *Ehe zur linken Hand* ('marriage with the left hand') is, of course, a bastard. Left-handedness also seems to be linked with the notion of an unclean hand and hence with masturbation. Freud's fears of homosexuality, masturbation and *coitus interruptus* are particularly intense and probably stem as much from the Old Testament injunction not to cast one's seed on the ground as from nineteenth-century hysteria and homophobia. It is, then, revealing to find Freud nine months later, on 9 October 1898, suggesting to Fliess: 'Leonardo, of whom no love-affair is recorded, was perhaps the most famous case of left-handedness. Can you use him?' (1954: 268). Leonardo is perhaps the ultimate in left-handedness since he actually developed a completely left-handed script, the famous mirror-writing, but he also personifies *par excellence*, while reinvesting them with new meaning by his perfection, the negative connotations of the sinister in the true sense of the word.

Leonardo combines in one imagined person some of Freud's deepest fears, such as that of homosexuality, and deepest desires, such as finding the key to genius by renouncing sexual activity. For example, the trace of his famous statement to Fliess of 31 October 1897, 'Also sexual excitation is of no more use to a person like me' (ibid.: 227), is present in his remarkable insistence that Leonardo, as a precondition of his scientific research and artistic production, must have forsworn sex, which flies in the face of the evidence. A distaste for heterosexual copulation and reproduction is not, as no one knew better than Freud, the equivalent of abstinence, yet that is how he persists in reading the matter, in spite of Leonardo's trial on a charge of sodomy and his subsequent lavish gifts over many years to the young men he protected. The assumption (with no evidence to support it) that Leonardo's homosexuality was almost completely sublimated and limited to the contemplation of the beautiful boys he employed in his workshop is the pure wishful thinking of one unwilling to admit that a great genius could also be an active homosexual, but also eager to justify his own choice of sexual abstinence.[3] It is vital to Freud to be able to see scientific research as the result of sublimation:

> Thus a person of this sort would, for example, pursue research with the same passionate devotion that another would give to his love, and he would be able to investigate instead of loving.
>
> (SE XI: 77)

The sublimation theory was a way of justifying the fact that Freud was finding considerably more emotional satisfaction in his research and in the intense homosocial relationship with Fliess than in mandatory sex with his philoprogenitive Martha.

Mothers deified and defiled

Freud's romanticising of bastardy contrasts with his homophobia, and yet the two are linked by a strange ambivalence about the single mother. His compelling narrative of the fatherless maternal paradise that he imagines Leonardo to have shared with his young mother, Caterina, we have already seen to be factually invalidated and firmly based in his secret desires. *Leonardo da Vinci and a Memory of his Childhood* is revealing not only of the power of the creative urge but of the role of fantasy in Freudian wish-fulfilment. The curious ambivalence of the text may be felt in its choice of icons: on the one hand, the *Santa Anna Metterza*, which celebrates a double immaculate conception and females miraculously free of the taint of sex, and, on the other, the double icons of sexual penetration, the drawing of the engorged and embedded penis and the memory of the bird's tail in the baby's mouth. The ambiguity is central to Freud's self-analysis. Equally central thematically to the whole analysis is the actual childhood *memory*, Freud's version of which was, as you recall:

> It seems that I was always destined to be so deeply concerned with vultures [should be hawks or kites]; for I recall as one of my very earliest memories that while I was

in my cradle a vulture [hawk] came down to me, and opened my mouth with its tail, and struck me many times with the tail against [should be within] my lips.

But we can also see how this functions as *mise-en-abyme* of a sort of coming from behind. Freud takes his own first 'left-handed' and obvious interpretation of the penetrating tail as *fellatio* and transforms it into a second, 'right-handed' pre-Oedipal repressed memory of a nipple brushing a baby's lips. This imposition of mastery by the appropriation of the text is re-enacted many times in the whole study.

Perhaps as important to this self-analysis as to the potential analysis of the *St Anne with Virgin and Child* is the figure we have already found to be missing from that paradisal text, that of the old woman. I speculated in Chapter 2 about the image of the missing grandmother, who has been replaced (and re-pressed?) by the youthful St Anne of both the cartoon and the painting. Other discoveries recorded by Freud in the letters to Fliess 3–15 October 1897 (just before the left-handedness debate) are not only his infantile sexual attraction to his mother but his realisation of the importance of a figure hitherto completely repressed, that of his 'double mother' – his old nurse: 'my "primary originator" [of neurosis] was an ugly, elderly but clever woman who told me a great deal about God and hell, and gave me a high opinion of my own capacities' (1954: 219). This old nurse turned out to be a thief, stealing 'all the shiny Kreuzers and Zehners and toys that had been given you [Freud's mother is speaking]' (ibid.: 221–2), and was sent to jail. Freud had completely repressed this figure, and she first surfaced in a dream, in which:

> She was my instructress in sexual matters, and chided me for being clumsy and not being able to do anything . . . . Also she washed me in reddish water in which she had previously washed herself . . . and she encouraged me to steal 'Zehners' to give to her.
>
> (ibid.: 220)

We can link this dream with Freud's later interest in the extremely bad copy (P: 67–73) of Leonardo's sketch of copulation, found in a professional journal by his disciple Reitler in 1916. He really did not need to produce it as evidence to prove his point that Leonardo was disgusted by the act of procreation (SE XI: 69–73).[4] Even more marked in the original drawing than in the copy, but still apparent there, is the fact that the headless female torso which is being penetrated is much older than the male (drooping breasts, wrinkled abdomen). This fact might have suggested (though not, I think, in a way that Freud would have consciously acknowledged) that the drawing also contained a very ambiguous fantasy of intercourse with the mother. In Freud's case – and perhaps in Leonardo's? – the headless female figure would seem to be linked with the 'grandmaternal' fantasy of the 'instructress in sexual matters' who evoked both disgust and desire. The disgust which Freud sees in the copy, and which is not at all present in the original, would also work against using the drawing to support his Oedipal theories, since a manifest repulsion involved in a fantasy of the penetration of the maternal body would scarcely advance the counter-fantasy of paradisal union.

Freud's whole argument is interesting, if only because of its emotional capacity to involve the reader and to invoke a counter-interpretation of the very scanty straws which go to construct the edifice. Even with its manifest display of prejudice it was still the first study of Leonardo to raise some very important questions. The relationship of sexuality to science and art and that of the illegitimate to the person and name of the mother were areas which had scarcely been touched at the turn of the century. Freud's text is a creative act. It has all the positive side-effects of such acts, not only in its production of an ingenious theory, but, more importantly, in the construction of the writer's own identity at a key point in his emotional and intellectual development. A narrative and a kind of poetry have to be created so that Freud can attain the desired and hidden synthesis between himself and the Leonardo he fantasises. Freud delegitimated himself in the eyes of his contemporaries by besmirching, as they thought, the memory of a genius. He relegitimated himself in his own estimation by identifying himself with aspects of that genius. The double movement is characteristic of the performance of exclusion by proxy.

SARTRE

'On the Fine Arts considered as Murder'

When we move on some fifty years to our next example, the social stakes are different. While a certain prudishness, which could be exploited in the interests of delegitimation, still characterised the post-war literary world,[5] psychoanalysis was no longer in question, nor the right of critics to discuss sexual propensities and repressions. Delegitimation by proxy could no longer be achieved by the exploration of infantile sexuality, even that of a genius. Identification with homosexuality had already received critical relegitimation in the canonisation of Proust and Gide. The stakes were raised. So if, as pseudo-bastard, you still had to find the fault line between criticism and the establishment, where could you turn? The wartime appearance of the first works of Jean Genet, flaunting the absolute inversion of morality which we glimpsed in the last chapter, and Cocteau's campaign to free this self-taught poet from the prison he hymned, gave a new focus to Jean-Paul Sartre's blend of criticism and philosophy. Textual identification with this inverted self, whose thievery was opposed to Sartre's strong financial morality, whose peasant upbringing was opposed to the other's bourgeois background, as was his gay to the other's straight, and his bastardy to the other's legitimacy, provoked an amazing outburst of critical creativity in Sartre.

We have already seen, in his 1947 study of Baudelaire – which, symptomatically, was dedicated to Genet – how Sartre, forging an identity through self-analysis, needed to use an *alter ego* as a mirror (see Pacaly, 1980). However, the question provoked by *Saint Genet: Actor and Martyr* (1952) concerns the use of criticism as a form of vampirism. Genet was no dead and enshrined genius when the book appeared, but 42 years old and at the height of his powers. One might well ask what effect such a comprehensive piece of textual appropriation might have had on his future production. Indeed, Genet wrote to Cocteau: 'You and Sartre have turned me into a monument. I am somebody else, and this somebody must find something to say' (cit. Cohen-Salal, 1987: 317).

Sartre has, of course forestalled this question, just as he, and not I, thought to invert the title of De Quincey's *On Murder considered as one of the Fine Arts*, though he did not intend to have it applied to *Saint Genet*. He has an ingenious response to those who say: 'when one writes so much about a living person, it is because one wants to bury him'. He replies: 'Why should *I* want to bury him? He doesn't bother me. The fact is that a certain Genet has just died and that Jean Genet has asked me to deliver the funeral oration' (SGAM: 574).[6] And, of course, it is true that Genet constantly proclaimed, with each new book, that he was giving up writing forever, until the prophecy became self-fulfilling. However, Sartre's remark that Genet is virtually indulging in self- interment by allowing his *Complete Works* to appear seems rather disingenuous when one reflects that Sartre's *Saint Genet*, in an occurrence unique in my recollection, actually appears as volume I of Genet's *Complete Works* in the Gallimard edition. It thus pre-empts discussion and critical appraisal, seeming to bear the author's own *imprimatur*. Sartre's text becomes the enigma which must be solved, the labyrinth which must be penetrated, and which will control our reading. It allows subversion, but subversion in approved terms.

This piece of paratextual appropriation is matched by an even more insidious piece of intratextual appropriation. In the 600-odd pages of text, there is massive quotation from all Genet's extant works at the time. Yet many of these quotations are not even attributed to a particular book, and none of them has page-references.[7] The result is that selections from Genet's texts become, as it were, part of the Sartrean master discourse for all but the few readers totally conversant with the works in question. One generally renounces the hunt for the elusive context, and Genet's words are reterritorialised by the discourse of existentialism. For this is the thrust of this enormous work, which takes its place as a case study beside *Being and Nothingness*. It belongs to that period of Sartrean thought, dating from the heady post-war days of the existentialist vogue, when pronouncements of our absolute personal liberty and personal responsibility in constructing both our own lives and society were unquestioned. Both idealism and a latent puritanism were present in the attempts of Marxism and existentialism to create a new world and a new morality. How challenging and how insidious we found the cry 'freedom alone can account for a person in his totality' (SGAM: 584). Yet setting out Genet's 'thought' in the theses and counter-theses of philosophy effectively removes that very freedom.[8]

In the same way there is an apparent freedom in a variant of the challenge which had already appeared in *The Second Sex*: 'One is not born a woman, one becomes one.' But in *Saint Genet* this is transformed into a dogmatic statement about homosexuality, based on some strange assumptions:

> A person is not born homosexual or normal. He becomes one or the other, according to the accidents of his history and to his own reaction to these accidents. I maintain that inversion is the effect of neither a prenatal choice nor an endocrinian malformation nor even the passive and determined result of complexes. It is an outlet that a child discovers when he is suffocating.
>
> (SGAM: 78)

Sartre's words make it impossible to read this text as a statement first of biology, then of social gendering, as de Beauvoir's statement about woman is generally read. Not only do the words 'normal' and 'inversion' pre-empt any discussion of the status of the large proportion of males who are gay, but the argument simply discards the views of Genet himself, who repeatedly asserted that a recognition of his homosexuality was one of the earliest impulses he could remember.

Nobody's son

Now this is not at all irrelevant to my main preoccupation, which is how Sartre deals with Genet's bastardy and the role of his missing mother. One is, after all, *born* illegitimate, although, as I have shown, one can choose the path of relegitimation or of a confirmation of delegitimation thereafter. Sartre has to perform the most extraordinary contortions in order to minimise this inscribed necessity and assert the liberty of the individual. He must do so to justify his own existential choice to write himself out of the bourgeoisie, his own symbolic delegitimation. This is the choice we see fully developed in *Les Mots*, as Jean-Paul elects himself pseudo-bastard: *he* is not born one but becomes one. Thus he escapes the awful possibility that essence may be written on to the very register that precedes and inaugurates civil existence. To help forward the analysis of the other as self-analysis,

Genet, though inescapably a victim of social contingency, is rather viewed as the product of a social vacuum, 'nobody's son' (SGAM: 8), motherless, fatherless and, above all, propertyless:[9]

> Genet has neither mother nor heritage – how could he be innocent? By virtue of his mere existence he disturbs the natural order and the social order. A human institution with its birth register and its bureaucracy has come between the species and himself. He is a fake child. No doubt he was born of a woman, but this origin has not been noted by the social memory. As far as everyone and, consequently, he himself are concerned, he appeared one fine day without having been carried in any known womb: he is a synthetic product. He is obscurely aware that he belongs legally to administrative bodies and laboratories, and so there is nothing surprising in the fact that he will later feel elective affinities with reformatories and prisons. Being a fabricated creature, he will find his truth in sophism; being a child of miracle, he will be mineral or spirit; but he does not belong to the intermediate kingdom: to life.
>
> (SGAM: 7)

It is not only Genet who finds 'truth in sophism', as is shown by this attempt to exploit the myths of bastardy while at the same time producing it as an existential blank page on which the essence of the bastard can be written; whereas, as I have endeavoured to show, bastardy itself informs the positive or negative choices which follow. Genet is presented, a little further on in the book, as a believer in the most extreme negative mythology of bastardy:

> He seizes upon the curse which goes back to the depths of his past, of his mother's past, and which has continued to the very present, and he projects it before him: it will be his future. It was a constraint; he makes of it his mission. He saw it as the raw fact of a tainted heredity; it becomes a value, an imperative.
>
> (SGAM: 50)

His problem, if this is true, is an excess of 'social memory', not a lack of it. However, not even the inverted morality of *Journal du voleur* labours under such antiquated discourse as 'curse' and 'tainted heredity'.

Sartre has taken over from Genet himself, and developed, the anti-myth of the miraculous birth, seen here in the words 'no doubt he was born of woman', though the God who presides at the conception is seen as none other than 'the great barbaric goddess, Genet, the Mother, Genemesis' (SGAM: 477), since nobody's son engenders himself. Subsequently, in *Les Mots*, which contains, ten years after *Saint Genet*, in-numerable verbal echoes of it, Jean-Paul too will see himself as 'present at [*his*] *nativity* between the ox and the ass' (TJ: 69), as he develops his vision of himself as *enfant du miracle* or divine (miraculous) child (see p. 159). The only difference is that the foundling is seen as free to create himself *ab nihilo*, whereas the bourgeois orphan has to accommodate a mother, who, however, as we saw in Chapter 8, is easily fitted into the role of the maculate virgin. In *Saint Genet*, the ambiguous love/hatred of the foundling for the mother who abandoned him is fused with the resentment of the adored divine son whose mother betrayed her role of virginal vessel by remarrying. The cultivation of an identity as self-made bastard in fact means a fusion with the identity of the Other: Sartre too will create himself as 'nobody's son'.

The 'raped child'

Like Freud, Sartre uses as *mise-en-abyme* of his writing of bastardy an extraordinary fantasy of sexual penetration. This is the period of Sartre's most extreme horror of the gaze of others,[10] which he combines with his terror of feminisation to produce, in Book II of *Saint Genet,* one of the most startling texts of combined homophobia and misogyny. The moment when, at 10 years old (SGAM: 17), the guilty child is unmasked as a thief by someone who enters the room behind him, serves Sartre as a basis for a very Derridean allegory of coming from behind:

> Genet has now been deflowered; an iron embrace has made him a woman. All that is left for him is to put up with *being*. He is the village whore; everyone can have him at will. Undressed by the eyes of decent folk as women are by those of males, he carries his fault as they do their breasts and behind. Many women loathe their

backside, that blind and public mass which belongs to everyone before belonging to them. When they are grazed from behind, their excitement and their shame will mount together. The same holds for Genet. Having been caught stealing *from behind*, his back opens when he steals; it is with his back that he awaits human gazes and catastrophe. Why be surprised if, after that, he feels more like an object by virtue of his back and behind and if he has a kind of sexual reverence for them?

(SGAM: 79–80)

While having extremely dubious validity as interpretation, this passage, developed over a number of pages, is immensely revealing of Sartre's private fears and desires. His fear of the unheralded rape to which the gaze of the other submits us, and more especially submits those 'village whores', writers who bare their wares to the public gaze – a fear which is, however, countered by his desire for the sexual thrill of such penetration – provides a guide to his own acts as reader. By reading those fears and desires in others he can enjoy them by proxy.

Sartre's works are often dominated by the image of the voyeur; and the voyeur, by the very fact of non-participation in the acts on which he spies, turns others into signs, to be arbitrarily read. Thus the voyeur reads that other voyeurism, the detection of those petty thefts, as rape:

Sexually, Genet is first of all a raped child. This first rape was the gaze of the other, who took him by surprise, penetrated him, transformed him forever into an object. Let there be no misunderstanding: I am not saying that his original crisis *resembles* a rape, I say that it *is* one.

(SGAM: 79)

Well, I am saying that Sartre's reading of Genet's childhood not only resembles a rape, but is one. In *Saint Genet* the text functions to turn the other into an object, a monument, as Genet says. It is an exercise in the very reification that Sartre condemns as one of the worst forms of self-deception. One of the aims of this rape is to acquire for his own the power he sees in Genet: 'Child without a mother, effect without a cause, the victim of misfortune carries out, proudly and rebelliously, the superb project of being self-caused' (SGAM: 69). Both *enfants du miracle*, children of a virgin birth, rich in the absence of a father, they will generate themselves. The delegitimation is, in effect, a relegitimation. It puts into practice the Sartrean maxim of 'qui perd gagne', or 'loser takes all'. By the *tour de force* of fitting his existential creed of liberty, choice and responsibility to the most unlikely subject possible, Sartre reaffirms both the poetic genius of Genet and his own role of John the Baptist to this inverted Christ figure.

Delegitimation in tandem

One can, I think, better appreciate the function of delegitimation by proxy in the construction – and deconstruction – of the subject if one compares the two extraordinary relationships which developed in tandem: that of Sartre with Genet, and that of Simone de Beauvoir with Violette Leduc. The parallelism is marked, the coincidence enormous. Not twelve months after Sartre and Le Castor[11] had met Genet, in 1945, de Beauvoir was given the manuscript of what was to become *L'Asphyxie* to read. She admired the subject-matter and style, and would probably have recommended the manuscript to *Les Temps modernes* in any case, but meeting with Leduc must have made the patronage almost irresistible. Here was a female Genet. A self-proclaimed lesbian, of peasant stock, living on the edges of criminality, a bastard, outrageous in dress and total disregard for convention, with a poetic flair for language, she provided de Beauvoir with a counter and a complement to Sartre's new enthusiasm.

The fact that Leduc fell immediately and desperately in love with this new friend and patron added further challenge to the relationship. The danger of such passions was not unknown to de Beauvoir, who had for years delegitimated herself socially by intense and often lesbian friendships with girls excluded from her stuffy bourgeois background by being foreigners, Jewish, artists, her own students, or all of these. This flirting with danger actually culminated in her being dismissed from her teaching job.[12] It was as though delegitimation by proxy provided a freedom for those expressions and feelings which had been inhibited by the rigid social and intellectual training that de Beauvoir had undergone. She was not an original stylist and never could write in anything but an 'acceptable' French prose, but she could admire innovation in others.

In their personal relationships with friends and lovers, it was as though she and Sartre could experience intellectually but, like the princess in the fairy tale, were incapable of feeling. They were, all their lives, extremely generous with money and professional encouragement, but apparently uncomprehending of the emotional effects on others of their sexual and social experiments. De Beauvoir had learned caution by the time of her relationship with Leduc and, although generous with advice and money – even paying for long psychiatric hospitalisation – rationed personal contact to a fortnightly meeting in the Café de Flore.[13]

The difference from Sartre is that de Beauvoir never attempts to appropriate Leduc, or to make the other over into her own image, except perhaps in her perception of the child's attitude towards her father, which is strongly coloured by her own experience. This emerges from her introduction to *La Bâtarde* (B: 14). Of course, she is no literary critic; indeed this twenty-page introduction was almost her only venture into the field. She has little feeling for texts as artefacts, for their narrative structure for instance, but only for their ideological impact and her own capacity for identification with them. This identification is what she values:

> Most writers, when they confess to evil thoughts, manage to remove the stings from them by the very frankness of their admissions. She [Leduc] forces us to feel them, with all their corrosive bitterness, both in herself and in ourselves. She remains a faithful accomplice to her desires, to her rancour, to her petty traits; in this way she takes ours upon her too and delivers us from shame: no one is monstrous unless we are all so.
>
> (BA: xxii–xxiii)[14]

The very parallelism, what one might call the his and hers aspect, of the relationships with Genet and Leduc, makes it easier to distinguish the two forms of delegitimation by proxy: in the first (the Sartrean) not only 'I is another', to quote Sartre's chapter heading taken from Rimbaud (SG: 159–72), but the other becomes I, appropriated and reterritorialised in the construction of the critic as subject; in the second (that chosen by de Beauvoir) the textual other maintains its integrity, but the mere display of existential and critical preference for the excluded serves to differentiate the critic from the establishment.

DERRIDA

The bastard path

When we move on another twenty years from *Saint Genet*, and ten years from the scandal of *La Bâtarde* and de Beauvoir's sponsorship of it in 1964, we also move into an era in which the innocence of criticism has been irretrievably deflowered. When Derrida writes *Glas* (1974),[15] he elaborates it in the full awareness that, in deconstructing Hegel and Genet, he is constructing the signature of Jacques Derrida. He is as aware as Sartre that he may be 'murdering' Genet, even suggests that Genet may wish him dead, or at least throw him up:

> Anyhow, he will vomit all that {*ça*} for me, he will not read, will not be able to read.

> Do I write *for him*? What would I like to do to him? do to his 'work'? Ruin it by erecting it, perhaps.

> So that one reads it no more? So that one only reads it starting from here, from the moment I myself consign and countersign it?
>
> (GE: 200)[16]

Yet, in signing and consigning, he is hedging his bets. In order to do so he doubles and redoubles his text in parallel columns, themselves then proliferating inserts, frames and windows. In, as he puts it, avoiding the 'empirico-chronological delay of the narrative' and the name of the father, he pursues 'a bastard course' ('*démarche bâtarde*') (GE: 6). This is a criss-crossing, tricksy manoeuvre, one which will throw the hounds of reception off the scent. One of the many ambiguities of 'the bastard path . . . that will have to feign to follow naturally the circle of the family in order to enter it' (GE: 6)[17] is that it leads one left-handedly into the column that discusses the accepted and legitimate Hegel, whereas taking the right-handed path leads one to the pariah and illegitimate Genet. Each column, declared as phallic, is then further 'invaginated' by textual inserts, which confer that sexual/textual androgyny often associated, as we have seen, with the bastard path.[18]

So long as these multiple texts remain incomplete, as they do, actually finishing in mid-sentence and refusing closure, the author's signature, so very close in nature to the Sartrean essence, cannot be finally grasped. Since both signature and essence are as much a death warrant as a guarantee of eternal life, Derrida's avowed intent, in the following address to the narratee, to frustrate the reader's construction of the text is a matter of self-preservation:

> Why, at least, write two texts at once? What scene is being played? What is desired? In other words, what is there to be afraid of? Who is afraid? Of whom? There is a wish to make writing ungraspable, of course. When your head is full of the matters here [on the right], you are reminded that the law of the text is in the other [on the left], and so on endlessly. By knocking up [impregnating] the margin – (no) more margin, (no) more frame – one annuls it, blurs the line, takes back from you the standard rule {règle droite} that would enable you to delimit, to cut up {découper}, to dominate.
>
> (GE: 64–5)[19]

Derrida and Sartre have very different ways of seducing their readers, and thereby acquiring authority over them. This can perhaps be seen most clearly, and relevantly, in their discussions of the only passage in *Journal du voleur* in which Genet describes a real woman, an old thief newly out of prison, whom he thinks of as his mother. Remember the passage we looked at in Chapter 9:

> I know nothing of her who abandoned me in the cradle, but I hoped it was that old thief who begged in the night. 'What if it were she?' I thought, moving away from the old woman. Ah, if it were, I would cover her with flowers, with gladiolus [*sic*] and roses, and with kisses! I would weep with tenderness over those moon-fish eyes, over that round and foolish face! 'And why', I went on, 'why weep over it?' It did not take my mind long to replace the customary marks of tenderness by some other gesture, even the vilest and most contemptible, which I empowered to mean as much as the kisses, or the tears or the flowers.
>
> 'I'd be glad to slobber all over her', I thought, over-flowing with love. (Did the word *glaïeul* [gladiolus] mentioned above suggest the word *glaviaux* [gobs of spit]?) To

slobber over her hair or vomit into her hands. But I would adore that thief who is my mother.

(TJ: 17)[20]

Sartre sees the passage as a trap for the 'just man' (SGAM: 506–8), a very hypothetical reader, representative of that very class from which Sartre wants to distance himself. This just man, postulated by Sartre to be the Genetian narratee, is a man of straw. Sartre alone creates him, inspired by the anti-bourgeois prejudice of the bourgeois, and the search for an ideology or, at least, an anti-ideology to fit this prejudice. On reading of the meeting with the old thief the just man is to be first touched by the thrilling of the bastard to maternal love, then gratified by his choice of a humble object for that love, and finally approving of the 'customary marks' of tenderness. Theoretically, he begins to identify with the speaker, and the trap closes: 'And there we have the decent man in the act of puking on his old mother.' The Sartrean interpretation is constructed as a condemnation of social hypocrisy, then as an exposition of his philosophical views; one can hear the very terms by which he imposes his own thinking on that of Genet:

> Genet requires no more: he has captured the just man's *freedom* and has forced it to give a *semblance of existence to the false* as a parasite of the true, to the *impossible as a transcendence of all possibles* . . . . And the reader, who is drawn by the thief's art into the pursuit of the *impossible adequation of nothingness with Being*, of privation with abundance, realises, in Genet's stead, the asceticism of the Black Saint.
>
> (SGAM: 508; my emphasis)[21]

Derrida's approach is totally different, but just as characteristic of a mind-set and a territorialisation. Language itself has taken the place of ideology, or, rather, is an ideology which controls both text and reader. In the discussion of the passage, he takes up Genet's suggestion that phonemes produce a network of attraction, that they 'call' one another, an idea first promoted by Rimbaud. Thirty-seven pages of *Glas* (G: 200–37), ranging from etymology to poetry, form an extended reflection and free association on the [gl] of the *glaïeul/glaviaux* attraction mentioned by Genet in the description of the old

205

woman. The appearance of the mother figure herself is seen as an efflorescence of the signifier, even if not completely devoid of semantic content:

> as always semantic necessity, giving rise to a hermeneutics, a semiotics, verily a psychoanalysis, remains undecidably suspended from the chance of an agglutination called formal or signifying. The flight, the theft {vol} of this suspense, and its necessity, derails semanticism as well as formalism. *Voleuse* takes up *veilleuse* in mid-flight {au vol} and fixes it a little further on in *vieille voleuse*. Marvellous {merveilleuse} writing. Incredibly precious.
>
> (GE: 146)[22]

It seems strange that the phonemes [v] [s] [l] [i] are not further linked at this point to the 'abject' tube of V*aseline* (the badge of homosexuality), discovered at the police station, in the experience of profound humiliation which immediately preceded the midnight meeting with the 'mother'. The Vaseline evoked the memory of 'the most cherished mother' (JV: 22), because, on the police desk, it lay exposed all night to that scorn which is 'the inverse of a Perpetual Adoration'. The text of *Glas* in fact goes on to play with the equivalence between the hymning of being 'despised and rejected' and the evocation of the virgin birth.

The immaculate conception

Derrida, again like Sartre, has taken over from Genet the fantasy of self-generation, and more particularly of male self-generation. Like Sartre, he follows with fascination Genet's replay of the myth of the divine son. He even warns his narratee, in one of his marginal, redoubled columns:

> Double gaze. Cross-eyed {bigle: Bi-gl} reading. While keeping an eye on the corner column {la colonne d'angle} (the contraband), read this as a new testament. But also as a genesis. *The Thief's Journal* that is soon going to decline its identity, as one declines one's responsibility, is presented as 'my book, become my Genesis'. Elsewhere, as '*my nativity*'.
> And if the reading of the Bible is not as familiar to

you as it is to a slightly vicious choirboy, it is useless
to continue.

(GE: 113–14)[23]

But he is far more concerned than Sartre with self-generation
through language, and more particularly through the power of
the name. The name is a rebus, which is to say it is a puzzle,
a play on words, but also, more importantly, a play on things, a
means of transforming things into names, or of reifying names
into things, which can then assume a life of their own (GE: 5).
Both parts of the name Jean Genet, for instance, have multiple
readings. The phonemes of the sign Genet are also heard as 'je
nais' ('I am born'). Among his other incarnations, he is reborn in
a biblical form as Jean/John, in an all-important trinity: as
another John the Baptist, he is the fruit himself of an immaculate
conception who announces the coming of a further divine child;
as another John the evangelist, he announces the primacy of the
word; and as another John of Patmos, he reveals the rule of evil
in the world (GE: 194–8).

Again like Sartre, but much more openly and consciously,
Derrida uses delegitimation by proxy to merge himself with the
Genet he creates. The first stage of this enterprise is the manipulation of discourse in the first person. Whereas Sartre merely
uses the God-given academic right to reify his subject in the
third-person, Derrida uses the more insidious approach of
deliberately merging his own discourse, and indeed his own
experience, with that of Genet:

> And it is true [he says] that I will have done nothing if I
> have not succeeded in ... making you sensitive, trans-
> forming you, beyond all that is combined here, out of the
> most proper affect of this text.

> But is there any? And of what text? of his? of mine?
>
> (GE: 104–5)[24]

Throughout *Glas*, a game with the first person is constant in the
right-hand (Genet) column, whereas the discourse of the left
(Hegel) column is much more consciously academic. On the right,
one is often left deliberately unsure whether the voice we hear is
Genet speaking, or whether it is that of Jacques Derrida using him
as a *porte parole*. How can we tell *who* is speaking in this
interpretation of the episode of the adolescent's flight to freedom

through a Polish rye field, a *mise-en-abyme* to both writers, when the young Genet first becomes aware that one can penetrate into a country as one would into an image, and vice-versa, in other words becomes conscious of his poetic vocation (JV: 50–1)?

> I give birth to myself {*je m'accouche*}, and I write myself {*je m'écris*} because of that. In plainsong. In the open field. I listen to myself {*Je m'écoute*}.
>
> That's where – here {*ici*} – I siglum ryeself or eagle myself {*je seigle ou m'aigle*}.
>
> (GE: 193)[25]

In fact, Derrida is deliberately practising precisely that form of textual coming from behind which he was later to describe so well in *La Carte postale*, where the disciple insidiously dominates the master. This rape/buggery is evoked by the figure of the eagle from the same passage of *Journal du voleur*, which, in a curious parallel to Leonardo's hawk:

> comes swooping down (on you), falling above you or hanging over {*surplomber*} you. It is a phallic sun, a lead {*plombé*} coffin, a heavy and rigid excrement that crashes down and plunges into you from behind, just as, come from above, Ganymede's eagle. (Or the angel Gabriel, flying–trying–stealing {*volant*} to make a child behind your back.)
>
> (GE: 194)[26]

The angel Gabriel is chosen to represent this coming from behind because he is the messenger of the virgin birth, another form of immaculate conception, which fascinates Derrida even more than it did Sartre, but for the same basic reason: it permits an escape from the name and the law of the Father (see Hartman, 1981: 105–6). Obviously, this is a far cry from the Christian version of the event, which, as we know, is destined to reinforce both transcendental and social patriarchy. As we saw in Chapter 2, in the official Gospel version the social lineage which traced Jesus back to the line of David was just as important as the divine paternity. Derrida has a much more radical programme in mind when he sees Genet's adoption of the name of the mother as a way of dispensing with both father and mother as a form of auto-genesis:

The name of the person who seems to affix, append here his *seing* (Genet) is the name, as we know (but how and from where do we know?), of his mother. Who then would have given birth according to a kind of immaculate conception . . . .

If all his literature sings and weaves a funerary hymen to nomination, Genet never sets any value, noblesse oblige, on anything but naming himself.

(GE: 34–5)[27]

One needs to think about that term 'weaves a funerary hymen'. The hymen, to Derrida, is the key to both sexual and textual life. It is the text/tissue which must first be woven and then penetrated. It is the mystery of birth, of intercourse, and of poesis: veil of the temple, and eventually shroud of the corpse and the corpus. By social convention, when the male penetrates this mystery, he becomes a potential father and earns the right to name the results, whether they be the offspring of the penis or of the pen. In an immaculate conception, however, there has been no penetration. It is the child, the son of course, who breaks the veil of the hymen as he emerges from the holy of holies. He is thus his own begetter, replacing both the father's erection and the mother's corresponding invagination, and he too is reversible and double in nature as are the angels. Whereas Derrida uses the imagery of the flower (*genêt*, broom; see pp. 175–6 and G: 65–6) as a metaphor of Genet's accession to this state of miraculous grace, he also uses *Glas* to trace an even more circuitous route and rebus with his own name. The text is the prosthesis that enables him to delegitimate the name legitimately conferred on him. Deriving from the phonemes of the names/signs Jacques Derrida he reads the mystery of the hymen, and of the text: he who signs Derrida is *derrière le rideau* ('behind the curtain'). Situated behind the woven veil by this linguistic sleight of hand, he has, of course, the right of the immaculately conceived, to break the hymen in giving birth to himself. However, as Derrida, Jacques, in the other form in which his signature will be enshrined in those metatextual graveyards known as bibliographies, the phonemes no longer suggest behind, *derrière*, but already, *déjà*. The written text is necessarily past, *déjà*, and its writer, text-enshrouded, is returned to his essential dust like his namesake

J.D., the lover whose obituary Genet writes in *Pompes funèbres* (Funeral Rites).[28]

'Remain(s) – the mother'

However one exploits the myth of immaculate conception, and even if one reverses it as anti-myth, it entails certain consequences. Derrida explodes it in a fireworks of paradox. Yet he also clings to it to the extent that he, as certain Fathers of the Church did for Mary, metaphorically restores the intact hymen that has been ruptured by childbirth, thus enforcing on the mother a renewable virginity: 'the mother (whatever forename or pronoun she may be given) stands beyond sexual opposition. Above all, she is not a woman. She only lets herself, detached, be represented by the attributes of sex'(GE: 134).[29] The problem is that this asexual mother, presented as empty vessel and mystic rose, is fated by the transcendental imperative of the narrative to preside over the sacrifice and death of the divine child. He is crucified, she remains. Both Genet and Derrida are haunted by the image of the *pietà*, the mother cradling the body of her dead son:

> I am {I follow} the mother. The text. The mother is *behind* [*derrière*] – all that I follow, am, do, seem – the mother follows. As she follows absolutely, a future that will never have been presentable, she always survives what she will have engendered [she is] present, impassible, fascinating and provoking, at the burial of that whose death she has foreseen.
> (GE: 116–17)[30]

The price of being the saviour or Messiah is this moment of female domination. Even if the death of the son is followed by resurrection and ascension, again the Fathers of the Church have inconveniently sanctioned that other ascension, whereby the mother becomes Queen of Heaven. Decidedly, she has a case to answer:

> Subject of denunciation: I call myself my mother who calls herself (in) me. To give, to accuse. Dative, accusative. I bear my mother's name, I am {following} my mother's name, I call my mother to myself, I call my mother for

myself, I call my mother in myself, recall myself to my
mother. I decline the same subjugation in all cases.

(GE: 117)[31]

The most cursory look at this schoolboy game with the hated
task of Latin declension, on a model such as 'Amo, amas, I love
a lass', will show the Derridean ambivalence to the name of the
mother. No matter what case he uses, when he seems to give he
also accuses. If the declension spells out the multiplicity of the
mother, in the same breath her power, even her name, is
declined. If there is declension, there is no conjugation: every
active verb except one (who *calls* herself me) is in the first person
singular. In fact, as always when Derrida invokes the name of
the mother, the true work of subjugation is that of the male
negating that obtrusive negative, the female. Swallowing her
whole, as Zeus swallowed Metis, he calls his mother in himself,
for himself and to himself. Two negatives, in fact, produce a
positive, and a man/woman is born fully armed, like Athena,
from the brain of the writer.

Since Freud (see Schneider, 1985), Sartre and Derrida – in
spite of the differences in their thought, which lead at times to
open attack, by Sartre on Freud and by Derrida on Sartre (G:
18–20,302–10) – share this preoccupation with masculine self-
generation, it is, I think, fair to ask if this is one way of writing
illegitimacy. Freud (see above), Sartre (see Chapter 8), and
Derrida (see Bennington, 1991) all document their own Oedipus
complexes. Each suggests in a different way delegitimation as an
escape from the law of the Father. Each replays the dream of
union with the virgin mother. However, each, in the end,
returns to male domination, either to the patriarchal world-view
or to that of the masculine androgyne, of whom Leonardo and
Genet are the models. Each should make the confession found in
Glas: 'I wormed my way in as a third party, between his mother
and himself. I gave him/her. I betrayed him/her' (GE: 203).[32]
Each uses delegitimation and the dream of the divine, miraculous
child as a means of eventual relegitimation in the transcendent
world of art and the mind. Genius can assert itself by reshaping
the genius of the other in its own image.

11

Conclusion

As my study has progressed, I have been constantly surprised not only by my own findings, but by the intensity of the reactions they have provoked in others. I started with the intention of examining a particular relationship between personal writing, the name and the signature. I had not anticipated that the investigation of the matronym would also lead towards the discovery that a whole field of human behaviour, that linked with illegitimacy, had been so extensively governed, and to a large extent continues to be governed, by myth and mythopoesis. These are myths of excess. In the recorded annals of bastardy there is no middle way: success must be resounding or failure ignominious.

We have seen the dichotomy of the classical myths. On the one hand the divine child, the saviour, the founder of cities; on the other the exile, revengeful, criminal, spurned and spurning, against whom every man's hand is turned. What is less obvious is the way in which these myths continue to operate in the maternal psyche. Both maternal fears and maternal desires, exacerbated by the stresses of defying convention, can produce excess, often a primary need for recognition and relegitimation at any price, sometimes an almost caricatural virilisation or feminisation,[1] and a kind of 'with your shield or on it' approach to success. One must remember these maternal drives as one looks at the personal myths which are embedded in the life and writing of the great bastards, and see how their phantasms of being queen, saviour, creator, utopian remain dreams of excess and success even at their most revolutionary. Rebellion is the other constant factor in these lives and autographies: the dream of excess is also one of sacrifice and justice

212

for the excluded. The sub-text is that the mother, through her child, will have her wrongs righted and even achieve her apotheosis.

In the case of the delegitimation that works by the proclamation of bastardy, either real or assumed, public reception is also intensified and influenced by mythologisation. The monster or the hybrid, king/commoner, man/woman, Messiah/whore, is credited with the power to produce social mutation, and this mutation or hybridity is both needed and feared. Public perception simplifies and exaggerates, believing the intellectual or emotional fantasies found in delegitimatory writing to be realities, and either hailing the outsider as saviour or, more frequently, 'cleansing' the body politic or the family group by the sacrifice or exile of the scapegoat. These ambivalent reactions are the stuff from which the signature emerges.

Of course, the signature is ambivalent in itself, produced as it is both by the writer's choices and by the public's perceptions, and it becomes doubly ambivalent when the very name it employs is called into question. But the ability to tap into the mythology of bastardy is only given to a few, and there is an even more notorious difficulty of access to the positive power of such myths. In our early examples, such as Elizabeth I or Maurice de Saxe, the exploitation of positive myth is most conspicuously available to those who combined royal parentage with brains and determination. But, with the spread of literacy, another enabling possibility emerges. This resides in the control of the master tongue and the force of the symbolic; and Elizabeth most conspicuously used this potential as well as the mere advantage of her royal blood.

Access to education is what permits writing, and it is only through writing their illegitimacy and having the texts published that the proclamation of delegitimation and the resultant signature become a possibility for social outcasts. This may be enabled by historical accident (if one can so call a revolution), as in the pamphlets of Olympe de Gouges; by the fervour of true believers, as in the utopian schemes of Flora Tristan; or by the curiosity of the newly literate about a life of unusual heroism, as in the case of Louise Michel. The very chance to be remembered, the possibility that the personal myth will relive as the writing emerges from oblivion, is denied to all but a handful. The lives of the rest remain in darkness, dominated by the negative

213

mythology and the social exclusion catalogued by historians like Laslett and Mitterauer.

Those who succeed in proclaiming their delegitimation by laying public claim to bastardy and who use the name of the mother as the sign of their emancipation from the law of the Father constitute, as we have seen, a form of noise in the system – sometimes the social, sometimes the political or literary system. It is in the interest of stability that this noise should be silenced. But the noise makers have something going for them. The more powerful and public the initial delegitimation, the stronger will be the forces of the eventual relegitimation. When cumulative noise has produced a mutation in the system, working, as Serres puts it, like the grit in the oyster, then the inevitable reterritorialisation will take place. The only reason we know some of these texts, even ones which are now canonical, like Stendhal's journal or Baudelaire's letters, is because of those shifts in feeling and taste which reterritorialise and even canonise what has previously been banned, silenced or execrated. How much more rare and remarkable must be the relegitimation of those who were triply excluded: female, socially unacceptable and illegitimate. Yet, like the royal or divine pariah eventually recuperated by myth or ideology, the fate of the few whose texts survive is to be recuperated into the law of the Father, or that of the Mother in the form of the new feminist canon.

The sheer extent of silencing and the overwhelming distortion of social reality in the service of ideology that such conscious or unconscious censorship produces have perhaps been the greatest revelation. The study of family histories and of genealogies put together in conformity with the principle of descent through the name of the father has made me realise just how our view of the family has been falsified by the omission of 'left-handed connections' and of children born 'on the wrong side of the blanket'. This realisation has been confirmed by a form of fieldwork I had not anticipated. Whenever I lecture on aspects of this study I am approached by people anxious to tell me their family history: the oral history which does not reach the books. Theirs are not just the poignant stories springing from the thousands of forced adoptions, but also tales of the courage and ingenuity of mothers and grandmothers determined to keep the child. These episodes of the young 'widow' helped or exploited as she endeavoured to support her child, or the heroic shifts of mother or sister, sometimes faking months of pregnancy to pretend the bastard was their own offspring, are tales not only of tragedy and heroism but of censorship and repression. One thing I hope this book will do is to encourage readers to re-examine their own family history in terms of a 'female gen-ealogy', and to release these hidden narratives from silence, stigma and repression.

The distortion in social records produced by the official inscription of legitimate genealogies is paralleled by the psycho-logical distortion produced by the many endeavours to uni-versalise the Oedipus complex beyond the period and the gender to which it belongs. As I did the research into my case studies, I realised the importance of all the different family models sub-sumed and reduced in importance by the excessive generalisation of those who try to make the Oedipus complex a shoe to fit all feet. Behind the writers I deal with is a history not merely of single motherhood but of alternative family structures. In fact, in the cases I look at, upbringing by the mother alone is unusual. Parenting is doubled or extended: brothers, sisters and a com-plicated network of carers (or abusers) in the form of wet-nurses, family servants, tutors and governesses often play a far greater part in the formation of the writer's shifting identity than does the father or even the mother.

But the thing that surprised me most was to discover the absolutely vital role played by grandparents in permitting so many of these children's access to the symbolic. It is not just a question of material care, though this is obviously important, but of the fact that the crucial structure behind the develop-ment of so many gifted children is one of double mothering or fathering or both. When a child is brought up across the generations, as the autobiographies of George Sand, Louise Michel, Jean-Paul Sartre and Thomas Bernhard attest, the internalised conflict may be merely that of attitudes and genera-tions or also one of classes and cultures. Sometimes apparently traumatic, such an upbringing produces a layering, a depth of understanding and often a depth of revolt, which can be an invaluable stimulus to writing, and more particularly to opposi-tional writing. While, in each of these particular cases, a cultivated grandparent provides the educative stimulus (or tyranny), there can exist at the same time, for Sand and Michel

215

as for Violette Leduc, the enabling access to an oral tradition provided by peasant or working-class grandparents. The important thing is the mix, the hybridity, which parallels that of the birth itself.[2]

What they perceive as the hybridity of their birth leads these writers to take advantage of the fluidity of the resulting identity. When they create themselves through autobiography there ensues an exciting multiplicity of narratives, particularly in the case of positive mythologisation. I would include as positive even such an apparently negative choice of personal myths of abasement and revenge as that made by Genet and Leduc, because they always see their self-accusation and indeed demonisation as justified by their role as authors and creators, and they are never in any doubt of the power of the word and the genius that springs from it. My studies have also shown ample evidence of that other fluidity, the fluidity of naming of which one mark is the assumption of the name of the mother, and another the use of the pseudonym. The effects of the extended family and multiple upbringing, but also of the demand for greater social justice common to the illegitimate, are marked, as I hope to have shown, by the shifting and multiple voices to be heard in their writings. These are writings which constantly display a dialogism of gender, of age, of class, of race and of language.

This capacity for the creation of the self *ab nihilo*, a fluidity of identity, a kind of androgyny of the mind and soul, are what give the writing of illegitimacy its power of subversion. It is this power that the pseudo-bastards and the delegitimators by proxy are seeking when they adopt the name of the mother or the identity of the other. In this other verbal existence the sexist, like Baudelaire, can play the woman; the straight, like Sartre, can try on being gay; and the bourgeois, like Derrida, can adopt the bastards' revenge on the society which obstinately refuses to reject them in their true personae. But in the end they suffer the fate of those scientists Stanislaw Lem, in his great novel *Solaris*, called 'the knights of the holy contact'. Seeking to take advantage of the secrets of alterity, the penetrators become the penetrated. By taking the circuitous 'bastard path', they achieve multiplicity, but this very multiplicity deprives them of ultimate control. By dabbling in the sinister they call into question their very dexterity in wearing the mask of the other. Thus, once again, the writing of illegitimacy becomes the noise in the system.

For example, Derrida's attempt to theorise and reterritorialise the name of the mother escapes from his control. In spite of the verbal sleight of hand by which he attempts to give birth to himself through the 'immaculate conception' of Jean Genet, in the last resort, as he says himself, 'the mother remains'.

The last and most unexpected outcome of my research was that it actually taught me the name of the mother. I have to thank Louise Michel for giving a meaning to the name Myriam. Myriam is a potent trinity. She stands at once for the revolution that will bring equality and social justice, for the bonds between mother and daughter, and for the love between friend and friend, all three stronger than death. I opened my book by dedicating it to my mother. I close it, as did Michel, by evoking Myriam, the name of the mother.

Notes

1 PERFORMANCES OF EXCLUSION

1 I am taking myth to be a narrative, or narrative corpus, which is underpinned, at either the public or the personal level, by a deep structure of belief. It is not, in my parlance, mere fraud or fiction. See Chapter 2 for further discussion.

2 I certainly do not subscribe to Jung's more extreme positions, but it is a fact that, for example, an archetype of the 'shadow', or dark double, exists in all cultures, and, in European society, tends to graft itself to prejudices about the 'bar sinister'.

3 Stendhal says this of his own autobiography, *Life of Henry Brulard* (1973: 380). See also p.427: 'My memory is only a novel composed for this purpose.'

4 See Michel Serres, *Le Parasite* (1980) for the implications of the concept of noise in communication theory in the study of literature.

5 I have endeavoured to capitalise Father in the expression law of the Father when using it in a Lacanian sense as a whole societal system of symbolisation and control, and not merely individual patriarchal structures or family constraints.

6 Gilbert and Gubar (1984: 26) extend this notion of impropriety to the whole system of female nomination: 'Her "proper" name, therefore, is always in a way *im*proper because it is not, in the French sense, *propre*, her own, either to have or to give.'

7 All translations are my own, unless otherwise indicated.

8 Chapters 3 and 4 of Geoffrey Hartman's *Saving the Text* (1981) contain a useful discussion of these theories of Derrida and their link with Lacanian thought.

9 This was made easier by the Spanish system of naming, which mentions both matronym and patronym.

10 Another myth which yields an interesting maternal sub-text is that of the titan Antaeus, who was invincible as long as he remained in contact with his mother, Gaia, the Earth.

11 See Nicole Loraux, *Les Expériences de Tirésias* (1989) for an account of the role of myths of the feminine in Greek culture.

218

12 *Dictionnaire de la conversation et de la lecture*, t. IV (1833), article '*Bâtard* et *Abâtardissement*', signé J.-J. Virey.

13 It should be remembered that Leonardo, a bastard in dispute with his legitimate brothers, is scarcely a dispassionate witness, but he is quoting popular wisdom.

14 She mentioned the 'testament de la paria' in a letter to the Abbé Constant of 3 March 1844 (1980: 194). He gathered together her ideas and reworked them in his own, more hysterical, style after her premature death.

15 In a conversation, M. Marin mentioned the life of Angélique Arnaud as an example of the authenticating narrative.

2 MYTH AND PSYCHOANALYSIS: LEGITIMATE AND ILLEGITIMATE

1 Compare the ambivalence of myths of Satan and their use as anti-myths in, for example, Baudelaire's poems entitled 'Révolte' (OC I: 121–5).

2 According to Marina Warner, in *Alone of All Her Sex: The Myth and Cult of the Virgin Mary*: 'For Matthew the Virgin birth was a symbol that gave Jesus legitimacy as a God, and was not inconsistent with his legitimacy as a social being with an official socially recognized father' (1976: 21).

3 This theme has engendered many literary variations, most notably Margaret Atwood's *The Handmaid's Tale*.

4 Jean-Pierre Vernant, for example, reads Sophocles' version in its original context of the Athens of the fifth century BC (Vernant and Vidal-Naquet, 1972).

5 SE stands hereafter for the 1981 Standard Edition of the *Complete Works* of Freud.

6 He certainly protests rather much, first placing the dream under the heading 'absurd dreams', and then arguing 'per contrario' that since the dream is about his father, his father cannot possibly be the subject of the dream (SE V: 436).

7 I will also be using the Pontalis edition of the text (Freud, 1987), for which P will be used hereafter.

8 The reading of *The Novel of Leonardo da Vinci* by the Russian writer Dmitry Merezhkovsky triggered Freud's interest in Leonardo.

9 Though Eissler (1961: 114) claims he may have stayed with her longer, and figured on his grandfather's return as a tax deduction!

10 See Leclaire, 1968: 52 for an account of possible associations and repressions in connection with *Geier*.

11 It is symptomatic that Rank does not comment on the biblical story, but merely quotes the Gospels (1909: 46).

12 This is in the original in the text, showing the link with the Oedipal reading of *Hamlet*.

13 This is supported by recent evidence from black communities. Heilbrun suggests that the father's absence, the 'failure to perform

a nuclear or Freudian role has aided daughters, and where the mother had sufficient strength and support, even the sons. That is not a conclusion likely to be granted by many' (Boose and Flowers, 1989: 421).

14 Compare the case study of Jean Genet.

15 Eissler's study is interesting, since he goes out of his way to support the findings of his mentor, Freud, and yet he scrupulously records the massive evidence which militates against them.

16 Most old women in Leonardo's work are depicted as viragos and harpies.

17 Freud states (SE: 112) that the representation of St Anne, the Virgin and Child was unusual in Italian art, whereas in fact the *Santa Anna Metterza* was a very common theme (see Maïdani-Gérard in P: 183–90). It is true, however, that the youth of the St Anne figure in Leonardo's various versions is unusual. This is the rarity, not the theme itself.

18 For a really detailed study of both manuscript and iconic evidence of the true Leonardo obscured by the Freudian text, see Michael Holly's 'Writing Leonardo Backwards' (1992).

19 See, however, *Beyond the Pleasure Principle*: 'His own attempt to make a baby himself, carried out with tragic seriousness, fails shamefully' (SE XVIII: 21).

20 It also more than compensates for her annoyance that she is unable to urinate in a standing position, the principal reaction of 2- and 3-year-old girls to their 'organic inferiority', to use Freud's expression (cit. Anzieu, 1977: 253).

21 See Brenkman, 1992: 949, and also Chapter 10 below, where Freud's missing double mother, his old nurse, is discussed.

22 Womb envy does not adequately translate Olivier's *envie du sein*, which is both womb envy and desire for the breast and for power of reproduction. *Sein* = both womb and breast.

23 See Maclean, 1974 for a discussion of this point.

24 See Mozet, 1988 and van Rossum-Guyon, 1990. Schneider, 1986 also has an interesting account of the ambivalence of Freud's own attitudes towards sexual reproduction and textual reproduction.

25 I owe my information here to Leah Marcus, 'Erasing the Stigma of Daughterhood' (Boose and Flowers, 1989: 400–17).

3   MYTHICAL HISTORIES, HISTORICAL MYTHS

1 Yet another definition of myth, which equates it much more closely to ideology, is to be found in Roland Barthes, *Mythologies* (1957).

2 For a very interesting discussion of the implications and their relation to the mythology of male birth-giving, see Warner, 1987: 117–24.

3 Thanks to Ross Chambers for this piece of recondite information.

4 Cf. Le Doeuff, 1989: 306. Since 1970, the woman can still only declare the child hers and her lover's if the husband agrees, or if she

can prove he could not have engendered it. The husband, however, can recognise a child conceived extra-maritally without the consent of his wife.

5 The type of double familial structure, with legitimate children and natural children sharing a household and all bearing the father's name, common among the feudal and Renaissance nobility, is still quite normal in many societies. One example is that of Fidel Castro, who was the second child of his father's second family, begotten from the family cook. He then perpetuated this double family of the left hand and right hand in his own generation, in a way typical of Caribbean society. Of course, in many of these cases, the father refuses responsibility and the offspring bear the matronym. Indeed, in some societies, such as those of the Caribbean, the norm changes as illegitimate births outnumber legitimate ones (Hartley, 1980). It is interesting to speculate on the forms taken by the inscription of the self in a society where the bastard becomes the unmarked social norm, and the right-handed bearer of the family line the marked exception.

6 The expression 'an infant Hercules' is also used in England in the 1790s to describe Colonel George Fitzclarence, Mrs Jordan's bastard son by the Duke of Clarence (Kelly, 1980: 119).

7 A possibility which suggests itself, and is less far-fetched than one might suppose, is that the real mother might have been Eugène's 17-year-old sister. Such substitutions are not uncommon in united families; the poet Aragon, for instance, believed his grandmother was his mother and his mother was his sister until he was in his teens.

8 Another tradition makes Esmeria Anne's mother, see Warner, 1976:47.

9 For an historical account of such structures, see Peter Laslett's theory of bastardy-prone sub-sets. Laslett tends to find these in lower socio-economic strata in England, though there is an active sub-set among English men of letters in the eighteenth and nineteenth centuries (1980: 231).

10 Paul-Lévy (1981: 63) mentions the recurring model of bastard families among both peasants and aristocracy and quotes René Pillorget's *La Tige et le rameau*, Paris: Calman-Lévy, 1979.

11 Ambrière will be hereafter A.

12 David Garrioch has pointed out to me that 'studies based on legal authorities often forget that these authorities are interpreting and imposing their own readings. Of course, the attempt by male jurists to tighten up the law in this way still supports the basic argument about a shift in attitudes, but it is part of a dialogue, a struggle.'

13 And in a series of plays and novels, ranging from Diderot's *Le Fils naturel* (1757) and Restif de la Bretonne's *La Fille naturelle* (1769) to the *Le Fils naturel* (1858) of Alexandre Dumas fils and *La Bâtarde* of Xavier de Montepin.

14 'George said, he [Wringim] seemed to have some demon for a familiar. Dal answered, that he did not wonder a bit at that, for the young spark was the third in a direct line who had all been children

of adultery; and it was well known that all such were born half deils [devils] themselves, and nothing was more likely than that they should hold intercourse with their fellows' (Hogg, 1969:67).

15 According to Partridge's *Dictionary of Slang*, 'ring', to change illicitly, dates from *c*. 1785, and 'ring-in', to insert or substitute fraudulently, from *c*. 1810.

16 For a history of this concept and of female iconography and idealisation generally, see Warner, 1987.

17 Enfantin, while willing to breed children, was notoriously unwilling to take responsibility for them. His 'liberation' of women was purely on his own terms (Grogan, 1992: 132).

4 A FEMALE GENEALOGY: THE EN-GENDERING OF GEORGE SAND

1 All factual material on Sand's life and family is taken from the text and notes of Georges Lubin's excellent edition of Sand's *Oeuvres autobiographiques,* I and II (Sand, 1970 and 1971). This text will hereafter be referred to as OA I and II.

2 This may be contrasted with the noble lady who regularly climbed four flights of stairs to see her great-great-grandchildren (OA I: 676).

3 Her parents were married on 5 June 1804 and she was born on 1 July.

4 Suleiman (1985) gives a particularly telling account and analysis of a story dealing with a similar relationship, Rosellen Brown's *Autobiography of My Mother*, where grandmother and mother battle for a child. In this case the story has an unhappy ending.

5 The other possible answer is the fear of marital rape, another unspoken shadow over many marriages, especially of child brides, but not exclusively, as texts as different as Balzac's *Physiologie du mariage* (The Physiology of Marriage) and Sartre's *Les Mots* bear witness. However, since Aurore was already 16 or 17, quite normal for a bride at the time, this seems unlikely. It is unusual that her brother was actually called on to intervene. See OA I: 1243–4.

6 There has been a series of studies taking this attitude, e.g. Danahy, 1978 and even, to some extent, Rea, 1985. They seem to stem from the views of Hélène Deutsch in *The Psychology of Women* (1945), which sees Fadette's 'low self-esteem' as springing from her lack of identification with the acceptable social model.

7 The same pattern is repeated in the old beggar-woman of '*Le Chêne parlant*' ('The Talking Oak'), which was one of the last things Sand published. She also leaves immense wealth to her protégé.

8 I have decided, rather against my will, to omit a discussion of the first formation and formulation of fantasy in the little Aurore by her creation of a divinity called Corambé, and narrating to herself long epics concerning him/her. This is because the literature on this subject is already too vast to be easily summarised. Berthier and

Vareille in Vierne, 1983, give some indication of recent thinking.

9 The most comprehensive attack on Sand ever made is that in *Mon coeur mis à nu* (OC I: 686–7). One little-remarked facet of this attack on Sand's 'vulgarity' and 'prolixity' is that it includes in the heads of accusation 'What she said about her mother', which comes oddly from a writer who attacked his own mother both publicly and privately. It shows the impact that an honest female assessment of the stages of a mother–daughter relationship could have, and highlights the swings between idealisation and denigration which characterise an equally intense mother–son bond.

10 'Mais le génie n'est que l'*enfance retrouvée* à volonté, l'enfance douée maintenant, pour s'exprimer, d'organes viriles [!] et de l'esprit analytique qui lui permet d'ordonner la somme de matériaux involontairement amassée' (OC II: 690).

11 'Je revins sur la terrasse et j'appelai ma mère; la voix répéta le mot d'une voix très douce mais très nette, et cela me donna beaucoup à penser. Je grossis ma voix, j'appelai mon propre nom, qui me fut rendu aussitôt, mais plus confusément. . . . L'impression la plus étrange pour moi était d'entendre mon propre nom répété avec ma propre voix. Alors il me vint à l'esprit une explication bizarre. C'est que j'étais double, et qu'il y avait autour de moi un autre *moi* que je ne pouvais pas voir, mais qui me voyait toujours, puisqu'il me répondait toujours. . . . J'en conclus que toutes choses et toutes gens avaient leur reflet, leur double, leur autre *moi*, et je souhaitai vivement voir le mien' (OA I: 573–4).

12 'C'est dans ce refuge que naît l'écriture: refuge doublement uterin, puisque le boudoir de la grand-mère est visité par le grillon, substitut de l'oiseau maternel: ainsi sont enfin réconciliées les deux mères, et l'identité recouvrée permet la création' (1977: 567).

13 The speculations on Sand's choice of name are enormous, particularly because of her appropriation of the first syllable of her lover's name, Sandeau, as her own. Busine, 1984, takes an interesting stand, firmly gendered masculine, as does Vareille, 1983. Laugaa, 1989, produces a fairly speculative view of the unconscious motivation of the signifier. Perhaps the most convincing is Freadman, 1988.

14 'On m'a baptisée, obscure et insouciante, entre le manuscrit d'*Indiana*, qui était alors tout mon avenir, et un billet de mille francs qui était en ce moment-là toute ma fortune. Ce fut un contrat, un nouveau mariage entre le pauvre apprenti poète que j'étais et l'humble muse qui m'avait consolée dans mes peines. Dieu me garde de rien déranger à ce que j'ai laissé faire à la destinée. Qu'est-ce qu'un nom dans notre monde révolutionné et révolutionnaire? Un numéro pour ceux qui ne font rien, une enseigne ou une devise pour ceux qui travaillent ou combattent. Celui qu'on m'a donné, je l'ai fait moi-même et moi seule après coup, par mon labeur' (OA II: 140).

15 'Imaginez-vous, à me lire, que je fais mon portrait? Patience: c'est seulement mon modèle' (1928:6).

16 Note that we are dealing with a toponym this time, but the archbishop had an aristocratic mother (OA I: 1064).

17 'C'était le compagnon de mes premières années; c'était le bâtard né heureux, c'est-à-dire l'enfant gâté de chez nous . . . . Dans certains milieux, l'enfant de l'amour inspire un tel intérêt qu'il arrive à être, sinon le roi de la famille, celui qui ose tout et à qui l'on passe tout, parce que les entrailles ont besoin de le dédommager de l'abandon de la société. Par le fait, n'étant rien officiellement, et ne pouvant prétendre à rien légalement dans mon intérieur, Hippolyte y avait toujours fait dominer son caractère turbulent, son bon coeur et sa mauvaise tête' (OA II: 432).

18 I was appalled enough at the casual account of daily cruelty to re-read Freud's 'A Child is Beaten' (SE XVII), and was struck by the curious reluctance here, as in his volte-face on the incidence of incestuous child abuse, to face the fact that these were not mere fantasies, but that gaining sexual satisfaction by beating children was a commonplace.

19 It is very revealing that she feels compelled to tell her readers that, for the first fifteen years of her life, she actually believed family gossip that she might have been a ring-in, born in 1802 or 1803, and substituted for a child born in 1804 who died shortly after (OA I: 468).

20 '"De quelles billevesées embarrasses-tu ta pauvre cervelle, rejeton dégénéré de ma race orgueilleuse? De quelle chimère d'égalité remplis-tu tes rêves? L'amour n'est pas ce que tu crois; les hommes ne seront jamais ce que tu espères. Ils ne sont faits que pour être trompés par les rois, par les femmes et par eux-mêmes"' (OA I: 31).

21 See Suleiman, 1985, for a very illuminating discussion of such relationships.

5 OPPOSITION AND REVOLUTION: OLYMPE DE GOUGES AND THE RIGHTS OF THE DISPOSSESSED

1 I use the term 'oppositional' in the way defined by Michel de Certeau in 'On the Oppositional Practices of Everyday Life' (1980).

2 As de Certeau says: 'Theoretical questioning . . . does *not forget* [would that it were true!], cannot forget that in addition to the relationship of these scientific discourses to one another, there is also their common relation with what they have taken care to exclude from their field in order to constitute it' (1984: 61).

3 In taking the work of Olympe de Gouges as my main example, I quote extensively from Olympe de Gouges, *Oeuvres*, edited and introduced by Benoîte Groult (1986), in the series 'Mille et une femmes', hereafter G. Unless otherwise referenced, de Gouges texts come from this edition. All translations are my own.

4 'Tenter une deuxième révolution dans la révolution semblait dément et complètement chimérique.'

5 See, for example, Charles Baudelaire, 'Portraits de Maîtresses' in *Petits poèmes en prose* (OC I).

6 'Les femmes ont fait plus de mal que de bien. La contrainte et la dissimulation ont été leur partage. Ce que la force leur avait ravi, la ruse leur a rendu; elles ont eu recours à toutes les ressources de leurs charmes, et le plus irréprochable ne leur résistait pas. Le poison, le fer, tout leur était soumis; elles commandaient au crime comme à la vertu. Le gouvernement français, surtout, a dépendu, pendant des siècles, de l'administration nocturne des femmes; le cabinet n'avait point de secret pour leur indiscrétion; ambassade, commandement, ministère, présidence, pontificat, cardinalat, enfin tout ce qui caractérise la sottise des hommes, profane et sacré, tout a été soumis à la cupidité et à l'ambition de ce sexe autrefois méprisable et respecté, et depuis la révolution, respectable et méprisé' (G: 107).

7 Olympe was her mother's second Christian name, and Gouze (not Gouges) the name of her mother's husband.

8 'L'homme de génie, l'homme éclairé, ne dédaigne jamais le fruit littéraire qu'a produit le seul jeu de la Nature. Je peux me dire même un de ses enfants favoris. Elle a tout fait pour moi . . .' (cit. Blanc, 1989: 14).

9 'Si les personnes de votre sexe deviennent conséquentes et profondes dans leurs ouvrages, que deviendrons-nous, nous autres hommes, aujourd'hui si superficiels et légers? Adieu la supériorité dont nous étions si orgueilleux. Les dames nous feront la loi.... Cette révolution sera dangereuse .... Les femmes peuvent écrire mais il leur est défendu, pour le bonheur du monde, de s'y livrer avec prétention' (G: 20).

10 'Quelquefois je demande des avis, que je ne suis jamais; cependant je vous donne pour épigraphe un vers latin; moi, du latin! moi qui à peine sais épeler le français!' ('Sometimes I ask for advice, which I never follow; yet I give you for epigraph a line of Latin; me, using Latin! when I can scarcely spell French!') (de Gouges, 1790: 35).

11 'Il faut que j'obtienne une indulgence plénière pour toutes mes fautes qui sont plus graves que légères: fautes de français, fautes de construction, fautes de style, fautes de savoir, fautes d'intéresser, fautes d'esprit, fautes de génie .... En effet, on ne m'a rien appris. Elevée dans un pays où l'on parle mal le français, je ne connais pas les principes, je ne sais rien. Je fais trophée de mon ignorance, je dicte avec mon âme, jamais avec mon esprit' (G: 20).

12 The whole question of the use of a scribe, and his or her modification of the printed text, is given insufficient weight in consideration of documents, particularly pre-1800. I suspect that Olympe's voluminous verbal production, and indeed her style, must have been considerably edited by the sheer necessities of transcription.

13 Paule-Marie Duhet remarks on the marginality and lack of social stability common to the backgrounds of the four outspoken heroines of the Revolution, Théroigne de Méricourt, Etta Palm, Claire Lacombe and Olympe de Gouges (1971: 78).

In the high-school student revolts of 1990 in Paris, a girl, Audrey, emerged as spokesperson, who had exactly the same profile, poor background, single mother, exceptional intelligence and burning determination to right the wrongs of her peers. 'The third of a family of five children, she never knew her father ... and was brought up by a mother who came from a state orphanage and is a charwoman. "I'm very strict about school", says the mother. "At 14, the director of the orphanage took me away from school to apprentice me."' *Libération*, 13 November 1990.

14 Employers generally prefer to allow union activity rather than admit employees to boards of management. The history of Australia shows that the 'free' propertied classes would admit the 'currency' to real economic power, but that attempts by the convict-bred to gain seats on the Legislative Council were seen as attacking the establishment and hence, in my terms, as revolutionary.

15 'On a raison d'exclure les femmes des affaires publiques et civiles. Rien n'est plus opposé à leur vocation naturelle.'

16 'Nous ne voulons d'empire que par les coeurs et de trône que dans vos coeurs.'

17 Théroigne de Méricourt, a *demi-mondaine* who also assumed an aristocratic pseudonym, became a standard-bearer of the revolution, the heroine of the Faubourg Saint-Antoine. She was subjected to the ultimate indignity for 'women who thought they were men', the public *fessée,* upending and beating on the naked behind. She finally endured the 'fate worse than death' of revolutionary women, incarceration for twenty-four years in an insane asylum.

18 See especially the *supplément* of wall posters in *Les Femmes dans la révolution française*, 1982.

19 In *Les femmes dans la révolution française*, 1982.

20 'Tout m'assure, Madame, qu'éloignée de tout conseil pernicieux, seule, recueillie avec vous-même, vous sentez dans votre coeur tout ce qui se passe dans le mien, tout ce que peut éprouver un individu sans reproches.' This comes from a series of pamphlets without date or publisher's name kept in the Bibliothèque Nationale, but appears from its context to belong to 1790.

21 Page 3 of the undated pamphlet with no name of publisher which is reprinted in *Les Femmes dans la révolution française* (henceforward DF).

22 Blanc (1989: 44) maintains that Olympe puts herself on stage, often as illegitimate heroine or repenting courtesan, in nearly all her many plays.

23 'Je ne sais si la Religion, et si Dieu même a commandé d'étouffer les cris du sang illégitime, mais la voix de la Nature parle en moi, elle me dit que sa loi est celle que Dieu lui-même a préscrite à l'homme.'

24 Benoîte Groult gives a hilarious example of a doctor who in 1904 decided that Olympe de Gouges suffered from *paranoia reformatoria* (G:62).

25 'L'homme seul s'est fagoté un principe de cette exception.'

26 'La liberté et la justice consistent à rendre tout ce qui appartient à autrui.'

27 'la femme a le droit de monter sur l'échafaud; elle doit avoir également celui de monter à la Tribune'.

28 'la constitution est nulle, si la majorité des individus qui composent la Nation, n'a pas coopéré à sa rédaction'.

29 'Dans les siècles de corruption vous n'avez régné que sur la faiblesse des hommes ... quelles que soient les barrières que l'on vous oppose, il est en votre pouvoir de vous affranchir; vous n'avez qu'à le vouloir.'

30 'Le mariage est le tombeau de la confiance et de l'amour. La femme mariée peut impunément donner des bâtards à son mari, et la fortune qui ne leur appartient pas. Celle qui ne l'est pas, n'a qu'un faible droit: les lois anciennes et inhumaines lui refusoient ce droit sur le nom & sur le bien de leur père, pour ses enfans, et l'on n'a pas fait de nouveaux lois sur cette matière' (DF: 16).

31 This was again way ahead of its time in its perception of the damage done by slavery and colonisation. Even today the figures for illegitimacy, and single maternity in conditions of extreme poverty, reach epidemic proportions in former slave societies. See Hartley, 1980.

32 'Rappelez-vous cette femme hautaine, la Roland, qui se crut propre à gouverner la République et qui courut à sa perte . . . .

Rappelez-vous cette virago, cette femme-homme, l'impudente Olympe de Gouges, qui abandonna tous les soins de son ménage, voulut politiquer et commit des crimes . . . . Cet oubli des vertus de son sexe l'a conduite à l'échafaud.

Tous ces êtres immoraux ont été anéantis sous le fer vengeur des lois. Et vous voudriez les imiter? Non! Vous sentirez que vous ne serez vraiment intéressantes et dignes d'estime que lorsque vous serez ce que la Nature a voulu que vous fussiez. Nous voulons que les femmes soient respectées, c'est pourquoi nous les forcerons à se respecter elles-mêmes'(G: 59).

6   THE MALE/FEMALE MESSIAH: FLORA TRISTAN

1 See Desanti, 1972 and Grogan, 1992.

2 For the iconography of this figure, and a fuller history, see Warner, 1987.

3 Perhaps because the mother did not stand up to her brother when he said that Flora should go back to her husband.

4 'Longtemps nous avons voyagé *seule*, et étrangère, nous connaissons, par conséquent, tout le malheur de cette cruelle situation. Nous nous sommes trouvée étrangère à Paris, dans des villes de province, dans des villages, aux eaux. Nous avons parcouru aussi plusieurs contrées d'Angleterre et son immense capitale. Nous avons visité une grande partie de l'Amérique, et nos paroles ne seront que le retentissement de notre ame [sic]; car nous ne savons parler que de choses que nous avons éprouvées nous-même' (1835:4).

5 'La maîtresse d'hôtel le craindra, les personnes qui habitent chez elle n'en douteront pas, et enfin les domestiques s'en porteront garants' (ibid.: 6).

6 I find it very odd that Desanti (1972: 165) should accuse her of frigidity and inhibition. In the light of the time and context, I should have thought the reason for her refusal of intercourse was clear.

7 Hereafter P.

8 'Ensuite je ne vois pas pourquoi vous vous occupez du style sous un autre rapport que sous celui des règles grammaticales Je signe mes articles, des lors j en assume la responsabilité. Que si les *fins connaissances* y trouvent des fautes, qu'ils m'attaquent je saurai motiver mes réponses. Tout mon ouvrage est parsemé de ce que vous nommez des hardiesses qui me font sortir de la monotonie du *goût académicien*, ce sont elles qui feront de moi ce que Dieu a voulu que je fus, un être à part'(1980: 69). The misspellings and lack of punctuation are in the original text.

9 'Au surplus, avant de commencer ce livre, j'ai examiné attentivement toutes les conséquences possibles de ma narration, et, quelque pénibles que fussent les devoirs que ma conscience m'imposait, ma foi d'apôtre n'a pas chancelé; je n'ai pas reculé devant leur accomplissement' (P: 60).

10 '"Insensés! Je vous plains et ne vous hais pas; vos dédains me font mal, mais ne troublent pas ma conscience. Les mêmes lois et les mêmes préjugés dont je suis victime remplissent également votre vie d'amertume; n'ayant pas le courage de vous soustraire à leur joug, vous vous en rendez les serviles instruments. Ah! si vous traitez de la sorte ceux que l'élévation de leur âme, la générosité de leur coeur porteraient à se dévouer à votre cause, je vous le prédis, vous resterez encore longtemps dans votre phase de malheur."

Cet élan me rendit mon courage, je me sentis plus calme; Dieu, à mon insu, était venu habiter en moi' (P: 8).

11 It is notable that, many years later, Tristan tells her new disciple, Eléonore Blanc, 'You shall be my Saint John' (Desanti, 1972: 280).

12 'Le peuple était dans l'ivresse; il battait des mains, sautait de joie et criait de toute sa force: Vive Jésus Christ! Vive la sainte Vierge! Vive notre seigneur *don José*! Vive notre seigneurissime le pape! Viva! Viva! Viva!' (P: 146).

13 Hereafter ME I and II.

14 'La femme de Lima, dans toutes les positions de la vie, est toujours *elle*; jamais elle ne subit aucune contrainte: jeune fille, elle échappe à la domination de ses parents par la liberté que lui donne sa costume; quand elle se marie, elle ne prend pas le nom de son mari, garde le sien et toujours reste maîtresse chez elle' (P: 338).

15 Like Zamyatin some hundred years later, in *We* (1924).

16 Cf. 'Denn die einen sind im Dunkeln / Und die andern sind im Licht. / Und man siehet die im Lichte / Die im Dunkeln sieht man nicht' ('For some are in the darkness / And others in the light, / And one sees those in the light / Those in darkness are not seen') (Brecht, 1955: 109).

17 According to Shoshana Felman, it also means an effeminate man (cit. Kadish, 1991: 56).

18 'Notre instinct est précisément ce qui nous rend si parfaites. Ce que vous apprenez, vous autres, nous le sentons, nous.'

19 For the political implications of this hybridisation, see Kadish, 1991: 52–63.

20 This curious divinity, which becomes more and more a personal manifestation, is influenced not only by Enfantin, but even more by the spurious prophet, Ganneau, who preached a maternal/paternal divinity called Mapa (Desanti, 1972: 185).

21 Phalansteries were the utopian communities which the Saint-Simonians endeavoured to set up.

22 'C'est l'historique de la Passion, sans l'omission d'aucune circonstance, mis en action; le tout accompagné de chants, de récitatifs: puis arrive la mort du Christ; les cierges s'éteignent, les ténèbres règnent. . . . La descente de croix est la seconde pièce: une foule confuse d'hommes, de femmes de race blanche, indienne et nègre assiègent le *calvaire* en poussant des cris lamentables; bientôt les arbres déracinés, les roches enlevées au sol sont dans leurs mains; ils expulsent les soldats, s'emparent de la croix, en détachent le corps; le sang découle des plaies de ce Christ de carton, les hurlements de la foule redoublent'(1983: 164–5).

23 'Il y a aujourd'hui 8 jours à pareille heure que je suis montée sur mon Calvaire – j'ai été crucifiée, comme mon maître, entre deux larrons femelles . . . le peuple de Paris [était] aussi stupide, aussi méchant que celui de Jérusalème (7 février 1839) (1980: 96).

24 This was not published until 1973, when J.-L. Puech completed a long-standing act of editorial devotion.

25 Actually, I wonder if this story is apocryphal, since there is no mention of it in the entry for 7 July in *Le Tour de France*. If it is, it merely shows the rapid work of mythologisation.

7 MY MOTHER THE REVOLUTION: LOUISE MICHEL

1 M refers to the Maspero 1983 edition of *Mémoires* hereafter.

2 The prosecutor's reading of the story we are telling is revealing. I will simply translate: 'What is the motive that drove Louise Michel on the fatal path of politics and revolution?

Obviously, pride.

An illegitimate daughter brought up by charity, instead of thanking Providence which had given her a higher education and the means to live happily with her mother, she gives way to her wild imagination, to her irascible character, and, after breaking with her benefactors, goes off to seek adventure in Paris.

The wind of Revolution is beginning to blow: Victor Noir has just died.

It's the moment to come on stage; but a minor part is not good enough for Louise Michel; her name must grasp public attention

and figure at the head of deceitful proclamations and advertise-
ments' (M: 316).

3 Her sense of equality was viewed as eccentricity when she equated
animal suffering with human suffering. Indeed, her empathy with
animals highlighted her drastic remedies for human ills, which
would spare neither fire nor sword to eradicate a decadent society.

4 The difference in revolutionary climate may be gauged by the fact
that Olympe assumed the *particule* (*de*), both in her *nom de plume*
and in the name, de Valmont, which covered her fictionalised
persona in *Mémoire de Madame de Valmont*. Michel, on the other
hand, eschewed the name Demahis, which she could have used, if
she wished.

5   MYRIAM!!!

Myriam! the name of them both:

My mother!

My friend!

   Go, my book, to the tombs where they sleep!

   May my life soon be over so that I may soon sleep near her!

   And now, if by chance my activity were to produce some
good, do not thank me, all of you who judge on facts: I am
merely drunk on words.

   World-weariness possesses me. Having nothing to hope nor
to fear, I hasten towards the goal, like those who throw away
the goblet with the dregs.

6 Not only the name of Michel's mother bears this out, but we will
note in the next chapter Marion as the name of Stendhal's nurse and
Mariette as that of Baudelaire's.

7 This is the conventional reading of male writers on the Commune,
and is even echoed, rather to my surprise, by Paule Lejeune in her
feminist life of Michel (1975), for the edition Des Femmes.

8 Although she comments herself on the tendency in France 'to
attribute to a *pathological case* any rather virile woman's character'
(M: 192), I would not presume to consider her a practising lesbian.
Her physical sexuality seems to have been completely sublimated in
the cause of anarchism, but further probing seems to me both
indiscreet and unimportant.

9 'Pauvre Marie!

   Elle dort dans un grand châle rouge qu'on m'avait donné
pour faire au besoin une bannière; il a fait un linceul; pour
nous c'est la même chose maintenant . . . .

   Je croyais mourir après ce coup terrible; ma mère me restait,
ma mère et la Révolution. Maintenant je n'ai plus que la
Révolution' (M: 253–4).

   As an example of the heteroglossia I mention later, note how this
text is echoed in popular communism: 'The peoples' flag is deepest
red,/It shrouded oft our martyred dead.'

10 'si je prends pour ma pensée et ma plume le droit de vagabondage,
on conviendra que je l'ai bien payé' (M: 17).

11 See, for example, Deleuze and Parnet, 1987: 43–4, and Deleuze and

Guattari, 1975, on the relationship between woman–becoming and minority–becoming.

12 See Todorov, 1981: 67–93, for a good summing-up of the Bakhtinian notion of heteroglossia.

13 'Lorsque *monsieur le maître*, comme nous disions, du haut de son grand fauteuil de bois, *la chaire*, avait bien *recommandé* d'écrire exactement les dictées, j'avais soin d'ajouter à ce qui devait être écrit tout ce qui n'était pas destiné à l'être. Cela faisait quelque chose de ce genre:

"Les Romains étaient les maîtres du monde (*Louise, ne tenez pas votre plume comme un bâton; – point virgule*). – mais la Gaule résista longtemps. (*Les enfants du haut de Quérot, vous venez bien tard; – un point. Ferdinand, mouchez-vous. – Les enfants du moulin, chauffez-vous les pieds*). César en écrivit l'histoire, etc."

J'ajoutais même des choses que monsieur le maître ne disait pas, ne perdant pas une minute, griffonant avec zèle' (M: 94).

14 'L'argot rouge, l'argot noir, l'argot blanc se mêlent pareils à des grouillements de monstres, où se trouveraient enlacées de formes charmantes, car l'argot est vivant, il fait image sanglante ou naïve. L'argot subit d'éternelles fluctuations, il a des remous rapides comme le destin de ceux qui s'en servent. L'argot blanc, c'est la tenue blanche des mots; la plupart sont encore inconnues au néophyte, les circonstances les lui apprendront. L'argot rouge et l'argot noir sont goguenards dans leurs histoires de morgue. Il y a encore l'argot des filles. Celui-là, parfois, fleurit dans la boue des ruisseaux ou les pavés sanglants de la place de la Roquette. Il a des coquetteries, des grâces de mort' (cit. Durand, 1987: 151).

15 'L'*écrégne* [sic.], dans nos villages, est la maison où, les soirs d'hiver, se réunissent les femmes et les jeunes filles pour filer, tricoter, et surtout pour raconter ou écouter les vieilles histoires du *feullot* qui danse en robe de flamme dans les *prèles* (prairies) et les nouvelles histoires de ce qui se passe chez l'un ou chez l'autre' (M: 51).

16 'It seemed to me that if he had come in I should have leapt at his throat to bite him and I said all that; I was indignant that they should believe that everyone couldn't have bread everyday; this stupidity of the herd outraged me.

– *Mustn't* talk like that, *littley*! said the woman. *It makes the good Lord cry.*'

17 'Pendant que certains reporters causaient avec moi dans une maison où *je n'étais pas*, d'autres me voyaient *en partie de plaisir au Bois* où je n'étais pas non plus. J'habitais dans les familles de mes amis Vaughan et Meusy, d'où je me rendais, vêtue en homme, chez ma pauvre mère.

J'aurais pu, sous ce costume, ne pas quitter Paris, ou emmener ma mère à l'étranger.

J'aurais pu, même, continuer à faire de la propagande. Combien de fois suis-je allée dans les réunions d'où les femmes sont exclues! Combien de fois, au temps de la Commune, suis-je allée, en garde national ou en lignard, à des endroits où on n'a guère cru avoir affaire à une femme!' (M: 275).

18 'Il y a peut-être beaucoup de vers dans mes Mémoires; mais c'est la forme qui rend le mieux certaines impressions, et où aura-t-on le droit d'être soi-même et d'exprimer ce qu'on éprouve, si ce n'est dans des Mémoires?' (M: 100).

19 'From those red carnations that we each held as a way of recognising one another, be reborn, red flowers. Others will use you again in the times to come, and they will be the victors.'

20 'Que de fleurs dans ma vie: les roses rouges du fond du clos toutes chargées d'abeilles, le lilas blanc que Marie voulut sur son cercueil, et les roses couleur de chair tachées de gouttes de sang que j'envoyais de Clermont à ma mère!' (M: 114).

8   SYMBOLIC DELEGITIMATION

1 OC I and II stand hereafter for the 1975–6 Pichois edition of the complete works of Baudelaire.

2 His father is actually called 'the bastard' in the letters to his sister Pauline from 9 June 1813 onwards, in French, not in English, though I imagine the English usage played its part.

3 However, he did at least once indulge in the daydream of being the son of a great prince: HB: 256. HB will be used hereafter for *Vie de Henry Brulard*, ed. B. Didier, 1973.

4 'Je me regardais comme Gagnon et je ne pensais jamais aux Beyle qu'avec une répugnance qui dure encore en 1835' (HB: 92–3).

5 Cf. Derrida, 1978 (cit. 1982: 131): 'Il n'y a pas d'essence de la femme' ('There is no essence of woman').

6 Quotations given are from this translation by B. Archer (Starobinski, 1962).

7 The first, very imperfect publication is in 1890. For details, see HB: 446–9.

8 'Mon oncle plaisantait sa soeur Henriette (ma mère) sur ma laideur. Il paraît que j'avais une tête énorme, sans cheveux, et que je ressemblais au Père Brulard, un moine adroit, un bon vivant et à grande influence dans son couvent, mon oncle ou grand-oncle avant moi' (HB: 67).

9 '*Par ainsi*, comme disent les enfants, je suis si loin d'être blasé sur leurs ruses et petites grâces qu'à mon âge, cinquante-deux ans, et, en écrivant ceci, je suis encore tout charmé d'une longue *chiacchierata* qu'Amalia a eue hier soir avec moi au Théâtre Valle.

Pour les considérer le plus philosophiquement possible et tâcher ainsi de les dépouiller de l'auréole qui me fait *aller les yeux*, qui m'éblouit et m'ôte la faculté de voir distinctement, *j'ordonnerai* ces dames (langage mathématique) selon leurs diverses qualités' (HB: 39–40)

10 I find it instructive to compare the recent negative reactions to Michel's heteroglossia and her high-handed fragmentation of time,

place and genre, discussed in the previous chapter, with the positive judgement made on those of Stendhal. Brombert's judgement is quite characteristic:

> In these two books [*Souvenirs d'égotisme* and *Vie de Henry Brulard*] the autobiographer rises to the level of artist. Their real interest lies not, however, in the many vivid details, peppery anecdotes, and memories they provide, nor even in the subtle nuances with which Stendhal diagnoses his sensibility. What counts here is the *manner* of the exploration, the state of innocence with which Stendhal faces himself, the problematical nature of his approach. Influenced by Rousseau's *Confessions*, these texts differ sharply, however, in their fundamental angle of vision: they are written not to justify a man, but to discover him. The telescoping of past and present, the almost Proustian insistence on an uncontrolled and uncerebral memory, are all aimed at a discovery *in time* of a fluid psychic reality.
>
> (Brombert, 1962: 6)

Michel, of course, has never been given canonical status, which subtly alters critical perspectives.

11 'Si donc tout nom est le nom du mort, ou d'un vivant dont il peut se passer, à ce moment-là, si on écrit à destination de noms, pour appeler des noms, on écrit aussi pour des morts. Peut-être pas des morts en général, comme dit Genet. Genet dit à peu près: "J'écris pour des morts, ou j'ai fait un théâtre destiné à des morts." Mais pour *tel* mort, et peut-être dans tout texte y a-t-il à chercher le mort ou la morte, la figure singulière de la mort à laquelle un texte est destiné, et qui signe' (1982: 74–5).

12 See the Lemaitre edition of the Complete Works (1966), hereafter N, for a discussion of the syncretic possibilities of the name: Nerva, the Roman emperor; Avernus, the underworld; the other local place names ending in *-val*; etc.

13 See, for example, the vituperative outpourings of Baudelaire on George Sand (OC I: 686–7), or the judgement of the revolutionary tribunal on Madame Roland and Olympe de Gouges (see pp. 104–5).

14 When Michel Butor wrote his *Histoire extraordinaire* (1961), a study of this dream, he too was unaware of the childhood trauma. CI stands hereafter for the Pichois and Ziegler 1973 edition of the *Correspondance*.

15 'Dans une foule de petits cadres, je vois des desseins, des miniatures, des épreuves photographiques. Cela représente des oiseaux coloriés avec des plumages très brillants, dont l'oeil est *vivant*. Quelquefois, *il n'y a que des moitiés d'oiseaux.* – Cela représente quelquefois des images d'êtres bizarres, monstrueux, presque *amorphes*, comme des *aérolithes*. Dans un coin de chaque dessein, il y a une note. – *La fille une telle, âgée de . . . a donné le jour à ce foetus en telle année*; et d'autres notes de ce genre'(C I: 339).

16 Van Rossum-Guyon, 1990, for example, studies the topos in the work of Balzac.

17 'Malheur, trois fois malheur aux pères infirmes qui nous ont faits rachitiques et mal venus, prédestinés que nous sommes à n'enfanter que des morts-nés!' (OC I: 560).

18 'Il était à la fois tous les artistes qu'il avait étudiés et tous les livres qu'il avait lus, et cependant, en dépit de cette faculté comédienne, restait profondément original. Il était toujours le doux, le fantasque, le paresseux, le terrible, le savant, l'ignorant, le débraillé, le coquet Samuel Cramer, la romantique Manuela de Monteverde' (OC I: 555).

19 Johnson (1979) has made a remarkable study of this play on words.

20 'Fais-moi le plaisir de lire ce manuscrit, qui est achevé. . . . Tu ne connais pas la fin; lis-le et dis-moi sincèrement *l'effet produit sur toi*' (C I: 103).

21 He also turns the knife in the wound by praise of the 'good mother', 'the good hearted servant', Mariette (OC I: 100). Her role as double mother is eventually given an almost sacred signification as he prays to his dead father and the ghostly Mariette, both more wish-fulfilment than reality (OC I: 673).

22 'Si je veux raconter ma vie, eh bien, c'est une destinataire, c'est un "je" marqué au féminin qui va signer et qui sera donc – je ne dirais pas l'auteur parce que le mot détruit tout immédiatement – mais qui sera le lieu depuis lequel quelque chose comme ma biographie, mon autobiographie sera signé. Autrement dit, ce ne sera naturellement pas une autobiographie mais une hétérobiographie. . . . Donc, l'autobiographie de la femme, la sienne, ou d'elle, descendant d'elle, comme héritée d'elle, d'une femme, de la femme' (1982: 108).

23 'Il n'y avait là qu'un foyer, qu'une famille, qu'un couple incestueux. "J'étais toujours vivant en toi, lui écrira-t-il plus tard, tu étais uniquement à moi. Tu étais à la fois une idole et un camarade"'(1947: 18–19).

24 'Il y avait, dans son existence, un événement qu'il n'avait pu supporter: le second mariage de sa mère. Sur ce sujet, il était inépuisable et sa terrible logique se résumait toujours ainsi: "Quand on a un fils comme moi – comme moi était sous-entendu – on ne se remarie pas"'(ibid.: 19–20).

25 W. stands hereafter for *Words,* tr. I. Clephane (Sartre, 1967).

'Pendant plusieurs années, j'ai pu voir, au-dessus de mon lit, le portrait d'un petit officier aux yeux candides, au crane rond et dégarni, avec de fortes moustaches: quand ma mère s'est remariée, le portrait a disparu' (Sartre, 1964: 12).

26 'elle eût aimé, je pense, que je fusse une fille . . . . Le ciel ne l'ayant pas exaucé, elle s'arrangea: j'aurais le sexe des anges, indéterminé mais féminin sur les bords' (1964: 83–4).

27 'On me montre une jeune géante, on me dit que c'est ma mère. De moi-même, je la prendrais plutôt pour une soeur aînée. Cette vierge en résidence surveillée, soumise à tous, je vois bien qu'elle est là pour me servir. Je l'aime: mais comment la respecterais-je, si personne ne la respecte? Il y a trois chambres dans notre maison:

celle de mon grand-père, celle de ma grand-mère, celle des "enfants". Les "enfants" c'est nous: pareillement mineurs et pareillement entretenus' (ibid.: 13).

28 'Au propriétaire, les biens de ce monde reflètent ce qu'il est; ils m'enseignaient ce que je n'étais pas: *je n'étais pas* consistant ni permanent; *je n'étais pas* le continuateur futur de l'oeuvre paternelle, *je n'étais pas* nécessaire à la production de l'acier: en un mot je n'avais pas d'âme' (ibid.: 71).

29 'mon grand-père, du haut de sa gloire, laissa tomber un verdict qui me frappa au coeur: "Il y a quelqu'un qui manque ici: c'est Simonnot." Je . . . me réfugiai dans un coin, les invités disparurent; au centre d'un anneau tumultueux, je vis une colonne: M. Simonnot lui-même, absent en chair et en os. Cette absence prodigieuse le transfigura . . . . Seul, M. Simonnot *manquait*' (ibid.: 73).

30 'un gémissement parcourait le désert et les rochers disaient au sable: "Il y a quelqu'un qui manque ici: c'est Sartre"' (ibid.: 93).

31 'la reproduction comme un vice de l'amour, la grossesse comme une maladie d'araignée' (OC I: 577).

32 'la signature ne sera effective, performée, performante, non pas au moment où apparemment elle a lieu, mais seulement plus tard, quand des oreilles auront pu recevoir le message' (1982: 71).

33 'D'autres consciences m'ont pris en charge. On *me* lit, je saute aux yeux; on *me* parle, je suis dans toutes les bouches, langue universelle et singulière . . . je n'existe plus nulle part, je *suis*, enfin! je suis partout' (1964: 162).

34 'Dans les salons d'Arras, un jeune avocat froid et minaudier porte sa tête sous son bras parce qu'il est feu Robespierre, cette tête dégoutte de sang mais ne tache pas le tapis; pas un des convives ne la remarque et nous ne voyons qu'elle; il s'en faut de cinq ans qu'elle est roulée dans le panier et pourtant la voilà, coupée, qui dit des madrigaux malgré sa machoire qui pend' (ibid.: 167).

9   'BETTER TO REIGN IN HELL . . .'

1 Chapter 10 will examine the relationship between the writing of illegitimacy and what I call delegitimation by proxy, paying special attention to the Sartre–Genet–de Beauvoir–Leduc relationship.

2 This is Genet's version. In fact, according to Albert Dichy and Pascal Fouché in *Jean Genet: Essais de chronologie 1910–1944*, he was abandoned thirty weeks after his birth, and his adoptive parents were not peasants. I thank Sue Marson for the information.

3 This version of events may be influenced by Leduc's self-mythologisation, and owe more to the writing than to the facts.

4 'Un bâtard ça doit mentir, un bâtard c'est le fruit de la fuite et du mensonge, un bâtard c'est le stock des irrégularités' (B: 75).
References to the works of Leduc hereafter:

A = *L'Asphyxie* (1946) B = *La Bâtarde* (1964) BA = *La Bâtarde* (tr.

1985) FT = *La Folie en tête* (1970) MP = *Mad in Pursuit* (tr. 1971) CH = *La Chasse à l'amour* (1973).

5 'Abandonné par ma famille il me semblait déjà naturel d'aggraver cela par l'amour des garçons et cet amour par le vol, et le vol par le crime ou le complaisance au crime. Ainsi refusai-je décidément un monde qui m'avait refusé' (JV: 92).

References to the works of Genet hereafter:

ND = *Notre-Dame-des-Fleurs* (1948) JV = *Le Journal du voleur* (1949) TJ = *The Thief's Journal* (tr. 1973) CA = *Un Captif amoureux* (1986).

6 'Les bâtards sont maudits: un ami me l'a dit. Les bâtards sont maudits .... Pourquoi les bâtards ne s'entraident-ils pas. Pourquoi se fuient-ils? Pourquoi se détestent-ils? Pourquoi ne forment-ils pas une confrérie? Ils devraient se pardonner puisqu'ils ont en commun ce qu'il y a de plus précieux, de plus fragile, de plus fort, de plus sombre en eux: une enfance tordue comme un vieux pommier' (B: 70).

7 I use the name Violette throughout for the first-person narrator, the protagonist in the text, and Leduc for the author/writer. *Pace* Lejeune, they are far from identical.

8 'Je crois, je croirai toujours au dédain des domestiques à mon égard. Ils me reprochent d'avoir mis ma mère au monde, d'en avoir fait une femme de chambre' (FT: 140).

9 To measure the depth of this wound, one must note its obsessive return in later work, particularly in *La Chasse à l'amour*: 'Ma mère m'attendait dans la gare .... Elle donnait la main à sa petite-fille. Elle ne m'a jamais donné la main. Affligeante comparaison. Privation éternelle, privation lancinante' ('My mother was waiting at the station for me .... She was holding her granddaughter's hand. She never held my hand. Distressing comparison. Eternal deprivation, piercing deprivation') (CA: 304).

10 'Les oiseaux soudain se taisaient pendant que je suçais mon porte-plume: le plaisir de prévoir que ma grandmère allait renaître, que je la mettrais au monde, le plaisir de prévoir que je serais le créateur de celle que j'adorais, de celle qui m'adorait. Ecrire . . .' (B: 549).

11 See *La Folie en tête* for the insane passion for 'Jacques' and, more particularly, for Genet. The similar relationship to Cocteau never reaches the same level of intensity.

12 To her amazement he offers at one stage to impregnate her (B: 481), an offer she refuses, wanting to throw up, not at the sexual implications but rather at being offered a child as one throws a bone to a dog. Twenty years later, she still finds it impossible to comprehend.

13 'Cependant mon extrait de naissance me fascine. Ou bien me révolte. Ou bien m'ennuie. Je le relis du début à la fin chaque fois que j'en ai besoin, je me retrouve dans la longue galérie où se répercute le bruit des ciseaux du médecin accoucheur. J'écoute, je frissonne. Finis les vases communicants que nous étions lorsqu'elle

me portait. Me voici née sur un registre de salle de mairie, à la pointe de la plume d'un employé de mairie. Pas de saletés, pas de placenta: de l'écriture, un enregistrement' (B: 25–6).

14 'Tu deviens mon enfant, ma mère, quand vieille femme tu te souviens avec une précision d'horloger. Tu parles, je te reçois. Tu parles, je te porte dans ma tête. Oui, pour toi, mon ventre a une chaleur de volcan. Tu parles, je me tais. Je suis née porteuse de ton malheur comme on naît porteuse d'offrandes. Pour vivre, tu sais vivre dans le passé. Parfois j'en suis lasse jusqu'à tomber malade' (B: 26).

15 'Anémiée, presque rachitique à sa sortie de l'ouvroir, une jeune fille – ma mère – reçut une nourriture phénoménale dans ses entrailles: un môme. Aux millions de graines dans un jet de sperme, elle opposa pour sa fille des milliards de calories' (B: 301–2).

16 'Mon cas n'est pas unique; j'ai peur de mourir et je suis navrée d'être au monde. Je n'ai pas travaillé, je n'ai pas étudié. J'ai pleuré, j'ai crié' (B: 25).

17 '22 août 1963. Le mois d'août aujourd'hui, lecteur, est une rosace de chaleur. Je te l'offre, je te la donne. Une heure. Je rentre au village pour déjeuner. Forte du silence des pins et des châtaigners, je traverse sans fléchir la cathédrale brûlante de l'été. Il est grandiose et musical mon raidillon d'herbes folles. C'est du feu que la solitude pose sur ma bouche' (B: 634).

18
> Allons dans les bois, ma mignonette,
> Allons dans les bois du roi.
> Nous y cueillerons la douce violette . . .

> Non, Lucien, tu n'auras pas ma rose,
> Non, Lucien, tu ne l'auras pas.
> Monsieur le Curé a défendu la chose. . .

19 See, however, note 2 above.

20 Actually Camille Gabrielle; is this more angel making?

21 'Je suis né à Paris le 19 décembre 1910. Pupille de l'Assistance Publique, il me fut impossible de connaître autre chose de mon état civil. Quand j'eus vingt et un ans, j'obtins un acte de naissance. Ma mère s'appellait Gabrielle Genet. Mon père reste inconnu. J'étais venu au monde au 22 de la rue d'Assas.

– Je saurais donc quelques renseignements sur mon origine, me dis-je, et je me rendis rue d'Assas. Le 22 était occupé par la Maternité. On refusa de me renseigner. Je fus élevé dans le Morvan par des paysans. Quand je rencontre dans la lande – et singulièrement au crépuscule, au retour de ma visite des ruines de Tiffauges où vécut Gilles de Rais – des fleurs de genêt, j'éprouve à leur égard une sympathie profonde. Je les considère gravement, avec tendresse. Mon trouble semble commandé par toute la nature. Je suis seul au monde, et je ne suis pas sûr de n'être pas le roi – peut-être la fée de ces fleurs. Elles me rendent au passage un hommage, s'inclinent sans s'incliner mais me reconnaissent. Elles savent que je suis leur représentant vivant, mobile, agile, vainqueur du vent. Elles sont mon emblème naturel, mais j'ai des racines, par elles, dans ce sol de France nourri des os en poudre des enfants, des adolescents enfilés, massacrés, brûlés par Gilles de Rais' (JV: 46–7).

Gilles de Rais was an aristocratic serial killer in the sixteenth century, reputedly the source of the Blue Beard legend.

22 Leduc refers to the *genêts* again and again in all her works, combining a love of the countryside with an echo of an admiration so excessive that it reduced Genet to physical assault in order to free himself (MP: 127, 149–59).

23 'J'aspire à la Guyane .... Ce lieu semble contenir la sécheresse et l'aridité la plus cruelle et voici qu'il s'exprime par un thème de bonté: il suscite, et l'impose, l'image d'un sein maternel, chargé comme lui de puissance rassurante, d'où monte une odeur un peu nauséabonde, m'offrant une paix honteuse. La Vierge mère et la Guyane je les nomme Consolatrices des affligés' (JV: 269–70).

24 'Je ne sais rien de celle qui m'abandonna au berceau, mais j'espérai que c'était cette vieille voleuse qui mendiait la nuit .... J'irais pleurer de tendresse sur les yeux de ce poisson-lune, sur cette face ronde et sotte. Et pourquoi, me disais-je encore, pourquoi y pleurer? Il fallut peu de temps à mon esprit pour qu'il remplaçât ces marques habituelles de tendresse par n'importe quel geste et même par les plus décriés, par les plus vils, que je chargeais de signifier autant que les baisers, ou les larmes, ou les fleurs.

– Je me contenterais de baver ... sur ses cheveux ou de vomir dans ses mains. Mais j'adorerais cette voleuse qui est ma mère' (JV: 21–2).

25 'La tendresse qui les incline n'est pas féminité mais découverte de l'ambiguïté. Je crois qu'ils sont prêts à se féconder eux-mêmes, à pondre et à couver leur ponte sans que s'émousse l'aiguillon cruel des mâles' (JV: 268).

26 See Maclean, 1987.

27 See, for example, Mimica, 1991, in which almost the entire mythopoeic cosmogony of a New Guinea social group revolves around this fantasy.

28 'Enfin par elle dont je porte le nom le monde végétal m'est familier. Je peux sans pitié considérer toutes les fleurs, elles sont de ma famille. Si par elles je rejoins aux domaines inférieurs – mais c'est aux fougères arborescentes et à leurs marécages, aux algues, que je voulais descendre – je m'éloigne encore des hommes' (JV: 47). *Fougères arborescentes* is mistranslated as bracken in TJ. Genet's notes here refer to the *genêt ailé* or winged broom, and to the other meaning of jennet. Cocteau called him a *genêt d'Espagne*, thus combining both horse and flower.

29 'Pour vous faire comprendre mieux à quel point j'avais atteint une solitude me conférant la souveraineté, si j'utilise ce procédé de rhétorique c'est que me l'imposent une situation, une réussite avec les mots chargés d'exprimer le triomphe du siècle. Une parenté verbale traduit la parenté de ma gloire avec la gloire nobiliaire' (JV: 184–5).

30 'Sans me croire né magnifiquement, l'indécision de mon origine me

permettait de l'interpréter. J'y ajoutais la singularité de mes misères
. . . mon imagination d'enfant. . . m'inventait. . . des châteaux, des
parcs peuplés de gardes plus que de statues' (JV: 92).

31 'Mais c'est l'imagination amoureuse des fastes royaux, du gamin
abandonné, qui me permit de dorer ma honte, de la ciseler, d'en
faire un travail d'orfèvrerie dans le sens habituel de ce mot, jusqu'à
ce que, par l'usage peut-être et l'usure des mots la voilant, s'en
dégageât l'humilité' (JV: 95).

32 'Mon prénom et mon nom me suffisaient, ils remplissaient chaque
page. Mes yeux buvaient de l'absinthe. Je comptais et recomptais le
nombre de lettres de l'alphabet pour mon nom et mon prénom: moi
la voûtée, je me tenais droite huit fois, je me tenais droite cinq fois,
je me tenais droite treize fois. J'avais des astres pour doigts de pied.
Je couchais ma joue sur la page du magazine, pour voir si mon nom
et mon prénom étaient statiques. Ils l'étaient' (B: 439).

33 'J'étais exilée, je suis rapatriée. Mon quatrième doigt s'ennuie, il lui
faut son anneau ce petit. Si j'insistais, il me répondrait qu'il est
trahi. Tu l'auras ton alliance, je te le promets' (B: 398).

34 'Mercure, m'a-t-on dit, chez les anciens était le dieu des voleurs qui
savaient ainsi quelle puissance invoquer. Mais nous, nous n'avons
personne' ('Mercury, I'm told, in ancient times was the god of
thieves who thus knew what power to invoke. But *we* don't have
anyone') (JV: 224).

35 See also Violette's attempt to transfer the Hermetic role to René,
who declines it, in CA: 243.

36 Although one finds an interesting echo of *The Maids* in the
'Madame' of *L'Affamée*.

37 'Cette célébrité toute virtuelle m'ennoblit, comme un parchemin
que personne ne saurait déchiffrer, une naissance illustre gardée
secrète, une barre de bâtardise royale, un masque ou peut-être une
filiation divine' (ND: 342–3).

38 'J'étais au coeur de mon enfance, à son instant le plus précieusement
conservé. A un détour de route j'allais découvrir sous trois palmiers
cette crèche de Noël où je venais, enfant, assister à *ma nativité* entre
le boeuf et l'âne. J'étais le pauvre du monde le plus humble' (JV: 82).

39 'The hero who kills and is killed in glory, intensely admired by a
whole community, becomes, when the sign is changed, the criminal
of a black morality who kills to be killed and whose death may
become as legendary as that of a great captain' (Sartre, 1952:
103–4; my translation).

40 'Créer n'est pas un jeu quelque peu frivole. Le créateur s'est engagé
dans une aventure effrayante qui est d'assumer soi-même jusqu'au
bout les périls risqués par ses créatures. On ne peut supposer une
création n'ayant l'amour à l'origine. Comment mettre en face de soi
aussi fort que soi, ce qu'on devra mépriser ou haïr. Mais alors le
créateur se chargera du poids du péché de ses personnages. Jésus
devint homme. Il expie. Après, comme Dieu, les avoir créés, il
délivre de leurs péchés les hommes: on le flagelle, on lui crache au
visage, on le moque, on le cloue. Voilà le sens de l'expression: "Il

souffre dans sa chair." Négligeons les théologiens. "Prendre le poids du péché du monde" signifie très exactement: éprouver en puissance et en effets tous les péchés; avoir souscrit au mal' (JV: 220–1).

41 'Puisqu'il était cette nuit au combat, dans sa chambre et sur son lit je tenais la place et peut-être le rôle du fils. Pour une nuit et le temps d'un acte simple cependant nombreux, un vieillard plus âgé qu'elle devenait le fils de la mère car "j'étais avant qu'elle ne fût". Plus jeune que moi, durant cette action familière – familiale? – elle fut, demeurant celle de Hamza, ma mère'(CA: 230–1).

10   DELEGITIMATION BY PROXY

1 'The mental world GGGentlemen/ . . ./ Works arbitrarily/ Erecting for itself/ With so-called generosity in honour of the workers on the edifice/ An auto-monument/ Let us repeat GGGGGentlemen/ When it is left alone/ The mental world/ Lies/ Monumentally.'

2 For those who have forgotten, Mary McCarthy's novel dealt with an academic no-hoper, who managed to avoid losing his job by claiming to be a member of a politically persecuted minority.

3 Eissler (1961) has an extended and interesting discussion of the traces of active homosexuality in the notebooks and paintings. As we have seen, since it is based on a misreading of the facts, Freud's other assumption that Leonardo's homosexuality was the result of a too long and loving relationship with his natural mother in the absence of a father also does not stand up to scrutiny.

4 Whether it helped to prove that his genius 'represented a cool repudiation of sexuality' (SE XI: 69) is another matter again. Freud scarcely comments on the strange androgyny of the graceful female head placed on the copulating male body, which is a marked feature of the original.

5 Gallimard's refusal to publish Leduc's account of teenage lesbianism in *Ravages*, in 1955, gives a bench-mark of advanced French attitudes at the time.

6 SGAM stands hereafter for Frechtman's 1963 translation. I will not give the Sartre original unless I have doubts about the translation.

7 I acknowledge that this is a frequent and rather unfortunate French academic habit, which I would regard as generally appropriative.

8 The classic example occurs at SGAM: 334–8 (SG: 373–7).

9 See Chapter 8, p. 160 for Sartre's attempt to present himself in the same terms.

10 See especially *Huis clos* (No Exit) (1945).

11 Le Castor (the beaver) was de Beauvoir's nickname. *Journal du voleur* is dedicated to them both.

12 These affairs are described in the *Lettres à Sartre*, published posthumously in 1990.

13 Leduc's passionate anguish at the frustration of her love may be read in *L'Affamée*. In fact, the treatment was highly necessary to make her continue writing.

14 'La plupart des écrivains, quand ils confessent de mauvais senti-

ments, en ôtent les épines par leur franchise même. Elle nous oblige à les saisir, en elle, en nous, dans leur âcreté brûlante. Elle demeure complice de ses envies, de ses rancoeurs, de ses mesquineries; par là elle prend les nôtres en charge et nous délivre de la honte: personne n'est monstrueux si nous le sommes tous' (B: 21).

15 Since *Glas* is actually untranslatable, I will use John Leavey and Richard Rand's very praiseworthy attempt at the impossible task (hereafter GE), but will give the original text (G hereafter) in the notes. [ ] in the text indicate my comments or clarifications, as usual, while { } indicate French terms included by the translators.

16 'De toute façon il me vomira tout ça, il ne lira pas, ne pourra pas lire.

Est-ce *pour lui* que j'écris? Qu'est-ce que je voudrais lui faire? faire à son "oeuvre"? La ruiner en l'érigeant, peut-être.

Qu'on ne la lise plus? qu'on la lise seulement à partir d'ici, du moment où moi je la consigne et contresigne?' (G: 279–80).

Genet did not die until 1986, but he produced little after this except letters and the notes of his stay with the Palestinian guerrillas.

17 'Chemin bâtard, donc, qui devra feindre de suivre naturellement le cercle de la famille' (G: 8). The left and right pages are numbered identically in the 1981 edition.

18 In what follows, double indentation will indicate quotation from the marginal columns or inserts.

19 'Pourquoi, du moins, écrire deux textes à la fois? Quelle scène joue-t-on? Que désire-t-on? Autrement dit, de quoi a-t-on peur? qui? de qui? On veut rendre l'écriture imprenable, bien sûr. Quand vous avez la tête ici, on vous rappelle que la loi du texte est dans l'autre, et ainsi à n'en plus finir. A engrosser la marge – plus de marge, plus de cadre – on l'annule, on brouille la ligne, on vous reprend la règle droite qui vous permettrait de délimiter, découper, dominer' (G: 90).

20 'Je ne sais rien de celle qui m'abandonna au berceau, mais j'espérai que c'était cette vieille voleuse qui mendiait la nuit.

– Si c'était elle? me dis-je en m'éloignant de la vieille. Ah! Si c'était elle, J'irais la couvrir de fleurs, de glaïeuls et de roses, et de baisers! J'irais pleurer de tendresse sur les yeux de ce poisson-lune, sur cette face ronde et sotte. Et pourquoi, me disais-je encore, pourquoi y pleurer? Il fallut peu de temps à mon esprit pour qu'il remplaçât ces marques habituelles de tendresse par n'importe quel geste et même par les plus décriés, par les plus vils, que je chargeais de signifier autant que les baisers, ou les larmes, ou les fleurs.

– Je me contenterais de baver sur elle, pensais-je, débordant d'amour. (Le mot glaïeul prononcé plus haut appela-t-il le mot glaviaux?) De baver sur ses cheveux ou de vomir dans ses mains. Mais j'adorerais cette voleuse qui est ma mère' (JV: 21–2).

21 'Genet n'en demande pas davantage; il a captivé la liberté du juste et l'a contrainte à donner un semblant d'existence au faux comme parasite du vrai, à l'impossible comme au-delà de tous les possibles . . . .

Et le lecteur jeté par l'art du voleur à la poursuite de l'impossible adéquation du néant avec l'être, de la privation avec l'abondance réalise à la place de Genet l'ascétisme du Saint noir' (SG: 563).

22 'comme toujours la nécessité sémantique, donnant lieu à une herméneutique, à une sémiotique, voire à une psychanalytique, reste indécidablement suspendue à la chance d'une agglutination dite formelle ou signifiante. Le vol de ce suspens, et sa nécessité, déroute aussi bien le sémantisme que le formalisme. *Voleuse* reprend *vieilleuse* au vol et le fixe un peu plus bas dans *vieille voleuse*. Ecriture merveilleuse. Incroyablement précieuse'(G: 203–4).

23 'Double regard. Lecture bigle. En gardant l'oeil sur la colonne d'angle (la contrebande), lire ceci comme un nouveau testament.

Mais aussi comme une genèse. Le *Journal du voleur* qui va bientôt décliner son identité, comme on décline sa responsabilité, se présente comme "mon livre, devenu ma Genèse". Ailleurs, comme "ma nativité".

Et si la lecture de la bible ne vous est pas aussi familière qu'à un enfant de choeur un peu vicieux, inutile de continuer' (G: 160).

24 'Et il est vrai que je n'aurai rien fait si je n'ai pas réussi . . . à vous rendre sensible, à vous transformer, par delà tout ce qui se combine ici, depuis l'affect le plus propre de ce texte.

Mais y en a-t-il? Et de quel texte? du sien? du mien?' (G: 147).

25 The original is unnecessary here, but one should note that the pun of *en plain-chant* requires a double translation, and the triple play on *mec* is merely suggested.

26 'il vient toujours fondre (sur vous), vous tomber dessus ou vous surplomber. C'est un soleil phallique, un cercueil plombé, un excrément lourd et rigide qui s'abat et s'enfonce en vous par derrière comme, venu de plus haut, l'aigle de Ganymède (ou l'ange Gabriel volant vous faire un enfant dans le dos' (G: 270–1). It should be remarked that this excerpt appears in an insert marginal column and that it is followed by the entire biblical story of John the Baptist, beginning with the annunciation of his miraculous birth to Elisabeth and Zachariah. One should realise as well that *fondre* also means to melt, *tomber dessus* is to descend upon or to attack, *plombé* is weighted (as in the nasty surprise of a weighted cane), and *aigle* is a play on the name Hegel, mispronounced in this way in French. I cannot go into every play on words, but mention these to justify my claim that *Glas* is (deliberately) an untranslatable text. See GE: 120 for an overview of the other passages of aquiline rape in TJ.

27 'Le nom de celui qui paraît apposer ici son seing (Genet) est celui, on le sait (mais comment et d'où le sait-on?), de sa mère. Qui aurait donc enfanté selon une sorte d'immaculée conception. . . .

Si toute sa littérature chante et tisse un hymen funèbre à la nomination Genet ne fait jamais cas, noblesse oblige, que de s'appeler lui-même' (G: 47–8).

28 See Todd, 1983, for a much fuller account of these textual games with the name Jacques Derrida.

29 'C'est pourquoi la mère (quelque prénom ou pronom qu'on lui

donne) se tient au-delà de l'opposition sexuelle. Ce n'est surtout pas une femme. Elle se laisse surtout représenter, détachée, par le sexe' (G: 188). I have amended the GE translation here for greater accuracy.

30 'Je suis la mère. Le texte. La mère est *derrière* – tout ce que je suis, fais, parais – la mère suit. Comme elle suit absolument, elle survit toujours, futur qui n'aura jamais été présentable, à ce qu'elle aura engendré, assistant, impassible, fascinante et provocante, à la mise en terre de ce dont elle a prévu la mort' (G: 164). I have modified the translation.

This obsession makes all the more poignant the reversal of the narrative twenty years later, when the son finds himself cradling the living death of his mother. See Bennington, 1991.

31 'Sujet de la dénonciation: je m'appelle ma mère qui s'appelle (en) moi. Donner, accuser. Datif, accusatif. Je porte le nom de ma mère, je suis le nom de ma mère, j'appelle ma mère à moi, j'appelle ma mère pour moi, j'appelle ma mère en moi, me rappelle à ma mère. Je décline dans tous les cas la même subjugation' (G: 165).

32 'Je me suis introduit en tiers entre sa mère et lui. Je l'ai donné'(G: 284).

11 CONCLUSION

1 As an example of the maternal fostering of hypervirility as well as the drive to success the case of the novelist Romain Gary is exemplary. He also shows a typical fluidity of name and identity.

2 This is so even in Sartre's case, in the mix of Alsatian and French speakers, and of Protestant and Catholic.

Bibliography

(Translations are placed immediately after the text translated, regardless of date.)

Aeschylus (1965) *The Oresteian Trilogy*, tr. P. Vellacott, Harmondsworth: Penguin.

Agulhon, Maurice (1981) [1979] *Marianne into Battle: Republican Imagery and Symbolism in France 1789–1880*, tr. J. Lloyd, Cambridge: Cambridge University Press and Editions de la Maison des Sciences de l'Homme.

Ambrière, Francis (1992) *Mademoiselle Mars et Marie Dorval*, Paris: Seuil.

Anzieu, Didier (1966) *Oedipe avant le complexe, ou De l'interprétation psychanalytique des mythes*, Paris: Temps modernes.

—— *et al.* (1977) *L'Oedipe, un complexe universel*, Paris: Tchou.

Aragon, Louis (1981) *Le Mentir–Vrai*, Paris: Gallimard.

Ariès, Philippe (1973) *L'Enfant et la vie familiale sous l'ancien régime*, Paris: Seuil.

—— (1979) *Centuries of Childhood: A Social History of Family Life*, tr. R. Baldick, Harmondsworth: Penguin.

Armogathe, Daniel (ed.) (1982) *Colloque Louise Michel 1980*, Marseille: Service des publications Marseille, diffusion J. Lafitte.

Arnold, A. James, and Piriou, Jean Pierre (1973) *Genèse et critique d'une autobiographie: 'Les Mots' de Jean Paul Sartre*, Paris: Minard.

L'Autobiographie, special edition, *Poétique* 56 (1983).

L'Autoportrait, special edition, *Corps écrit* 5 (1983).

Baelen, Jean (1972) *La Vie de Flora Tristan: socialisme et féminisme au XIXe siècle*, Paris: Seuil.

Bakhtin, Mikhail (1968) [1965] *Rabelais and His World*, tr. H. Iwolsky, Cambridge, Mass.: M.I.T. Press.

—— (1973) [1963] *Problems of Dostoevsky's Poetics,* tr. R. Rotsel, Ann Arbor: Ardis.

—— (1985) [1975] *The Dialogic Imagination*, ed. M. Holquist, tr. C. Emerson and M. Holquist, Austin: University of Texas Press.

Balzac, Honoré de (1983) [1834] 'La fille aux yeux d'or', in *La Duchesse de Langeais*, Paris: Livre de Poche.

Barthes, Roland (1957) *Mythologies*, Paris: Seuil.
—— (1983) *Mythologies*, tr. A. Lavers, New York: Hill & Wang.
Bateson, Gregory, with Ruesch, J. (1968) *Communication: The Social Matrix of Psychiatry*, New York: Norton.
—— (1979) *Mind and Nature: A Necessary Unity*, London: Wildwood House.
Baudelaire, Charles (1973) *Correspondance Baudelaire*, eds C. Pichois and J. Ziegler, Paris: Gallimard.
—— (1975–6) *Oeuvres complètes*, 2 vols, ed. C. Pichois, Paris: Gallimard.
Beaugrande, Robert de (1988) *Critical Discourse*, New York: Ablex.
Beaujour, Michel (1980) *Miroirs d'encre: Rhétorique de l'autoportrait*, Paris: Seuil.
Beauvoir, Simone de (1960) *La Force de l'âge*, 2 vols, Paris: Gallimard.
—— (1973) *The Prime of Life*, tr. P. Green, Harmondsworth: Penguin.
—— (1972) *Tout compte fait*, Paris: Gallimard.
—— (1974) *All Said and Done*, tr. P. O'Brian, New York: Putnam.
—— (1981) *La Cérémonie des adieux*, suivi de *Entretien avec Sartre*, Paris: Gallimard.
—— (1984) *Adieux: A Farewell to Sartre*, tr. P. O'Brian, New York: Pantheon Books.
—— (1990) *Lettres à Sartre*, Paris: Gallimard.
—— (1991) *Letters to Sartre*, tr. Q. Hoare, London: Radius.
Benjamin, Jessica (1986) 'A Desire of One's Own: Psychoanalytic Feminism and Intersubjective Space', in *Feminist Studies/Critical Studies*, Bloomington and Indianapolis: Indiana University Press.
Bennington, Geoffrey, and Derrida, Jacques (1991) *Jacques Derrida*, Paris: Seuil.
Benstock, Shari (ed.) (1988) *The Private Self: Theory and Practice of Women's Autobiographical Writings*, London and New York: Routledge.
Bernhard, Thomas (1985) *Gathering Evidence: A Memoir*, tr. D. McLintock, New York: Alfred Knopf. [Comprises *Die Ursache* (1975), *Der Keller* (1976), *Der Atem* (1978), *Die Kälte* (1981), *Das Kind* (1982).]
Berthier, Philippe (1983) 'Corambé: interprétation d'un mythe', in *George Sand: Colloque de Cérisy*, ed. Simone Vierne, Paris: SEDES and CDU.
Bidelman, Patrick (1982) *Pariahs Stand Up: The Founding of the Liberal Feminist Movement in France, 1858–1889*, Westport, Conn., and London: Greenwood Press.
Blanc, Olivier (1985) *La Dernière lettre: prisons et condamnés de la Révolution 1793–1794*, Paris: Laffont.
—— (1987) *Last Letters: Prisons and Prisoners of the French Revolution, 1793–1794*, tr. Alan Sheridan, London: A. Deutsch.
—— (1989) *Olympe de Gouges: Une femme de libertés*, Paris: Syros/Alternatives.
Bloch, Ernst (1962) 'Uber Märchen, Colportage und Sage', in *Erbschaft dieser Zeit*, Frankfurt/Main: Suhrkamp.

Bogue, Ronald (1989) *Deleuze and Guattari*, London and New York: Routledge.

Bonnet, Catherine (1992) *Les Enfants du secret*, Paris: Jacob.

Boose, Lynda, and Flowers, Betty (eds) (1989) *Daughters and Fathers*, Baltimore: Johns Hopkins University Press.

Bouchardeau, Huguette (1990) *George Sand: La lune et les sabots*, Paris: Laffont.

Bozon-Scalzitti, Yvette (1984) 'Vérité de la fiction et fiction de la vérité dans *Histoire de ma vie*: le projet autobiographique de George Sand', *Nineteenth Century French Studies* 12/13: 95–118.

Brecht, Bertolt (1955) [1928] *Die Dreigroschenoper*, Berlin: Suhrkamp.

Brenkman, John (1992) 'Family, Community, Polis: The Freudian Structure of Feeling', *New Literary History* 23: 923–54.

Brennan, Teresa (ed.) (1989) *Between Feminism and Psychoanalysis*, London and New York: Routledge.

Brombert, Victor (ed.) (1962) *Stendhal*, Englewood Cliffs, NJ: Prentice-Hall (Twentieth Century Views).

Brooks, Peter (1984) *Reading for the Plot: Design and Intention in Narrative*, New York: Knopf.

Burton, Richard (1988) *Baudelaire in 1859*, Cambridge: Cambridge University Press.

Busine, Alain (1984) 'Matronymies', *Littérature* 54: 54–76.

Campbell, Joseph (1968) *The Hero with a Thousand Faces*, Princeton, NJ: Princeton University Press.

Castro, Eve de (1989) *Les Bâtards du soleil*, Paris: Presses Pocket.

Certeau, Michel de (1980) 'On the Oppositional Practices of Everyday Life', tr. F. Jameson and C. Lovitt, *Social Text* 3: 3–43.

—— (1984) [1980] *The Practice of Everyday Life*, tr. S. F. Rendall, Berkeley: University of California Press.

Chambers, Ross (1987) *Mélancolie et opposition*, Paris: Corti.

—— (1991) *Room for Maneuver: Reading (the) Oppositional (in) Narrative*, Chicago and London: University of Chicago Press.

—— (1992) 'The Etcetera Principle: Narrative and the Paradigmatic', forthcoming.

Charme, Stuart L. (1984) *Meaning and Myth in the Study of Lives: A Sartrean Perspective*, Philadelphia: University of Pennsylvania Press.

Chevaly, Maurice (1989) *Genet*, 2 vols, Volume 1: *L'Amour cannibale*; Volume 2: *L'Enfer à fleur de peau*, Marseille: Le Temps parallèle.

Child Bickel, Gisèle A. (1987) *Jean Genet: criminalité et transcendance*, Saratoga, Calif.: ANMA Libri.

Chodorow, Nancy (1978) *The Reproduction of Mothering: Psychoanalysis and the Sociology of Gender*, Berkeley: University of California Press.

Cobban, Alfred (1963) *A History of Modern France*, 3 vols, third edition, Volume 1: *1715–1799*, Harmondsworth: Penguin.

Cohen-Salal, Annie (1987) *Sartre: A Life*, tr. A. Cancogni, ed. N. MacAfee, New York: Pantheon Books.

Colette (1928) *La Naissance du jour*, Paris: Flammarion.

—— (1979) *The Break of Day*, tr. E. McLeod, London: Women's Press.

Colloque International Flora Tristan (1984) *Un Fabuleux destin: Flora Tristan*, Dijon: Editions universitaires de Dijon.

Constant, Abbé Alphonse-Louis (pseud. Eliphas Lévy) (1841) *L'Assomption de la femme, ou Le livre de l'amour*, Paris: A. Le Gallois.

—— (1844) *La Mère de Dieu: Epopée religieuse et humanitaire*, Paris: C. Gosselin.

Corbin, Alain (1982) *Les Filles de noce: Misère sexuelle et prostitution (19e siècle)*, Paris: Flammarion.

—— (1990) *Women for Hire: Prostitution and Sexuality in France after 1850*, tr. A. Sheridan, Cambridge, Mass.: Harvard University Press.

Courtivon, Isabelle de (1985) *Violette Leduc*, Boston, Mass.: Twayne.

—— (1986) 'From Bastard to Pilgrim: Rites and Writing for Madame', *Yale French Studies* 72: 133–48.

—— (1988) 'Violette Leduc: L'enfermée pèlerine', *Cahiers du GRIF*, 39: 49–53.

Daix, Pierre (1975) *Aragon: Une vie à changer*, Paris: Seuil.

Danahy, Michèle (1982) 'Growing up Female: George Sand's View in *La Petite Fadette*', in N. Datlof (ed.) *The George Sand Papers*, conference proceedings, 1978, Hofstra University, New York: AMS Press.

Delacroix, Eugène (1981) *Journal: 1822–1863*, pref. Hubert Danusch, Paris: Plon.

—— (1979) *The Journal of Eugène Delacroix*, tr. L. Norton, New York and London: Garland Publishing.

Delaisi de Parseval, Geneviève (1981) *La Part du père,* Paris: Seuil.

Deleuze, Gilles, and Guattari, Félix (1975) *Kafka: Pour une littérature mineure*, Paris: Minuit.

—— (1986) *Kafka: Toward a Minor Literature*, tr. D. Polan, Minneapolis: University of Minnesota Press.

—— (1980) *Mille plateaux*, Paris: Minuit.

—— (1988) *A Thousand Plateaus: Capitalism and Schizophrenia*, tr. and foreword B. Massumi, London: Athlone Press.

Deleuze, Gilles, and Parnet, Claire (1987) *Dialogues,* London: The Athlone Press.

Del Litto, V. (ed.) (1978) *Le Journal intime et ses formes littéraires: Actes du colloque de septembre 1975*, Geneva: Droz.

De Man, Paul (1979) 'Autobiography as De-facement', *Modern Language Notes* 94: 919–30.

Demeron, Pierre (1978) 'Interview with Violette Leduc', tr. H. Rowley, *Hecate* 4, 1: 47–56.

Depauw, Jacques (1972) 'Amour illégitime et société à Nantes au XVIIIe siècle', *Annales E.S.C.* 27: 1155–82.

Derrida, Jacques (1978) *Eperons: Les styles de Nietzsche*, Paris: Flammarion.

—— (1979) *Spurs: Nietzsche's Styles*, tr. B. Harlow, intro. S. Agosti, Chicago: Chicago University Press.

—— (1980) *La Carte postale: de Socrate à Freud et au-delà*, Paris: Flammarion.

—— (1987) *The Post Card: from Socrates to Freud and Beyond*, tr. A. Bass, Chicago, University of Chicago Press.

—— (1981) [1974] *Glas: Que reste-t-il du savoir absolu?*, 2 vols, Paris: Denoël/Gonthier.

—— (1986) *Glas*, tr. J. P. Leavey and R. Rand, Lincoln and London: University of Nebraska Press.

—— (1983) *Signéponge/Signsponge*, tr. R. Rand, New York: Columbia University Press.

—— (1990) *Mémoires d'aveugles: L'autoportrait et autres ruines*, Paris: Réunion des musées nationaux.

Derrida, Jacques, with C. Lévesque and C. McDonald (1982) *L'Oreille de l'autre: Otobiographies, transferts, traductions*, Montreal: VLB.

—— (1985) *The Ear of the Other: Otobiography, Transference, Translation: Texts and Discussions with Jacques Derrida*, ed. Christie McDonald, tr. Peggy Kamuf, New York: Schocken Books.

Desanti, Dominique (1972) *Flora Tristan: La femme révoltée*, Paris: Hachette.

—— (1976) *A Woman in Revolt: A Biography of Flora Tristan*, tr. Elizabeth Zelvin, New York: Crown Publishers.

—— (1983) 'Masquer son nom', *Corps écrit* 8: 91–8.

—— (1984) 'Flora ... Messie du temps des prophètes ou Messie parce que femme?', Colloque International Flora Tristan, *Un Fabuleux destin: Flora Tristan*, Dijon: Editions universitaires de Dijon, 209–20.

Deutelbaum, Wendy, and Huff, Cynthia (1985) 'Class, Gender, and the Family System: The Case of George Sand', in *The (M)other Tongue: Essays in Feminist Psychoanalytic Interpretation*, ed. S. Garner *et al.*, Ithaca, NY, and London: Cornell University Press.

Devereux, Georges (1982) *Femmes et mythes*, Paris: Flammarion.

Dichy, Albert, and Fouché, Pascal (1988) *Jean Genet: Essai de chronologie 1910–1944*, Paris: Bibliothèque de littérature française contemporaine de l'Université Paris 7.

Diderot, Denis (1965) [1757] *Le Fils naturel*, Bordeaux: SOBODI.

Didier, Béatrice (1977) 'Femme/Identité/Ecriture: à propos de l'*Histoire de ma vie* de George Sand', *Revue des sciences humaines* 168: 561–76.

—— (1981) *L'Ecriture femme*, Paris: PUF.

—— (1983) *Stendhal autobiographe*, Paris: PUF.

—— (1984) 'Rôles et figures du lecteur chez George Sand', *Etudes littéraires*, 17: 239–59.

—— (1989) *Ecrire la Révolution 1789–1799*, Paris: PUF.

Dinnerstein, Dorothy (1977) *The Mermaid and the Minotaur: Sexual Arrangements and Human Malaise*, New York: Harper & Row.

Doubrovsky, Serge (1988) *Autobiographiques: de Corneille à Sartre*, Paris: PUF.

Duhet, Paule-Marie (1971) *Les Femmes et la révolution*, Paris: Julliard.

—— (1981) 'Préface', *Cahiers de doléances des femmes et autres textes*, Paris: Des femmes.

Dundes, Alan (1965) *The Study of Folklore*, Englewood Cliffs, NJ: Prentice Hall.

Durand, Pierre (1987) *Louise Michel: La passion*, Paris: Messidor.

Eissler, Kurt (1961) *Leonardo da Vinci: Psychoanalytic Notes on the Enigma*, New York: International Universities Press.

Evans, Martha (1985) 'Writing as Difference in Violette Leduc's Autobiography *La Bâtarde*', in *The (M)other Tongue: Essays in Feminist Psychoanalytic Interpretation*, ed. S. Garner *et al.*, Ithaca, NY, and London: Cornell University Press.

Feldstein, Richard, and Sussman, Henry (eds) (1990) *Psychoanalysis and . . .*, London and New York: Routledge.

Fellows, Otis (1981) 'The Facets of Illegitimacy in the French Enlightenment', *Diderot Studies* 20: 77–97.

Les Femmes dans la révolution française (1982) 2 vols plus Supplément, Paris: Edhis.

Foucault, Michel (1961) *Histoire de la folie à l'âge classique*, Paris: Plon.

—— (1971) *Madness and Civilization: A History of Insanity in the Age of Reason*, tr. R. Howard, London: Tavistock Publications.

—— (1983) 'L'Ecriture de soi', *Corps écrit* 5: 3–26.

Fraenkel, Béatrice (1992) *La Signature: Génèse d'un signe*, Paris: Gallimard.

Freadman, Anne (1983) 'Sandpaper', *Southern Review* 16: 161–73.

—— (1988) 'Of Cats, Companions, and the Name of George Sand', in *Grafts,* ed. S. Sheridan, New York: Verso.

Freud, Sigmund (1954) *The Origins of Psychoanalysis: Letters to William Fliess, Drafts and Notes 1887–1902*, ed. M. Bonaparte, A. Freud, E. Kris, tr. E. Mosbacher, J. Strachey, London: Imago Publishing Co.

—— (1981) *Complete Works*, The Standard Edition, 24 vols, ed. and tr. James Strachey, with A. Freud, A. Strachey and A. Tyson, London: Hogarth Press and Institute of Psychoanalysis.

—— (1987) [1910] *Un Souvenir d'enfance de Léonard de Vinci*, tr. J. Altounian, A. and O. Bougignon, P. Cotet and A. Rauty, preface by J.-B. Pontalis, Paris: Gallimard.

Gary, Romain (1960) *La Promesse de l'aube*, Paris: Gallimard.

—— (1961) *Promise at Dawn*, tr. J. M. Beach, New York: Harper.

Gaudemar, Martine de (1982) 'Louise Michel, martyre? ou "Artiste révolutionnaire"?', in *Colloque Louise Michel 1980*, ed. Daniel Armogathe, Marseille: Service des publications Marseille, diffusion J. Lafitte.

Genet, Jean (1948) *Notre-Dame-des-Fleurs*, Paris: Marc Barbezat-L'Arbalète.

—— (1965) *Our Lady of the Flowers*, tr. B. Frechtman, London: Anthony Blond.

—— (1949) *Journal du voleur*, Paris: Gallimard.

—— (1973) *The Thief's Journal*, tr. B. Frechtman, London: Faber.

—— (1979) *Oeuvres complètes*, Vols I–IV, Paris: Gallimard.

—— (1986) *Un Captif amoureux*, Paris: Gallimard.

Gilbert, Sandra, and Gubar, Susan (1984) 'Ceremonies of the Alphabet: Female Grandmatologies and the Female Authorgraph', in *The Female Autograph*, ed. Domna Stanton and Jeanine Plottel, New York: New York Literary Forum.

Girard, Pièr (1986) *Oedipe masqué: Une lecture psychanalytique de 'L'Affamée' de Violette Leduc*, Paris: Des femmes.

Glasgow, Janis (1985) *George Sand: Collected Essays*, Troy, NY: Whitson.

Goubert, Pierre, and Denis, Michel (1964) *1789 les français ont la parole: Cahiers des doléances des Etats-Généraux*, Paris: Julliard.

Gouges, Olympe de (1788) *Mémoire de Madame de Valmont contre l'ingratitude et la cruauté de la famille des Flaucourt avec la Sienne dont les Sieurs de Flaucourt ont vécu tant de services*, in *Oeuvres de Mme de Gouges*, 3 vols, Paris: l'auteur et Cailleau.

—— (1790) *Départ de M. Necker et de Madame de Gouges ou Les Adieux de Madame de Gouges aux François et à M. Necker*, Paris: [no publisher].

—— (1975) *Le Couvent ou les voeux forcés* [three-act drama], Paris: Hachette.

—— (1982) [1791] 'Les Droits de la femme', in *Les Femmes dans la révolution française*. [Partly translated in *European Women: A Documentary History 1789–1945*, ed. Eleanor Riemer and John Fout, New York: Schocken Books.]

—— (1986) *Oeuvres*, ed. and intro. Benoîte Groult, Paris: Mercure de France.

—— (1989) [1788] *L'Esclavage des nègres ou L'Heureux naufrage* [three-act drama], ed. E. Varikas, Paris: Côté-femmes.

Grimmer, Claude (1983) *La Femme et le bâtard: Amours illégitimes et secrètes dans l'ancien régime*, Paris: Presses de la renaissance.

Grogan, Susan (1992) *French Socialism and Sexual Difference: Women and the New Society*, London: Macmillan.

Grosz, Elizabeth (1990) *Jacques Lacan: A Feminist Introduction*, London and New York: Routledge.

Groult, Benoîte (1977) *Le Féminisme au masculin*, Paris: Denoël/Gonthier.

Gunn, Daniel (1988) *Psychoanalysis and Fiction*, Cambridge: Cambridge University Press.

Hahn, Johann Georg von (1876) *Sagwissenschaftliche Studien*, Jena: E. Schenk.

Hartley, Shirley (1980) 'Illegitimacy in Jamaica', in *Bastardy and its Comparative History*, ed. Peter Laslett *et al.*, London: Edward Arnold.

Hartman, Geoffrey (1981) *Saving the Text: Literature, Derrida, Philosophy*, Baltimore: Johns Hopkins University Press.

Hirsch, Marianne (1989) *The Mother Daughter Plot*, Bloomington and Indianapolis: Indiana University Press.

Hogg, James (1969) [1823] *The Private Memoirs and Confessions of a Justified Sinner, written by himself, with a detail of curious traditionary facts and other evidence by the editor*, London and New York: Oxford University Press.

Holly, Michael (1992) 'Writing Leonardo Backwards', *New Literary History* 23: 173–210.

Holquist, Michael (1990) *Dialogism: Bakhtin and His World*, London and New York: Routledge.

Idt, Geneviève (1976) 'L'autoparodie dans *Les Mots* de Sartre', *Cahiers du vingtième siècle* 6: 53–86.

—— (1982) 'Des mots à l'enfance d'un chef: autobiographie et psychanalyse', in *Sartre et la mise en signe*, ed. M. Issacharoff and J.-C. Vilquin, Paris: Klincksieck.

Irigaray, Luce (1974) *Speculum, de l'autre femme*, Paris: Minuit.

—— (1985) *Speculum of the Other Woman*, tr. G. C. Gill, Ithaca, NY: Cornell University Press.

—— (1981) *Le corps à corps avec la mère*, Montreal: De la pleine lune.

—— (1987) *Sexes et parentés*, Paris: Minuit.

Jackson, Rosemary (1981) *Fantasy: The Literature of Subversion*, New York and London: Methuen.

Jameson, Fredric (1985) *Sartre after Sartre*, New Haven: Yale University Press.

Jeanson, Francis (1969) *Sartre par lui-même*, Paris: Seuil.

Johnson, Barbara (1979) *Défigurations du langage poétique: La seconde révolution Baudelairienne*, Paris: Flammarion.

—— (1982) 'My Monster/My Self', *Diacritics* 12: 2–10.

Jouve, Nicole Ward (1990) *White Woman Speaks With Forked Tongue: Criticism as Autobiography*, London and New York: Routledge.

Jung, Carl, and Kerenyi, Karl (1970) [1940] *Introduction to a Science of Mythology: The Myth of the Divine Child and the Mysteries of Eleusis*, tr. R. Hull, London: Routledge & Kegan Paul.

Jurgrau, Thelma (1988/9) 'Autobiography in General and George Sand's in Particular', *Nineteenth Century French Studies* 17: 196–207.

Kadish, D. Y. (1991) *Politicising Genders: Narrative Strategies in the Aftermath of the French Revolution*, New Brunswick, NJ: Rutgers University Press.

Kelly, Linda (1980) *The Kemble Era*, London: Bodley Head.

Kleinschmidt, B. (1930) *Die Heilige Anna: Ihre Verehrung in Geschichte, Kunst und Volkstum*, Düsseldorf.

Kofman, Sarah (1976) *Autobiogriffures*, Paris: Bourgois.

—— (1980) *L'Enigme de la femme: La femme dans les textes de Freud*, Paris: Galilée.

—— (1985) *The Enigma of Woman: Women in Freud's Writings*, tr. C. Porter, Ithaca, NY: Cornell University Press.

—— (1984) *Lectures de Derrida*, Paris: Galilée.

—— (1984a) 'Sartre: Fort ou Da?' *Diacritics* 14: 9–18.

—— (1986) *Paroles suffoquées*, Paris: Galilée.

—— (1990) *Séductions: de Sartre à Héraclite*, Paris: Galilée.

Kristeva, Julia (1977) 'L'autre du sexe', *Sorcières* 10: 37–41.

—— (1986) 'Stabat Mater', in *The Female Body in Western Culture: Contemporary Perspectives*, ed. Susan Suleiman, Cambridge, Mass.: Harvard University Press.

—— (1987) [1983] *Tales of Love*, tr. L. Roudiez, New York: Columbia University Press.

Lacan, Jacques (1966) *Ecrits*, Paris: Seuil.

—— (1977) *Ecrits: A Selection*, tr. A. Sheridan, London: Tavistock Publications.

—— (1975) *Encore*, Paris: Seuil.

Laplanche, Jean, and Pontalis, Jean-Baptiste (1964) 'Fantasme originaire, fantasmes des origines, origine du fantasme', *Les Temps modernes* 19, 215: 1833–68.

Laqueur, Thomas (1990) *Making Sex*, Cambridge, Mass.: Harvard University Press.

Laslett, Peter, *et al.* (ed.) (1980) *Bastardy and its Comparative History: Studies in the History of Illegitimacy and Marital Nonconformism in Britain, France, Germany, Sweden, the United States, Jamaica and Japan*, London: Edward Arnold.

Laugaa, Maurice (1986) *La Pensée du pseudonyme*, Paris: PUF.

—— (1989) 'Autobiographies d'un pseudonyme', *Textuel* 22: 111–35 [special issue, 'Images de l'écrivain'].

Laurentin, R. (1963) *La Question mariale*, Paris: Seuil.

Lecarme, J. (1975) 'Un cas-limite de l'autobiographie: Sartre', *RHLF* 6: 1058.

Leclaire, Serge (1968) *Psychanalyser: Un essai sur l'ordre de l'inconscient et la pratique de la lettre*, Paris: Seuil.

Le Doeuff, Michèle (1989) *L'Etude et le rouet*, Paris: Seuil.

Leduc, Violette (1946) *L'Asphyxie*, Paris: Gallimard.

—— (1970) *In the prison of her skin*, tr. D. Coltman, London: Hart-Davis.

—— (1948) *L'Affamée*, Paris: Gallimard.

—— (1964) *La Bâtarde*, Paris: Gallimard.

—— (1985) *La Bâtarde*, tr. D. Coltman, London: Virago.

—— (1970) *La Folie en tête*, Paris: Gallimard.

—— (1971) *Mad in Pursuit*, tr. D. Coltman, London: Panther.

—— (1973) *La Chasse à l'amour*, Paris: Gallimard.

Lejeune, Paule (1975) *Flora Tristan: Réalisations, oeuvres*, Paris: Le peuple prend la parole.

Lejeune, Philippe (1971) *L'Autobiographie en France*, Paris: Armand Colin.

—— (1975) *Le Pacte autobiographique*, Paris: Seuil.

—— (1980) *Je est un autre*, Paris: Seuil.

—— (1989) *On Autobiography*, ed. P. J. Eakin, tr. K. Leary, Minneapolis: University of Minnesota Press.

Lemaire, Anika (1979) *Jacques Lacan*, London and New York: Routledge & Kegan Paul.

Le Millour, Charlotte (1982) *La Maternité singulière: Récits de vie de mères célibataires*, Paris: R. Laffont.

Leprohon, Pierre (1979) *Flora Tristan*, Antony: Editions Corymbe.

Livingston, Beverly (1981) 'George Sand and Flora Tristan', *Topic* 35: 38–44.

Loraux, Nicole (1989) *Les Expériences de Tirésias*, Paris: Gallimard.

Lyotard, Jean-François (1983) *Le Différend*, Paris: Minuit.
—— (1988) *The Differend: Phases in Dispute*, tr. Georges Van Den Abbede, Minneapolis: University of Minnesota Press.
MacCannell, Juliet (1986) *Figuring Lacan: Criticism and the Cultural Unconscious*, London and New York: Routledge.
Maclean, Marie (1974) *Le Jeu suprême*, Paris: Corti.
—— (1982) 'Baudelaire and the Paradox of Procreation', *Studi francesi* 76: 87–98.
—— (1987) 'Oppositional Practice in Women's Traditional Narrative', *New Literary History* 19: 36–50.
—— (1988) *Narrative as Performance: The Baudelairean Experiment*, London and New York: Routledge.
—— (1989) 'Revolution and Opposition: Olympe de Gouges and the *Déclaration des droits de la femme*', in *Literature and Revolution*, ed. D. Bevan, The Hague: Rodopi.
Maidani-Gérard, Jean-Pierre (1987) *Léonard de Vinci, Sigmund Freud . . . : L''application' de la psychanalyse à une oeuvre du passé, validité*, Lille III: ANRT, 10 microfiches.
Makward, Christiane (1977) 'Le Nom du père: écritures féminines d'un siècle à l'autre', Third Annual Colloquium in 19th Century French Studies, October 1977, Columbus, Ohio.
Mannoni, Octave (1978) *Fictions freudiennes*, Paris: Seuil.
Marbeau-Cleirens, B. (1980) *Les Mères célibataires et l'inconscient*, Paris: J. P. Delarge.
Marcus, Leah (1989) 'Erasing the Stigma of Daughterhood: Mary I, Elizabeth I, and Henry VIII', in *Daughters and Fathers*, ed. Lynda Boose and Betty Flowers, Baltimore: Johns Hopkins University Press.
Marin, Louis (1981) 'On the Theory of Written Enunciation: The Notion of Interruption–Resumption in Autobiography', *Semiotica*, Special Supplement 1: 101–11.
Marini, Marcelle (1986) *Lacan*, Paris: Pierre Belfond.
Marson, Susan (1992) 'Le Temps du récit littéraire dans *L'Affamée* de Violette Leduc', unpublished thesis.
Mauron, Charles (1966) *Le Dernier Baudelaire*, Paris: Corti.
—— (1972) *Des Métaphores obsédantes au mythe personnel*, Paris: Corti.
Mehlmann, Jeffrey (1974) *A Structural Study of Autobiography: Proust, Leiris, Sartre, Lévi-Strauss*, Ithaca and London: Cornell University Press.
Mendus, Susan, and Rendall, Jane (eds) (1989) *Sexuality and Subordination: Interdisciplinary Studies of Gender in the Nineteenth Century*, London and New York: Routledge.
Mères-Femmes, special edition, *Cahiers du GRIF* 17/18 (1977).
Les Mères, special edition, *Nouvelle revue de psychanalyse* 45 (1992).
Meyer, Jean (1980) 'Illegitimates and Foundlings in Pre-Industrial France', in *Bastardy and its Comparative History*, ed. Peter Laslett *et al.*, London: Edward Arnold.
Michaud, Stéphane (1984) 'En miroir, Flora Tristan et George Sand',

Colloque International Flora Tristan, *Un Fabuleux destin: Flora Tristan*, Dijon: Editions universitaires de Dijon.

Michel, Louise (1888) *Le Monde nouveau*, Paris: E. Dentu.

—— (1905) *Oeuvres posthumes*, ed. and pref. L. Taillade, Alfortville: Librairie Internationaliste.

—— (1976) [1886] *Mémoires*, rev. edition, Paris: Maspero.

—— (1981) *The Red Virgin: Memoirs of Louise Michel*, ed. and tr. B. Lowry and E. Gunter, Alabama: University of Alabama Press.

—— (1983) [1905] *Souvenirs et aventures de ma vie*, Paris: Maspero.

Miething, Christoph (1983) *Saint Sartre: oder der autobiographische Gott*, Heidelberg: C. Winter.

Miles, Margaret (1986) 'The Virgin's One Bare Breast: Female Nudity and Religious Meaning in Tuscan Early Renaissance Culture', in *The Female Body in Western Culture: Contemporary Perspectives*, ed. Susan Suleiman, Cambridge, Mass.: Harvard University Press.

Miller, Nancy (1980) 'Women's Autobiography in France: For a Dialectics of Identification', in *Women and Language in Literature and Society*, ed. S. McConnell-Ginet *et al.*, New York: Praeger.

—— (ed.) (1986) *The Poetics of Gender*, New York: Columbia University Press.

—— (1990) *Subject to Change: Reading Feminist Writing*, New York: Columbia University Press.

Mimica, Jadran (1991) 'The Incest Passions: An Outline of the Logic of Iqwaye Social Organization', *Oceania* 62, 1: 34–58; 62, 2: 81–113.

Mitchison, Rosalind (1989) *Sexuality and Social Control: Scotland 1660–1780*, Oxford: Blackwell.

Mitterauer, Michael (1983) *Ledige Mütter. Zur Geschichte illegitimer Geburten in Europa,* Munich: C.H. Beck.

Montrelay, Michèle (1977) *L'Ombre du nom*, Paris: Minuit.

Moraly, Jean-Bernard (1988) *Jean Genet: La vie écrite*, Paris: Editions de la différence.

Morris, Jenny (ed.) (1992) *Alone Together: Voices of Single Mothers*, London: The Women's Press.

Mozet, Nicole (1988) '*Ursule Mirouët* (1841) ou le test du bâtard: quand l'Histoire prend la forme d'une vérité scientifique', in *Actes du colloque 'Balzac après 1840: le moment de "La Comédie humaine"'*, Paris: Université de Paris VIII.

Murphy, Sara (1991) 'Refusing to Confess: George Sand's *Histoire de ma vie* and the Novelization of Autobiographical Discourse', in *Selected Proceedings of the 16th Colloquium in 19th Century French Studies*, ed. K. Busby, Amsterdam and Atlanta, Ga: Rodopi.

Nathan, Michel (1981) *Le Ciel des fouriéristes*, Lyon: PU Lyon.

Nerval, Gérard de (1966) *Oeuvres*, ed. H. Lemaitre, Paris: Garnier.

—— (1957) *Selected Writings*, ed. and tr. G. Wagner, Ann Arbor: University of Michigan Press.

Nicole, Eugène (1983) 'L'Onomastique littéraire', *Poétique* 54: 233–53.

—— (1984) 'Personnage et rhétorique du nom', *Poétique* 46: 200–16.

Le Nom, special edition, *Corps écrit* 8 (1980).

Noms propres, special edition, *Cahiers du GRIF* 7 (1980).

Olivier, Christiane (1980) *Les Enfants de Jocaste: L'empreinte de la mère*, Paris: Denoël/Gonthier.

—— (1989) *Jocasta's Children: The Imprint of the Mother*, tr. G. Craig, London and New York: Routledge.

Olney, James (ed.) (1980) *Autobiography: Essays Theoretical and Critical*, Princeton, NJ: Princeton University Press.

Pacaly, Josette (1980) *Sartre au miroir*, Paris: Klincksieck.

Paul-Lévy, Françoise (1981) *L'Amour nomade: La mère et l'enfant, XV–XXe siècle*, Paris: Seuil.

Pauly, R.M. (1989) *Le Berceau et la bibliothèque: le paradoxe de l'écriture autobiographique*, Stanford, Calif.: ANMA Libri, (Stanford French and Italian Studies, 62).

Pellissier, Pierre (1985) *Emile de Girardin: Prince de la presse*, Paris: Denoël.

Planté, Christine (1985) 'Flora Tristan, écrivain méconnue', in *Actes du colloque Flora Tristan*, Dijon: Editions universitaires de Dijon.

Prévert, Jacques (1949) *Paroles*, Paris: Gallimard.

Prince, Gerald (1984) 'Sartre Resartus', *Diacritics* 22: 2–8.

Puech, J.-L. (1925) *La Vie et l'oeuvre de Flora Tristan*, Paris: Rivière.

Quesnel, Michel (1987) *Baudelaire solaire*, Paris: PUF.

Raglan, Lord [Fitzroy Somerset] (1934) 'The Hero of Tradition', *Folklore* 45: 212–31.

Rank, Otto (1909) *Der Mythus von der Geburt des Helden. Versuch einer psychologischen Mythendeutung*, Leipzig and Vienna: F. Deuticke.

—— (1970) *The Myth of the Birth of the Hero: A Psychological Interpretation of Mythology*, New York: Johnson Reprint Corporation.

Rea, Annabelle (1985) 'Toward a Definition of Women's Voice in Sand's Novels: The Siren and the Witch', in *George Sand: Collected Essays*, ed. Janis Glasgow, Troy, NY: Whitson.

Riemer, Eleanor and Fout, John (eds) (1980) *European Women: A Documentary History 1789–1945*, New York: Schocken Books.

Rimmon-Kenan, Shlomith (1987) *Discourse and Psychoanalysis in Literature*, London and New York: Routledge.

Robert, Marthe (1976) *Roman des origines et origines du roman*, Paris: Gallimard.

—— (1980) *Origins of the Novel*, tr. S. Rabinovitch, Bloomington: Indiana University Press.

Rosci, Marco (1977) *Leonardo*, tr. J. Gilbert, Sydney: Bay Books.

Roustang, François (1983) *Psychoanalysis Never Lets Go*, Baltimore, Md: Johns Hopkins University Press.

Sand, George (1958) *La Petite Fadette*, Paris: Garnier Frères.

—— (1977) *Fanchon the Cricket*, Chicago: Cassandra Editions.

—— (1960) *François le champi*, Paris: Garnier Frères.

—— (1960) *Contes de ma grand'mère*, Paris: Garnier Frères.

—— (1970) *Oeuvres autobiographiques, I*, ed. G. Lubin, Paris: Gallimard (La Pléiade).

—— (1971) *Oeuvres autobiographiques, II*, ed. G. Lubin, Paris: Gallimard (La Pléiade).

—— (1979) *My Life*, tr. and adap. D. Hofstadter, New York: Harper & Row.

Sartre, Jean-Paul (1939) 'L'enfance d'un chef', in *Le Mur*, Paris: Gallimard.

—— (1969) *The Wall (Intimacy) and Other Stories*, tr. L. Alexander, New York: New Direction.

—— (1947) *Baudelaire*, Paris: Gallimard.

—— (1949) *Baudelaire*, tr. M. Turnell, London: Horizon.

—— (1952) *Saint Genet: Comédien et martyr*, Paris: Gallimard.

—— (1963) *Saint Genet: Actor and Martyr*, tr. B. Frechtman, London: W. H. Allen.

—— (1964) *Les Mots*, Paris: Gallimard.

—— (1967) *Words*, tr. I. Clephane, Harmondsworth: Penguin.

—— (1986) *Lectures de Sartre*, Actes du colloque de l'Université Lyon.

Schapiro, Meyer (1956) 'Leonardo and Freud', *The Journal of History of Ideas* 17: 147–8.

Schérer, René (1989) *Pari sur l'impossible: Etudes fouriéristes*, Paris: PU Vincennes.

Schneider, Manfred (1986) *Die erkältete Herzensschrift. Der autobiographische Text im 20. Jahrhundert*, Munich: C. Hanser.

Schneider, Monique (1985) *'Père, ne vois-tu pas . . .?': Le père, le maître, le spectre dans 'L'Interprétation des rêves'*, Paris: Denoël.

Schoenfeld, Jean (1982) '*La Bâtarde*, or Why the Writer Writes', *French Forum* 7: 261–8.

Schor, Naomi (1985) 'Female Fetishism: The Case of George Sand', *Poetics Today* 6: 301–10.

—— (1986) 'Reading Double: Sand's Difference', in *The Poetics of Gender*, ed. Nancy Miller, New York: Columbia University Press.

—— (1987) *Reading in Detail: Aesthetics and the Feminine*, London and New York: Routledge.

Searle, John (1969) *Speech Acts: An Essay in the Philosophy of Language*, Cambridge: Cambridge University Press.

Segal, Naomi (1992) *The Adulteress's Child: Authorship and Desire in the Nineteenth Century Novel*, Cambridge: Polity Press.

Sénart, Philippe (1964) 'Jean Paul Sartre ou l'enfant du miracle', *La Table Ronde* 195.

Serres, Michel (1980) *Le Parasite*, Paris: Minuit.

—— (1982) *The Parasite*, tr. L. R. Schehr, Baltimore: Johns Hopkins University Press.

—— (1987) *Statues*, Paris: François Bourin.

Serullaz, Maurice (1989) *Delacroix*, Paris: Fayard.

Seurat, Georges (1987) *Notes sur Delacroix*, Caen: l'Echoppe.

Sowerwine, Charles (1978) *Les Femmes et le socialisme*, Paris: Presses de la fondation nationale des sciences politiques.

—— (1982) *Sisters or Citizens? Women and Socialism in France since 1876*, Cambridge: Cambridge University Press.

Spence, Donald (1982) *Narrative Truth and Historical Truth: Meaning and Interpretation in Psychoanalysis*, New York: W. W. Norton.

Spivak, Gayatri (1977) '*Glas*-Piece: A Compte-Rendu', *Diacritics* 7, 3: 22–43.

—— (1983) 'Displacement and the Discourse of Woman', in *Displacement: Derrida and After*, ed. M. Krupnik, Bloomington: Indiana University Press.

Stanton, Domna (1984) 'Autogynography: Is the Subject Different?', in *The Female Autograph*, ed. Domna Stanton and Jeanine Plottel, New York: New York Literary Forum.

—— (1986) 'Difference on Trial: A Critique of the Maternal Metaphor in Cixous, Irigaray and Kristeva', in *The Poetics of Gender*, ed. Nancy Miller, New York: Columbia University Press.

Stanton, Domna, and Plottel, Jeanine (eds) (1984) *The Female Autograph*, New York: New York Literary Forum.

Starobinski, Jean (1961) 'Stendhal pseudonyme', in *L'Oeil vivant*, Paris: Gallimard.

—— (1962) partly tr. B. Archer as 'Truth in Masquerade', in *Stendhal*, ed. V. Brombert, Englewood Cliffs, NJ: Prentice-Hall.

—— (1980) 'The Style of Autobiography', in *Autobiography: Essays Theoretical and Critical*, ed. James Olney, Princeton, NJ: Princeton University Press.

Stendhal (1908) *Correspondance: 1800–1842*, ed. A. Paupe and P.-A. Chéramy, Paris: Bosse.

—— (1973) *Vie de Henry Brulard*, ed. B. Didier, Paris: Gallimard.

—— (1973) *The Life of Henry Brulard*, tr. J. Stewart and B. Knight, Harmondsworth: Penguin.

—— (1983) *Souvenirs d'égotisme*, ed. B. Didier, Paris: Gallimard.

—— (1975) *Memoirs of an Egoist*, tr. D. Ellis, London: Chatto & Windus.

Suleiman, Susan (1985) 'Writing and Motherhood', in *The (M)other Tongue: Essays in Feminist Psychoanalytic Interpretation*, ed. S. Garner *et al.*, Ithaca, NY, and London: Cornell University Press.

—— (ed.) (1986) *The Female Body in Western Culture: Contemporary Perspectives*, Cambridge, Mass.: Harvard University Press.

Thiele-Knobloch, Gisela (1989) *Olympe de Gouges oder Menschenrechte auch für Frauen?*, Berlin: Zentraleinrichtung zur Förderung von Frauenstudien.

Thomas, Annie (1984) *Louise Michel, une femme libertaire*, Paris: Les lettres libres.

Thomas, Chantal (1988) 'Féminisme et Révolution: les causes perdues d'Olympe de Gouges', in *La Carmagnole des Muses*, ed. J.-Cl. Bonnet, Paris: A. Colin.

Todd, Jane (1983) 'Autobiographics in Freud and Derrida', thesis, Ann Arbor: U.M.I. Dissertation Services.

—— (1986) 'Autobiography and the Case of the Signature: Reading Derrida's *Glas*', *Comparative Literature* 38: 1–19.

Todorov, Tzvetan (1981) *Mikhaïl Bakhtine: Le principe dialogique*, Paris: Seuil.

—— (1984) *Mikhail Bakhtin: The Dialogical Principle*, tr. W. Godzich,

Minneapolis: University of Minnesota Press.

Tristan, Flora (1835) *Nécessité de faire bon accueil aux femmes étrangères par Mme F.T.*, Paris: Delaunay.

—— (1838) *Méphis*, 2 vols, Paris: Ladvocat.

—— (1846) *L'Emancipation de la femme, ou Le Testament de la paria*, posthumously reworked by A. Constant, Paris: au bureau de direction de 'La Vérité'.

—— (1983) [1838] *Les Pérégrinations d'une paria 1833–1834*, Paris: La Découverte/Maspero.

—— (1986) *Peregrinations of a Pariah: 1833–1834*, tr. and ed. J. Hawkes, London: Virago.

—— (1983a) [1840] *Promenades dans Londres*, ed. F. Bédarida, Paris: La Découverte/Maspero.

—— (1982) *The London Journal of Flora Tristan, 1842, or The Aristocracy and the Working Class of England*, tr. J. Hawkes, London: Virago.

—— (1967) [1843] *Union ouvrière*, 3rd, rev. edition, Paris: Editions d'Histoire sociale.

—— (1983b) *The Workers' Union*, tr. B. Livingston, Urbana: University of Illinois Press.

—— (1973) *Le Tour de France: Journal inédit 1843–1844*, pref. M. Collinet, ed. J.-L. Puech, Paris: Tête de Feuilles.

—— (1980) *Lettres*, ed. Stéphane Michaud, Paris: Seuil.

Van Rossum-Guyon, Françoise (1990) 'Mais produire, mais accoucher . . .', Colloque: *Lectures de la différence sexuelle*, Paris (Oct. 1990).

—— (1991) *George Sand: Une oeuvre multiforme*, Amsterdam and Atlanta, Ga: Rodopi.

Vareille, Jean-Claude (1983) 'Fantasmes de la fiction: fantasmes de l'écriture', in *George Sand: Colloque de Cérisy*, ed. Simone Vierne, Paris: SEDES and CDU.

Vernant, Jean-Pierre, and Vidal-Naquet, Pierre (1972) *Mythe et tragédie en Grèce ancienne*, Paris: Maspero.

—— (1981) *Tragedy and Myth in Ancient Greece*, tr. J. Lloyd, Brighton: Harvester.

Vickery, John (ed.) (1966) *Myth and Literature: Contemporary Theory and Practice*, Lincoln: University of Nebraska Press.

Vierne, Simone (ed.) (1983) *George Sand: Colloque de Cérisy*, Paris: SEDES and CDU.

Villelaux, A. (1964) 'Auto-Sartro-Graphie', *Les Lettres françaises*, 2 (20.2.1964).

Voyages, exils, errances, special edition, *Cahiers du GRIF*, 39 (1988).

Warner, Marina (1976) *Alone of All Her Sex: The Myth and Cult of the Virgin Mary*, New York: Vintage Books.

—— (1987) *Monuments and Maidens: The Allegory of the Female Form*, London: Pan Books.

Wolff, Reinhold (1980) 'Der Mythos von der Geburt des Helden. Jean-Paul Sartre oder *Les Mots* als Familienroman', *Lendemains, Zeitschrift für Frankreichforschung und Französischstudium* 17/18: 139–53.

Index